GENTLEMAN'S RELISH

(Photo: Country Life Picture Library)

Whitbourne Hall

GENTLEMAN'S RELISH

*A Landowner
in the Twentieth Century World*

EDWARD EVANS

SAPEY PRESS   1993

Sapey Press, Whitbourne, Worcester WR6 5SG

© Edward Evans 1993

ISBN 0 9521917 0 9 (hardback)
      0 9521917 1 7 (paperback)

British Library Cataloguing-in-Publication Data
A catalogue record for this book is available from the British Library.

Cover/Jacket photograph Angela Lloyd-James

Design and production Andrew Lamb, Book Production Services
Typeset by J&L Composition Ltd, Filey, North Yorkshire
Printed in Great Britain by SRP Exeter

Contents

Preface — vii

PART ONE – PREPARATION IN PEACE AND WAR
I Beginnings — 3
II The quiet revolution — 18
III Into industry — 38
IV World War II — 44
V Keren — 50
VI Behind the lines — 57
VII H.Q. Western Command — 66
VIII Erica — 74

PART TWO – DOWN TO BUSINESS
IX Gathering up the reins — 93
X The Vanishing Island — 109
XI The Captain — 117
XII Allies — 123
XIII Rozi's word — 132
XIV A world aim for farmers — 138
XV Farmers and friends — 148
XVI Return to Eritrea — 155
XVII Whose job to feed the hungry? — 164
XVIII Anything to declare? — 167
XIX Landowners and tenants — 176
XX The estate's second home — 189
XXI Forestry first — 197
XXII The richest country in the world — 207

Preface

THIS IS A record of one person's progress through the 20th century. To be exact, from 1910 to 1993 (so far). It is not an autobiography, just some memoirs. But they will be authentic, as far as they go.

I write them with a deep sense of thankfulness for the way my life's purpose has unfolded, and for my participation in an adventure beyond all expectations.

The idea of writing the story first occurred to me after my 80th birthday party in April 1990 – made possible by Erica my wife and by Bill and Chris my sons and their wives at Whitbourne Hall, our old family home. We celebrated the miracles of liberation in Eastern Europe and South Africa, remembered gratefully members of our family from our parents' time, and welcomed among our guests some of the new owners of Whitbourne Hall.

PART I
PREPARATION IN PEACE AND WAR

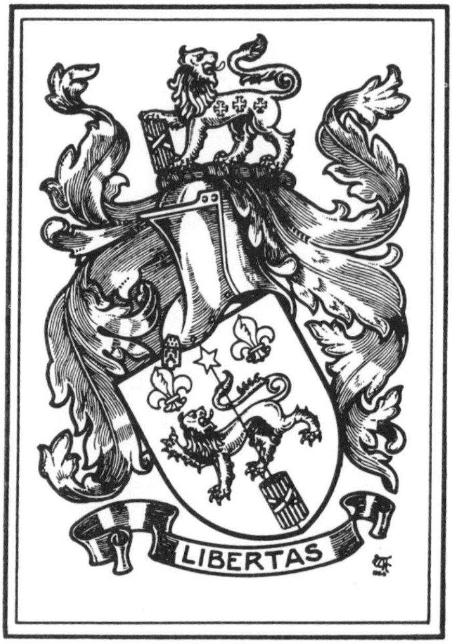
LIBERTAS

CHAPTER I
Beginnings

WHITBOURNE HALL, the family home which I was born into in 1910, is a massive place. It was built for our great grandfather, Edward Bickerton Evans, in 1860 and he moved in with his family in 1862. In front are six Ionic pillars on a pediment. The details are a copy of the Erechtheum (temple of Erechtheus) in Athens. This was great grandfather's wish. (The story goes that he went over one morning to inspect the work of the men laying the foundations, and said to them: 'It's too small. Double it.') The front door is also a replica of the Erechtheum. Inside is a vast hall with a patterned floor of coloured Italian tiles, a marble staircase, and more pillars (Corinthian this time) supporting an upstairs gallery. The whole house is built of a pleasant grey Bath stone, except for the pediment of the portico which is of harder Portland Stone, and the stable yard, inner yard and kitchen wing, which are of bricks made of clay from beneath the lake.

The lake itself, known to us always as 'The Pool', was dug by hand as part of the landscaping of the whole area. It covers about three acres, with an island, and lies some 50 feet below the Hall. There has always been a boat on it, a boat with a well-loved personality, throughout my life. It holds plentiful coarse fish, roach, perch and tench, tens of thousands of which have been netted and taken to restock the rivers in the Severn River Board area. My father later introduced carp.

Edward Bickerton Evans came from Worcester (his last house there is now the Eye Hospital) where his father Edward enjoyed an honoured position in the city; he was a leading Liberal on the City Council for several years and mayor of the city in 1840. Edward had arrived in Worcester in 1811 from Wales, where the Evans family had farmed for many years as tenants of the Earl of Powys. In partnership with William Hill, he made his fortune from the vinegar brewery of Hill, Evans and Co. on a five-acre site at Lowesmoor in the city. He had six daughters, but Edward Bickerton was his only son, and Edward lived to see him embark on a new life as a landowner at Whitbourne Hall.

Frank and Fanny Evans with Gwen (left), Edward and Rozi

Edward aged 3

Edward Bickerton built the Hall to form the centre of his new agricultural estate on the Hereford-Worcester border, systematically acquiring the surrounding land – about three thousand acres originally – through a large number of individual purchases. His elder son Edward Wallace, my grandfather, married Rhoda, née Somers Cocks, known to us as 'Grannie Rho'. She was an ample person, kind to us children and viewed by us with a kind of modified affection. After Edward Wallace's early death, she married again, but my parents felt great affection for her and had her to visit whenever they could. They also kept closely in touch with her brothers and sisters, whom we knew as Aunt Dorothy, Uncle Henry and Uncle Percy. Her second husband also died in due course and she spent her widowhood at the Rookery, near Newbury; I remember that Rozi and I, both undergraduates at Oxford at the time, went with our parents to her funeral.

Edward Wallace appears to have moved house several times during his marriage to Grannie Rho, from Wichenford to Alfrick to near Cheltenham – all places within range of Whitbourne and of the vinegar works in Worcester. He must have come to live at the Hall at the age of fifteen, when it was completed and his parents moved in; but they outlived him and he never inherited it.

On the death of Mrs Edward Bickerton Evans, the Worcestershire part of the estate (c1200 acres) passed to Mrs Patrick Evans, widow of her younger son, and formed what became known as the Harpley Estate.

My father inherited the Whitbourne estate (1800 acres, with Whitbourne Hall) on the death of his grandmother in 1910. Five years earlier he had married my mother, Fanny Brierley. She was the youngest of the seven children of Joseph Brierley, the much loved and respected rector of Whitbourne. The Brierleys came from Lancashire. Grannie Brierley, after her husband's death, came back to live near my parents in Whitbourne. I used regularly to be sent to have tea with her: she made delicious scones and cakes, and owned some beautiful red toy bricks with which I played contentedly. She also possessed a book about a boy called Robin Adair who did wonderful deeds for his King and Country. I wanted to be like him.

My father spoke very little about his father, who he referred to as 'the Governor'. He said equally little about his own young manhood. He went to Eton, then to Oxford for a spell, but was taken away in mid-course for, we understood, financial reasons. He did a stint in the militia (predecessor to the Territorials). He tried tea planting in

India for a period – an episode of which we got a glimpse when an old girl-friend of his turned up at Whitbourne Hall, who called him 'Toddy'. Both my father and mother were highly amused, and we were quite intrigued. He also served in the South African war. At some stage he took some training in a land agent's office. And then in 1905 he married, and got down to the management of Whitbourne estate. For the first five years or so he employed an agent, for whom he built a house in Whitbourne called Rosemore Grange.

One of Pa's favourite mottos was 'Anything for a quiet life'. I think this reflected his rather unquiet life before his marriage. In 1914 he volunteered for active service again and was wounded on the Somme – as a company commander at the ripe age of forty-three. In 1919 he was demobilised. He dispensed with the services of the agent, and settled for a 'quiet life' at Whitbourne Hall, managing the estate (now 1800 acres) and within it a small home farm of 66 acres.

In due course he became well-known locally as a landowner and a typical country squire. An ex-soldier, he kept a good cellar of port – the 1908 vintage sticks in my mind and respectful memory. He loved country sports and passed on this love to us his sons. At the age of six or seven I used to look forward eagerly to watching him fly-fishing for trout in the brook, always standing close up behind him so that his fly did not catch me on the backward cast. At ten I had my first fly-rod, at fourteen my first gun, a 16-bore. My father was the best shot at partridges and pheasants I have ever seen. He was also a J.P. and a County Councillor of Herefordshire, later to become County Alderman. He was Chairman of Bromyard Rural District Council for twenty-one years, and on retirement was presented by the members and officers of the Council with an oak chair made by local craftsmen. It stands now in our hall at Dial House. Of these activities of my father I as a schoolboy, and even while at University, knew little or nothing.

He employed a staff of three estate men for maintenance etc., two farm men and four gardeners under a head gardener. One of the farm men was waggoner, and looked after the two shire horses, called Dragon and Boxer. Their job was to do all the timber hauling out of the woods, as well as the ploughing and cultivating: there were no tractors then. The estate and farm worked together sawing up timber on a circular saw driven by a continuous belt powered by an engine fuelled by paraffin. They also worked together at corn threshing time. It took about eight people to man the threshing machine. (In my time we needed at least one outside man to make up the number.) The corn was cut by a reaper and binder – combines had not been invented. When tractors came in, we converted the binder to tractor-drawn, and carried on with it for several seasons.

The hay was cut by a mower with reciprocating knives, turned by hand with a pitchfork till dry, and pitched up onto a wagon moving slowly along the rows by men on each side. On the wagon stood two men, one at each end, also with forks. Their job was to tease out the hay as it arrived and pack it up level on the bed of the wagon, while themselves keeping their feet on top of it. Then they roped the whole load and took it to the rick where it was unloaded and the rick itself was built up to a height of perhaps fifteen to twenty feet – by hand, of course, there were no bales in those days. When bales did come in, I remember old Tom, one of our last farm workers from an older generation, saying that he felt sure bales of hay could never be as sweet as a 'keech' of loose hay, left loose. The bales were too compressed, he felt.

There was no spraying of crops in those days. Most years we had too many thistles in the corn. The accepted way of getting rid of them was to have a man walk up and down the rows with a 'thistle bodger' – a narrow push-hoe with a blade about two inches wide which you poked into each individual thistle just below ground level. I had a taste of thistle bodging in those early years. People like old Tom did it uncomplainingly for days on end. It was a sweet relief when spraying came in.

Agricultural wages were then about thirty shillings a week, or £1.50 in today's terms. Farm rents were at a maximum of £2.00 per acre per year.

The estate men's work was practically all maintenance. They fenced round every wood with a solid timber and wire fence. The timber, steeped in creosote by the 'hot and cold' method, was reckoned to last forty years – some of it is still good today after sixty. There was digging of drains, laying of concrete round farm yards, endless replacing of roof-tiles and battens, endless measures to cure and prevent damp in farmers' living-rooms and bedrooms. There were then perhaps forty dwellings on the estate, including 'tied cottages' which paid no rent. Very few tenants would tell you what needed doing; they preferred to wait till my father visited them. He did this steadily year in year out. 'I got round the Captain to build me a pigscot,' in the words of one tenant, sums up the give and take spirit which I think prevailed.

My father's accounts showed that his income from rents just

covered his expenditure on maintenance by about £150 a year. I don't think he ever took any money out of the estate for his personal use, in terms of salary or anything else. On the farm he regularly made a loss of a few hundred pounds, which could be set against income tax. His income to live on was practically all from shares in Hill, Evans and Co. Originally founded by his great grandfather, it was now a public company. He was a director and for many years, up to his death in 1958, chairman of the Company.

Just occasionally he would do something really striking on the estate. An example was his rehabilitation of Lower Poswick, a beautiful black-and-white half-timbered farmhouse some three hundred years old which had fallen into disuse, and was barely visible behind a mass of briars, nettles and old apple trees fallen down. He cleared the rubbish, cleaned it up, made it habitable, and then offered it with some ninety acres of land as a viable farm to a new tenant, taking the ninety acres off another farm whose tenant had just died and which my father thought was unnecessarily large. It was a case, to him, of getting more people properly settled on the land.

Another example was when he drained our lake in 1931 because the retaining wall at the sluice end needed repair. The water was eighteen feet deep. I cannot remember how thick the concrete was which replaced the bricks, or how our men got it to the site. What I do remember is my brother John standing at the bottom of the scaffolding by the exit-pipe trying his hand at spearing eels with an eel-spear as they went down the outflow pipe with the receding water.

As regards the woods, they were full of growing, semi-mature oak. My father kept saying to me time and time again 'That timber may be useful to you sometime, Edward.' How right he was.

To a small extent, the estate provided a 'farming ladder' up which people could climb to better things. My father gave Bob, our waggoner, the tenancy of one of our smaller farms. A good price for cherries in his first year helped him to pay the rent and ingoing expenses. Bob stayed on that farm till he died. His love of horses remained with him, and in his later years he trained a point-to-pointer and could be seen exercising him through the village, both horse and rider smartly turned out. One of his sons is tenant today of a larger farm. He became for several years chairman of the Parish Council, and a member of the Rural District Council. This son lost his wife to an illness while their large family were still growing up. Knowing she was going, she called each of the children in to her in turn and gave them her particular thought for what they might be. Another son, conscripted into the army early in World War II, became an officer in the Kings Shropshire Light Infantry, lost a leg, and came home after the war to a great welcoming reception in the village hall. He is now just retired after many years as Secretary of the Worcestershire branch of the N.F.U.

This kind of 'giving people a chance' was essentially a bit like the 'sustainable development' theme of the present day. The landlord tenant system was a stable framework in which it could happen. Provided, of course, the landlord had some money somewhere.

When my parents moved into Whitbourne Hall in 1910, they brought with them my two sisters Gwen (aged four) and Rozi (aged two). I was born at the Hall later in that year, followed in 1912 by my brother John. The four of us, Gwen, Rozi (Rosalind), Edward and John, grew up happily there until it was time for us to go to school. My father and mother took it for granted, I think, that all their children, boys and girls, should go to boarding school for their education. It never occurred to us that we might have gone to the village school.

At any rate I turned up at the Wells House, Malvern Wells, in September 1918, at the age of eight. I was told its way of life was modelled on the Scottish public school, Loretto. We went everywhere, winter and summer, in shirts open at the neck and shorts, with a sweater in winter. For the first couple of days at school I did not understand how to adjust the side buttons of my new white shorts. I followed a lively walking party at a distance, for over a mile keeping my hands in my pockets to keep my trousers up. Someone in the dormitory showed me how, and that was that.

One Sunday in my first term my mother came to take me out. My mother had prepared me for school, starting us all off on reading, writing and arithmetic at miniature school desks. For the last two weeks or so at home she made a point of talking to me by herself, mainly at bath times when I was temporarily 'promoted' from the nursery bathroom to my parents' bathroom, and introduced to the rubber sponge which I was to take to school with me. I was looking forward eagerly to seeing her again. I had understood that she was to take me out after chapel, where she was sitting at the back. But I had not been told when, so when all we boys streamed out of chapel first to go on the regulation walk along the hills, I could not somehow face being different and went along with them. As soon as we got back I was summoned to the head's study and to my great relief my mother was there waiting for me. She has never gone on record as to what her feelings were. At any rate she took me to a hotel in Malvern for lunch. The lunch happened to be fish, which I compared very unfavourably with the beef I knew we could have had at home. It was all a bit awkward. The sudden change back to my mother, from a month's learning to look after myself, had been too much for me.

However, it did not last. School suited me, and after two years I had made a reasonable start at both work and games.

E.P. Frederick, the headmaster, was a stoutly built man, well on in his sixties. We started the day, the whole school together, with prayers and a hymn, followed by 'Double'. Double was to me one of the times when I absorbed most; Freddie would discourse in a conversational way on any subject that came to his mind. He would talk about the virtues of cabbage, or of cold water; of the bad habit some of us had of rolling rocks down the Malvern Hills; occasionally of outside things like our victories in the war, or the engagement of his daughter Grace to an old Wells House boy. Very occasionally he would administer a public beating to a boy for some misdemeanour. (I was once the boy caned.) One of Freddie's guiding principles was 'trust the boys'. Any boy at any time could come and see him in his study. It was a rule that you did not knock, you walked straight in and made your point. You could also come in without permission and just sit or read quietly. Not many people used this privilege, but I never heard of anyone abusing it. Freddie never preached to us, except in chapel once a term. Then his sermons could be very moving. The general atmosphere of the school was cheerful and relaxed, yet quite spartan.

The masters, of course, played a part in this, led by the deputy head, A.M. Paterson – 'Dander' to us. Dander was an elderly Scot with a reputation for great athletic feats in his youth. He wrote the school plays and composed the lyrics and set them to music. *Alcestis* was a memorable one, which all of us loved who took part in it.

Then there was E.A.D. White, History and Geography. 'Whito' was a formidable figure, carrying with him the ever-present threat of a few strokes from his slipper. His method of teaching history was to read out his longhand notes of various kings' reigns to us. I was miles away once in the middle of one of his lessons, when he suddenly stopped and asked me what he had just said. I goggled at him blankly. 'Well, dearie', he said, 'I'm, afraid you'll have to have one or two smacks.' So I bent down and received ten strokes with the slipper plus three small taps to round it off, which I always proudly chalked up as a record. Thirteen strokes from Whito!

There was also C.W. Bourne (Stately Bourne, or 'Chris Wig'). He stood out as the first person to teach us how to play strokes at cricket. He made you stand with raised bat, left elbow forward, and taught us how to do a proper off drive. He was in charge of the 'second game' and a true talent spotter among us boys. One boy, Peter Phelps, who came to the school at the late age of eleven, made 134 in his first innings under C.W.B., and was immediately promoted to the 'first game'. Later on, he played an occasional innings for Worcestershire. Casper and Charlesworth ('Charlie') were two popular games masters. Casper, ex-Durham University, was in charge of rugger. After our first game in the 1922 season he surprised me by saying 'Well played, Evans. First game of rugby I've seen you play.' He had seen me play the year before, but then I was having a certain lapse of conduct and confidence and had lost my previous place in the XV. Now I took heart and regained it. Rugger was a game I loved, and cricket second, though I enjoyed all games and sport. Whito also made an interesting point to me after watching the kicking competition. I had expected, and perhaps been expected, to win this, but the ball would not go where I meant it to; I got quite angry and it showed. Next day Whito asked me 'Have you ever seen anybody get rattled?' 'No, I don't think so, Sir,' I replied, 'I did, yesterday, down on the field,' he said, and he gave me a knowing grin. I took the point. It was a lesson, at any rate, in self-control. Later on, after I had been head boy for three terms and thought I had developed a pretty thick skin, Whito scored another bullseye. Wishing me well as I was leaving the school, he said: 'There is only one thing I am afraid of for you.' 'What's that, Sir?' 'That you won't have enough to say for yourself.' I felt in Whito the perceptiveness of a friend.

Fighting between boys was fairly common. The accepted way of handling it was that it had to take place in the bootroom only, and some senior boy or boys (I think) had to be present to see fair play. If you were challenged to a 'free fight' it was a point of honour to accept. Once a rather bigger boy made some rude remark about me, which I rejected in the presence of several others, and the next thing I knew was a cry of 'free fight! Evans against Blake.' A crowd gathered in the bootroom, with most of those present urging me on to teach Blake a lesson. I was inwardly afraid of him. I could not box; he could. However, perhaps with the support of the populace I could manage a lucky blow or two. So we started in (no rounds, just 'fight on'). He dotted me one or two in the face. At last I connected with a terrific swing from my right. It surprised him, and he took a step backward and hit a ledge in the bootroom floor and went down on his backside. Loud cheers! Blake had given in and I had won! It made not the slightest difference to our relationship, which was matter of fact and quite cordial.

There was a family at school called Prescott. A.E.C. Prescott (Tony), the eldest, was a hero of mine in my first term. He broke his collar-bone at rugger, and with his arm in a sling got me to tie up his bootlaces, talking rugger to me and so getting me keen on it. Later he played for Harlequins. Jack, the second brother, was also quite a friend. The Prescotts kept a goat, and I remember watching a tremendous 'free fight' between Jack and Christopher his younger brother – not in the bootroom this time but out on the path by the shed – over something to do with this goat. But it was Christopher who was the nearest to me in age. We had jokes together in the sickroom when I was in bed from over-indulgence in rabbit-food – I kept first rabbits and later ferrets at the school, though I was more interested in collecting birds' eggs. Prescott and another boy and I used to visit a farmer's son called Jason Dunn in Malvern Wells. It was a sort of open invitation, but usually the Dunns were not there and we would amuse ourselves in their yard. Once we caught a duck and launched it from a loft window to see how it would fly. It flew rather ponderously onto a lower roof across the yard, and looked stuck there. I went to rescue it up a water pipe, but fell into the water-butt and got soaked. There was no time to change, and I sat through the whole of afternoon school in my wet clothes without anyone noticing. Christopher Prescott was the sort of boy with whom you did that sort of thing. Known as 'Christo' by the P.T. instructor Sergeant Major Beeden, he was a merry boy, and a 'card'. I remember once Christopher and I were changing for a gym competition in one of the dormitories. When it was about time to go down, he sort of dawdled about, and appeared to be waiting for me to go. Finally he lost patience, said 'Excuse me' and knelt down by a bed and prayed. I knew at once that he was praying to win the gym competition (and he did). Years afterwards we remembered that incident together.

I mentioned that my mother had 'prepared' me for school. I got the impression from her that Jesus was a sort of special friend, invisible but always present, to whom I could turn if I was afraid or had a problem about anything. At home we were expected to say our prayers before going to bed. This fitted in well with Wells House, where it was the 'done thing' for each boy at bedtime to shout out 'Silence please' when he wanted to pray, and to pray kneeling at his bed for perhaps a minute or less with no one interrupting. This practice was taken for granted by all boys. I don't remember it ever being called in question or raised as an issue during my whole six years at the school.

My mother and father were both regular churchgoers, and we grew up to accept the routine. Sometimes on Sundays Mother used to read us books of religious instruction. One which stands out in my memory was about a young Christian knight called Fides who had to overcome the giants of Sloth, Selfishness, Hate and Pride. I was clear from then on that Pride was the worst of all sins. My mother employed a full-time nanny to look after her four children, Gwen, Rozi, myself and John, who arrived at two-yearly intervals before World War I. Robin, Mary and Pat followed after my father's return from the war. 'Nursie', as she was called, looked after us all and lived on with my parents in her own room in the nursery wing of the house until her death in 1939.

Mother radiated warmth and fun and happiness. She had the reputation of having been a daring rider (side-saddle) to hounds. Now in her later thirties she played plenty of games with us, both indoors and out. One Easter holidays she and my father played non-stop tennis with us after tea practically every evening. At the same time she was quite a disciplinarian. She beat me once with a long-handled brush from the store-room drawer for calling Rozi a liar. And when some cheeky village boys flung the cap of one of them under our car as she was driving it away from the church, she stopped the car, got out of it and gave them a terrific telling off.

Mother picked her moment when we were walking together one holidays and asked me if I was taking my religion seriously. She added that some people missed such a lot by not doing this. It was not long after this that it was my turn to get confirmed, with six or seven other boys, in Worcester Cathedral. I understood at my confirmation that I was now to be responsible for leading my own Christian life, and could no longer rely on parents and godparents to do it for me. I did take this very seriously for a while. Generally speaking, I seem to have 'taken in' some basic Christian standards during those prep-school years. But my interest in Bible Study can be gauged by the fact that at the end of one term I got 70 or 80 per cent for most main subjects like Latin and Maths, but only 6 per cent Scripture. An exception to this lack of interest was that I did like the singing of hymns and anthems in the school chapel. One boy in particular, Budge Jackson, had a very true treble voice, and his singing of 'As pants the hart for cooling streams' and 'Oh for the wings of a dove' introduced me to a world of religious music. The effect was enhanced by the fact that Budge was an expert rugger player, and one of the most likeable and generally popular boys in the school.

What part the beatings played in all this, I am not sure. They seemed to be woven into the tapestry of life. Certainly as head boy for the last four terms I gave plenty of beatings myself. And I won a reputation for firmness and fairness. I even beat my own brother John on one occasion. John was two years younger than me. In the holidays we were pretty close, but at school we kept our distance as seemed natural.

I have already mentioned what Whito said to me on saying goodbye on my leaving the Wells House. We also had to have a leaving interview with Freddie, whom I had been seeing every day for the last year. It was very brief. Practically all he said was: 'Well, old man, the one thing that matters is: be a Christian.' It was the only time he had personally put this challenge to me.

Such were my years at prep school. They were on the whole happy years. Freddie wrote in my report: 'His responsibilities are making a man of him.'

At Cheltenham, my public school, I had a very similar career to that at the Wells House; a good start, a rough patch in the middle, and finishing up as senior prefect, also just making the rugby XV. It was hard work. We had two hours' 'prep' in House every evening, and often got up early to catch up with other school work in our studies before breakfast. Again, I owed a lot to the friendship and encouragement of masters, such as G.M. Paterson, form master of Lower VI Classical, John Gurney my housemaster at Hazelwell, and the headmaster, H.H. Hardy.

H.H. Hardy was a commanding figure. I remember him sitting in his seat by the door while we all filed out of daily chapel, his eagle eye falling momentarily on each boy. He was memorising each of the six hundred boys as they went out. The process seemed to continue on Sundays, when people were standing around after chapel outside. Hardy's figure stood out as he beckoned to someone he wanted to talk to – boy, old boy, master or parent. It seemed to me all got the same treatment. And most of them moved smartly towards the headmaster, rather than wait for him to come to them!

Myself, aged 17, and friend, at the Duke of York's camp, New Romney, in 1927. The Duke of York, later to become H.M. King George VI, initiated these camps as a move towards breaking down class barriers, and always put in a visit himself, participating in the games and concerts. The 1927 camp had 400 boys, 200 from public school and 200 from industry. I enjoyed this camp. We let off plenty of steam in the concerts, and no one seemed to worry about class

A shooting party with our cousins at Harpley House

Running with the ball. Corpus Christi College v. University College, Oxford 1932. Paddy Herbert is on the extreme left of Corpus side. In the middle in a scrum-cap is R.R. MacGibbon, our only blue of the year; next to him the scrum half, Johnnie Creek, who has just passed me the ball

As his Senior Prefect for two terms (spring and summer 1929) I was specially privileged to see another side of him. In the spring term he was scheduled to come over once a week on Thursday mornings and take us in Upper VI Classical for one of our routine lessons. The first Thursday he forgot and never came, so I did my best to choose some work without him. Afterwards I told him of this, and he said: 'Why didn't you come and fetch me? If I forget again, you are to come over to College House and fetch me straight away.' He forgot again, and I walked over to College House and reminded him. It happened again, every week of the term. About half-way through the term, the weather froze solid, and it was impossible to play any games. On my routine visit to Hardy to remind him to come and teach Upper VI, he said: 'Aren't you going to ask me for a whole holiday for the College to go skating on Pittville?'

'No Sir,' I replied. 'But it would not be a bad idea.'

'Well, I cannot announce a special holiday without the support of the Senior Prefect.'

'Oh well, in that case, Sir, may we have a special holiday to go skating on Pittville?'

Hardy announced the holiday, making it sound as if I had pestered him for it, and of course putting up my popularity several notches at a stroke.

CHAPTER II
The quiet revolution

GOING UP TO OXFORD, after two quite exacting stints at school, I remember wondering how on earth I would make out with no one about to tell me what to do next! However that soon passed, and at the age of twenty-two, having finished 'Mods', I found myself in a comparatively relaxed period before serious work for 'Greats' had to begin.

It was 1932, the year before Hitler came to power in Germany. The world financial system was recovering after its collapse in 1929. Unemployment was rising. Noel Coward was popular. Agriculture was at a standstill.

My sister Rozi had just left Oxford with a degree in French. Gwen, the eldest of the family, had been to finishing school in Paris. I was at Corpus Christi College Oxford, in my third year, John was at Oxford in another college in his first year. Robin, Mary and Pat were at school. I was spending a good part of the vacations hunting, shooting, fishing and working for 'Greats' – and also some of the long vac. exploring in Poland, Germany and France. At times I would go for walks with my mother and try to explain to her my 'doubts' about religion.

Some time about now the word went round that a fellow called Kit Prescott had turned up at Worcester College and had 'got religion' and become what was then known as a 'Buchmanite'. My friends and I pictured Buchmanites as people who asked you if you were saved, were extreme and simplistic in their Christianity, and not very nice to know. We avoided them. I remember being asked my opinion of them once by a clergyman and my reply had been: 'I think they are fundamentally self-centred!' His comment was 'I think you have just about summed it up.' I had not met any of them at that time. All the same I had a sneaking admiration for their guts, and I did not want to avoid Kit, who, I had found out, was none other than the Christopher Prescott I had known ten years earlier at the Wells House. So when he suggested a walk up Boars Hill one Sunday afternoon, I brought along Paddy Herbert, one of my year at Corpus who had also been at the Wells House. Paddy and I enjoyed that walk with Kit. We teased him a bit but we laughed a lot. We could see he was genuine, and he was still fun to be with. So when he invited me to a meeting of the Oxford Group at Oriel College, I agreed to come and have a look.

It was a completely undergraduate affair, sitting around informally in someone's rooms. I remember two people in particular. One was Harry Addison, a man of working-class origins who spoke of how his parents had sacrificed to get him to Oxford, and gave a very humble and passionate account of how he was facing the four moral standards of absolute honesty, absolute purity, absolute unselfishness and absolute love in his life. The other was Francis Goulding, a public school man like myself, who described how he had tried to be the self-sufficient man, but had only found freedom from the need to retain other people's good opinion when he stopped seeking it and gave his life to Christ. After the meeting I asked: 'Would anyone like to try and convert me?' Francis said: 'Yes, I would.' We went out and sat on a bench in the quad. Francis said 'Let's have a quiet time.' We were quiet. Francis said: 'What did you get?' I said: 'Well, I was thinking about those four standards, honesty etc.' He said: 'I had three things about you: self-consciousness, impurity, and futility.' I thought: 'Well! Self-consciousness no doubt and impurity certainly up to a point, but futility – never!' Aloud I said, 'Well, I must be going now. Thank you for the talk. I'll think about it.' And out I went. Next morning, there was a knock on my door and Francis appeared: 'Good morning. Would you like to come to tea this afternoon and meet some more of my friends?' 'I'd rather be left alone,' I replied, only half turning round in my desk chair. He went. And so ended my first encounter with the Oxford Group. It might very well have been my last.

But there were other influences at work. The first of these was 'Greats'. Greats at Oxford took five terms, or the best part of two years. The subjects were history of the Greek and Roman civilisations, and philosophy from Plato and Aristotle to the present day. I loved philosophy. My tutor, W.F.R. (Frank) Hardie, who later became President of Corpus and an honoured figure in the Senior Common Room – he died in 1991 – helped me enormously to develop my own ideas. His method of teaching was usually to get his pupils to read aloud to him their latest essay. He would listen very carefully, expose any flaws in our argument, and suggest lines of thought which seemed tenable. At any rate, subjects like logic, metaphysics and the theory of knowledge lit up for me at times, especially Plato and Immanuel Kant. In the course of all this, I got a fairly thorough grounding in the intellectual arguments for and against the existence of God. I think there were twelve for and thirteen against – a very close thing! I am bound to say that even then I sometimes thought this elaborate study of God by the mind of man was a bit ridiculous. As God said to Job, 'Where were you when I laid the foundations of the earth?' Still I persisted, and where a theory of one of the philosophers seemed to square with my traditional picture of life here and life hereafter (such as in Kant's *Critique of Pure Reason*), I was excited. I really believed I could penetrate through philosophy to reality with God.

Another influence sprang from events at home. We had two or three visits from a farmer turned Anglo-Catholic priest, whom my mother had found. She thought he might help me. I liked Gilbert Shaw: he was an ascetic type, given to wearing a cassock at dinner when the rest of us were in dinner jackets or evening dress. But he smoked a pipe and knew how to converse in country society. And he could talk about philosophy. He was going to a conference of young clergy at Glasshampton in Worcestershire that summer, and he asked me if I would like to come. Our host, Father William of Glasshampton, was a Benedictine monk who had been a wine merchant as a young man, then got ordained, and had finally joined the Benedictine Order and received permission to come and live in the old stables at Glasshampton as a solitary. He allowed me to come amongst this small intimate bunch of Anglo-Catholics – six or seven Englishmen and one American – and see how I got on. I left that place with a deep sense of the wonder of God the Creator of all things. I even thought that I might have to become a parson. As a follow-up, I was invited for a short spell in a parish in City Road, Islington. I took some of my 'Greats' work with me, and stayed in the clergy house, making friends with the children in the street. I even took some of them for a ride in a train, and was reprimanded by the rector afterwards for making an ass of myself. Back to Whitbourne in time for the partridge shooting!

One of the things that time with the clergy did for me was to make me want to go the whole way with God. Probably also it helped me to digest the truths I had heard at my first meeting with the Oxford Group six months before. Anyway I went up to Oxford for my last year feeling ready for anything. Almost at once I was invited to another Oxford Group meeting and accepted happily. At it I felt challenged to try having a 'quiet time' to start my day. I tried it, really asking God to speak to me. Two thoughts came. The first was to stop smoking, and the second was to shave off my moustache. Well, I ask you! I spent an uncomfortable few hours asking myself if such trivial and non-moral thoughts could possibly come from God. Finally I realised that I had promised God I would do what He said, and that most of my objections were due to fear of what my friends would think; and that if they were trivial things, at least they would not hurt anybody, so why not get on with it? So I did. I quite enjoyed it when a friend asked me in the J.C.R., having been startled by my naked upper lip: 'Evvy, was it guidance?' A few days later I described what had happened to me in a light-hearted and, I thought, humorous way at an open meeting in Corpus. The editor of *Isis* was present and wrote a vitriolic article about the meeting, ending with the memorable sentence, 'As for those pimply introverts the Buchmanites themselves, we shall continue to ignore them.' However, I was utterly and completely delivered from the fear of what people would think. (In those days, by the way, smoking was fashionable. We did not foresee at all the times like today when it is almost outlawed).

Some time in my last year I was elected to the 'Wasps', the elite Corpus dining club, which was a pleasant surprise. Also I made many more friends outside the College than before. But the main thing was preparation for 'Greats'. The exams duly took place in the early summer. I felt I had done well, and was confident that I should get a Second. But when I went in to the *viva* a few days later, I was confronted by a body of friendly and faintly amused dons, who asked me two exotic history questions and seemed quite pleased when I could not answer them. 'Well, Mr Evans,' said one, 'your attention was given to more important things.' I smiled at him happily, and was dismissed after what must have been one of the shortest *vivas* on record. When the results came out I found I had got a First, with an alpha of sorts for every paper connected with philosophy. It was the sort of result which opened up the possibility of an academic career, something which I had never considered. A telegram came from Frank Hardie in his best laconic style. He had evidently not expected me to get a First at all. The telegram read: 'Congratulations and recantations.'

At home meanwhile, I had been trying to tell the family about my new experience with the Oxford Group. Rozi stood smoking a cigarette with one elbow on the mantelpiece and said coolly: 'It's immaturity. You'll grow out of it.' My mother was pleased I had changed, but I think hoped that Gilbert Shaw would help me to get over the Oxford Group. My father, whom I introduced to some of the team in Oxford, was relieved to find them more practical than emotional. Now in that summer of 1933 something quite important happened. My parents, Rozi, John and I all accepted an invitation to the annual 'house-party' of the Oxford Group at Oxford. Actually it was a three-week conference, attended by several hundred people, with much of the staff work being done by undergraduates (many of whom I knew). I had been wondering how the family would take it. I soon knew. Rozi came up to me one evening with Dorothy Prescott, Kit's sister, and said: 'Dorothy and I have been out on the river, and I have given my life to Jesus Christ. I am sorry I was so snooty with you about the Group.' She looked radiantly happy. I felt embarrassed, and murmured something like 'Thank God.' Dorothy said cheerfully: 'Don't be pious, Edward.' And there the encounter ended. Rozi took action immediately: she sent a telegram to Gwen, who at that time was training to be the Church of England's first woman missionary to Liberia. Gwen promptly came to Oxford the following weekend to see what was going on. My mother started intensively lobbying all the clergy she could find at the house-party, to see if they thought the Group was 'sound'. Apparently they all did. But one or two things that were said stung and challenged her. She found herself becoming quite angry with the Group. This, she thought, must be wrong for her, a devoted Christian and churchwoman, so she went home alone to think things over. She came back and told us that God had made it clear to her that these people in the Group were living a quality of life far beyond anything she had known before, and she must change too. She told me that she had wanted me to change, but in her way, not in God's way. Gwen meanwhile had been profoundly shaken by the difference in Rozi. She searched her heart as to why she had not been able to bring about in Rozi what the Group appeared to have accomplished in a few short days. She became honest about a painful love affair, now past but not forgotten, in which she had renounced her man for the sake of her conviction and her church. This gave her a liberation and a lightness of spirit, and also, progressively, perspective about her calling to be a missionary.

After the conference proper, Gwen, Rozi and I were invited to stay on for a few days of 'team training'. Frank Buchman, whom I had hardly seen before and never heard speak, led the opening meeting.

His first words to the perhaps two hundred of us present were: 'We're going to put a new car on the market. What shall we call it?' Various suggestions, from which Frank chose 'Revival'. 'What qualities will it have?' A hilarious few minutes followed, with various suggestions from the floor, including I remember, 'No brakes'. But it got us all thinking. The training we received was basically on how to bring about a revival of Christianity through changed lives. It was how, not whether. I only once spoke personally to Frank during that time. I was wandering along a corridor and he was walking briskly along behind and overtook me. He said 'Hullo.'

'Hullo,' I said.

'How are you getting on here?'

'Not too well.'

'What convicted you?'

'I just have not been doing the job.'

He passed on quietly. That was all. 'Doing the job' was shorthand for changing people, or more fundamentally letting God use you to change people. This was the 'job' I found difficult to grasp. Frank meant 'Convicted of sin' – another strange concept to me at the time, but it was all that he said. Perhaps it was because I looked on Jesus more as a person whose example I had to follow than as a living friend whom I could trust. Certainly I had no conception of how the Holy Spirit, whom He sent, could intervene in the ordinary affairs of men, not just important affairs but the ordinary everyday ones. So I naturally found it difficult to have a regular quiet time in the morning. I remember shedding tears at the difficulty of it – my first tears for a long time. But I persisted. It was a bit like turning again and becoming as a little child. Of course I was still pretty ignorant of human nature, including my own. My mind turns to a wedding I went to recently, at which the best man in his speech referred to the bridegroom, a Magdalen man, as 'the cream of the University – rich and thick'. I thought I qualified as the cream of the University. But I was beginning to realise that in the 'university of life' I was very much a beginner.

Gwen, Rozi and I drove home together. As soon as we arrived, Harry Griffiths, my father's groom, chauffeur, handyman and general foreman, said 'What on earth's happened to Miss Rozi? She's completely different – hardly recognisable.' And he said it to her too. It was not long before he became 'Harry' to us; hitherto it had been 'Griffiths'.

My mother's change was a revelation. She made a point of telling each of us older children what she had been like as a girl and young woman. She became a friend as well as a mother. In fact we all four found each other in quite a new way. My sisters had to me been just a part of my background. Now for the first time I saw them as interesting personalities in their own right. And I began to enjoy their company as comrades in a battle. Only John shut up like a clam in response to my efforts to change him! My father held his counsel and waited a little.

It was about then that I had the conviction to start going to the village pub. This was quite a bold move at that time. My father never went to the pub. He kept his drinks at home. It was unheard of for people in our social circle to go. But I felt the separation from the village and thought it might help to bring us together, so I went. I was dead scared the first time, but after the first minute of silent shock I was received with courtesy. The man who helped me most over this was Bob Jones, our gamekeeper, who was quite naturally one of the few men on the village I had a real contact with. We played billiards together, and had one or two drinks, but I was still painfully shy and never really got going. For one thing, it was a long walk down a mile of drive, after dark, before I got to the pub. The best times were when we walked home via Bob's cottage, and he would treat me to a diatribe on class. He would say: 'What's good for you isn't good for us. Take baths, for instance. We don't have any baths or running water in the house. You do.' Then he would say: 'We need you people because you bring money in. Capital – that's it.' Then he would praise my father. I persuaded him once to come to church with me at 8 a.m. on a Sunday, and he agreed, but when I got to his cottage to pick him up I drew a blank; he evidently was not coming. Not long afterwards I heard that Bob had given up drink for three days as a result of our talks, but people had teased him so unmercifully that he had given in and started again! There is no doubt we became a fertile source of gossip in the village.

Some time about now the question of my career came up. The possibility of being a parson had receded somewhat in my mind. What was more pressing was that I had applied for membership of the Sudan Political Service, having been recommended as a candidate by my former headmaster at Cheltenham, H.H. Hardy. Now I was summoned by them for an interview in London. I told the examining board about my change of direction through the Oxford Group, and they asked me if I would try to convert the natives. I replied that the short answer was yes, though I could not say how. They said: 'Well, your qualifications from school and university are excellent, but in view of what you have told us we think you might run into difficulties.' I did not hear any more from them for some time. But I knew that the Colonial Service was still open to be applied for. The Colonial Service, which I slightly preferred to the Sudan, had about twenty places to offer to an estimated six hundred or so candidates.

Meanwhile, through Kit Prescott, I received an invitation to work full-time with the Oxford Group. It was a total surprise. I had no idea where it would take me. But I knew it was a time of rapid expansion for the Group, and I got the notion that I might be able to do more good by working full-time with them than by filling a place in the Colonial Service when there were so many others ready and willing to take it. Which was I to choose? I went to Father William at Glasshampton to seek his advice. He said, to my astonishment: 'Let's toss up!' adding, when he saw my dismay, 'under guidance, of course!' I was only slightly amused. But I saw that I would have to decide myself. I decided to accept the offer to go full-time.

This, to me, momentous decision, which meant giving up all thought of a career and embarking without salary on an unknown future, did not meet with universal approval from our friends and relatives. There were painful times. My father showed me a letter he had had from a favourite cousin. 'It is bad luck about Edward,' he wrote; 'I myself had a bad period of Socialism at University, but luckily there was a job waiting for me when I left and it saved me.'

My full-time work began with a 'campaign to change London'. About two hundred of us, the vast majority under the age of thirty, converged on the Hotel Metropole in Northumberland Avenue. The Archbishop of Canterbury commissioned us in a solemn service in his private chapel at Lambeth Palace. There was a much bigger commissioning service at St Paul's, attended by thousands, including my father and mother and Bert Prosser our head gardener. There was a meeting at the Mansion House for a selected few. There were meetings in the city. And most mornings there were training meetings for the team. These training meetings were often taken by Loudon Hamilton, an ex-gunner officer of the war, 40-ish, one of the very few older men in our party. He it was who after all the turmoil I had been through taught me afresh to think: 'Out of self into Christ. Through Christ to other people. With other people to a new world order.' He kept emphasising that this was 'Bible Christianity'. One of the greatest sins was 'inferior thinking' – a lack of loving imaginative insight into what a person could become. 'The world is waiting to see what Jesus Christ can do in, by, for and with one person wholly committed to Him.' Those training times in particular began to paint a new picture in my heart and mind.

The nearest I got to 'changing London' was what happened next in East London. The vicar of St Mark's, Victoria Park, had asked Frank Buchman to send him a team who would help to 'change his parish'. I was one of a small group whom Frank selected. He called us together for a short talk before we began. He said: 'Now there is a lot of unemployment down there. You are not to give them any money. Your job is to change people.' Very brief. Off we went, wondering how the dickens it would work out. My team mate, Frank Bygott, and I slept at 4 Wallis Road, the home of the Pooles. Tom Poole was a navvy in a timber yard. He had a wife, a daughter aged fourteen and a son younger. They gave us breakfast, and tea most evenings I think. It was noticeable that apart from bread and butter and tea there was not much to eat or drink. But the Pooles could not have been more hospitable. We had to go to a pump at the bottom of the garden to get water for washing and shaving. It was a freezing, foggy December. We were left to ourselves to operate as we saw fit.

The vicar had fixed a Watch Night service in the church for the evening of 31 December 1933. This was to be the opening gun of our campaign in the parish. Of course we invited the Pooles. Then we felt we should go out into the highways and byways and try and rope in the populace. So Frank and I set off down Wallis Road one evening with no idea what to do. We immediately encountered four men singing raucously round a barrel on the other side of the road. Frank and I stopped and looked at one another. One of us said: 'Are you thinking what I'm thinking?' 'Yes, we ought to go and join them.' So we walked over, and with cheerful abandon started singing with them, until they stopped singing and looked at us. 'Who are you?' said one.

'We're the Oxford Group and we're having a meeting at the church on Sunday evening. Would you like to come?'

'What is the Oxford Group? Is it a fight?' they asked.

After the slightest of pauses, Frank answered 'Yes, it is a fight.'

'All right, we'll come.'

They came. One of them, Bill Robins, came afterwards to several meetings at the church hall as well. One evening he was part of a group whistling and making catcalls. When the meeting was over I went up to this group and said 'Does anyone want to talk about religion?' To my surprise, Bill replied: 'Yes, I do.' I said, 'Let's go into the Church,' and we went in. I put it to him to surrender his life to Jesus Christ. He said 'How do you do that?' I cannot remember exactly what I said but it was to the effect that you just kneel down and do it in your own words, and I would kneel too in support. We knelt. Then Bill got the giggles. I remember saying something like 'I am sure God is laughing with us.' Bill prayed. He gave his life and asked for a fresh start. He was not speaking to me, but direct to God.

We left the church, and Bill went home. He lived with his wife and two young children in one room - no lavatory, no bathroom, no washing facilities. She was a pretty young woman of about twenty-six, but prematurely aged. Next morning George Light, another of the older men on our team whose friendship was a help to me – he was Chairman of the Warwickshire Unemployed – called on the Robinses. Mrs Robins opened the door, recognised George as one of the team, and immediately flung her arms round his neck and kissed him. Bill had come home the night before and apologised for the beatings he had given her. They both did their best to clean up their room, and I was invited in to see it. Bill insisted that I come with him to a dairy where he had worked in Palmers Green for some time and had been in the habit of removing a milk bottle now and then to take home without leave. He wanted to put things right with the manager. The manager appeared less than pleased to see him, and Bill seemed to me a bit incoherent in the way he put things, but he seemed satisfied afterwards that he had managed to do it. Frank Bygott and I started a Bible study group in the front room at 4 Wallis Road for Bill and one or two others, hoping that it would help them grow in the faith.

Those days in East London taught me more about the Holy Spirit and how It works than any experience I had had before. They were a land-mark, or a turning point, or a revolutionary stride on the road. We were only to be there for a matter of weeks before moving on. Bill in due course got a job and moved with his family to Ely. Most of the parish of St Marks, Victoria Park, was laid flat by bombs during the war, including Wallis Road. But one more thing happened at one of those church meetings at St Marks, which I must describe. Hallen Viney, an engineer who had been ordained as a Church of England priest in his thirties, was just closing the meeting when my old friend Gilbert Shaw, who had arrived at the meeting unheralded and unannounced, stood up and said in a loud voice: 'I demand to know:

what is the Oxford Group's attitude to Communism, Pacifism, and War?' No one answered. Hallen continued down the aisle and engaged him I think in quiet talk. Nothing more was said. Father Shaw did not speak to me. And, which disquieted me a bit, I did not see him again.

This incident, coming as it did just after I had been learning what changing people could really mean, seemed to put a rivet into my new perspective on listening to God. Gilbert Shaw's intervention seemed to contrast to a listening Christianity, a Christianity of point of view.

I had one last fling at clinging on to the 'point of view' approach. It came during one of our busy conferences of 'taking stock'. I had the idea that it might be right for me to try for a junior Demyship at Magdalen which would enable me to continue and develop my thoughts on the philosophy of the Christian religion. I think Frank Hardie had suggested it as a way into the academic world, and he thought on my Greats results I had a possible chance of getting one. So I asked three people to help me decide. One was my sister Rozi, who knew me and knew Oxford, having been at St Hilda's College. Another was Basil Yates, a fellow full-time worker, who had been a tutor in Moral Philosophy at Liverpool University. The third was Frank Buchman. After I had outlined my idea, Frank said: 'I feel that if you do this, you are to go in there to change people. No discussion.' We were quiet together. I cannot remember what Basil had. Frank had: 'Edward decide on the basis of principle advanced.' I had, not to go on with it. Rozi had, with great conviction, 'You have too much to learn yet about life-changing. Do not do it.' It was all settled in twenty minutes. I never doubted the rightness of the decision.

But I went back to Oxford all the same, on my own initiative, as part of my full-time work. And I think it was at that time that I first paid a courtesy call on the new President of Corpus, Sir Richard Livingstone. He later came at my invitation to a meeting of the Oxford Group's summer house-party at Lady Margaret Hall, where he met Frank Buchman. Thanking me after the meeting, he said how impressed he had been by the sincerity of the speakers, and that he would never be a party to the negative talk about the Group which sometimes went on.

After that, it was Northern Ireland with the main body, followed by some weeks in Worcestershire with a team based on the rectory at Bredon. This team conceived the idea of a house-party at Malvern, and I remember our jubilation when we got the go-ahead from the Group's policy-making body with whom we had checked the idea. I was entrusted with some of the preliminary arrangements, such as booking accommodation in hotels, which involved explaining how the Group lived financially and asking for special all-in rates. Then I was entrusted to visit the Bishop of Worcester and tell him about the house-party and ask him if he would be patron of it. The Bishop, Dr Perowne, received me warmly and sent a message which we put on the invitation. As the time drew near for the house-party to begin – it was exactly a year after our entry into East London – I started consulting a few colleagues about who they thought ought to lead it. They all said they had assumed I would be leading it. So I did. And it was quite a lesson in leadership. About one hundred of the team met every morning with me as chairman to plan the day. We met for an hour at 7.30 a.m. before breakfast. I had to learn how to draw out from those hundred people what the theme for the day should be, who should speak, who should take charge of the various smaller meetings, and so on.

Next Frank Buchman took 250 of us to Denmark. This was the most international team I had yet travelled with. It was also the one most consciously aimed at making an impact on a whole nation. Frank decided to open his campaign with a series of big public meetings in the Oddfellow Palaets, Copenhagen's largest available hall. One immediate result was that we got sensational press coverage, most of it favourable. Yet all the time the emphasis remained on changing people one by one, and then training people to be life-changers themselves. This key work was done outside the big meetings, which were more an effort to shift public opinion through the evidence of changed lives which could be offered at them. My personal memories include being sent with George Daneel of South Africa to address the masters and boys of Soro Academy, the Eton of Denmark, during their Sunday service in the school chapel. I carried away a picture of the beauty and dignity of Soro, its buildings and its green playing fields in the early summer. Also of one of the masters there, Juul Mortensen, who gave me hospitality and took a lot of interest in our work. Then an afternoon on the estate of Count Daneskiold-Samso, where I met the Head Forester, Svend Kindt. Svend invited me in to meet his wife and their large, mostly teenage, family of boys and girls. The boys and I had a wild time kicking a football about on the lawn, I remember. We became friends, and Svend met others on the team and was a prominent speaker at our Whitsun house-party at Elsinore.

Another odd memory of Denmark stays with me. Quite by chance, in the middle of a busy time with the press and meetings on strategy, I found myself standing in a hotel lounge and Frank Buchman came into the room quite alone, obviously wondering what to do next. We both stood there quite companionably, without speaking. Then Frank murmured: 'H'm. Yes. Edward. You're the country.' I took it he meant that my ultimate sphere of work would be in the country. I sensed that he thought for me as he did for each of the other 250 members of his team.

But there were ten thousand people to hear Frank speak in Kronborg Castle, Elsinore, on Whit Sunday afternoon. He said: 'We accept as a commonplace a man's voice carried by radio to the uttermost parts of the earth. Why not the voice of the living God as an active, creative force in every home, every business, every parliament? Men listen to a king when he speaks to his people over the air. Why not to the King of Kings? He is alive, and constantly broadcasting.' Ten thousand seemed an awfully big crowd to most of us at the time. But next year at the British Industries Fair, Birmingham, there were twenty-five thousand. Many of them came in special trains from the far corners of the British Isles.

During the year immediately following that first Oxford house-party, my father's attitude of caution about the Group gave way to one first of reassurance, and then of active interest in some people whom he met in it. One was a South African, an Afrikaaner who had kept the blood-stained shirt of an uncle killed in the Boer War just as it was in a cupboard, to keep alive his hatred of the British. Another was a Sussex poultry farmer, John Meekings, who had been wounded in World War I, and was one of my father's own generation. John Meekings helped my father to accept that he could change too. Pa came up to me, flipped me on the arm and said 'I've decided to come in.' He said that he and John had thought that they had already 'faced their Gethsemane', and could not stomach another major change in their lives, but had decided that they must. He also confessed that he had been guilty of 'leaving religion to the parson'. He had been Rector's Churchwarden for years in our church at Whitbourne, and this continued for many years more. But he felt he had not been pulling his weight on the spiritual side.

Pa's decision did not prevent him from continuing to express resistance to our propensity as a family to have 'crocks' to stay with us at Whitbourne. 'Damn it,' he would say, 'You're turning it into some sort of rest home for invalids.' Sometimes he was right. There

Some of the group on board the S.S. Europa *bound for the U.S.A. in May 1936. They include: on extreme left; George Light. Seated, back row left; Jimmy Watt, former Communist from Fife. Seated, back row middle; Dr Duys, Dutch M.P. Behind him, in centre, Loudon Hamilton and his wife Beatrice (seated, centre). With striped tie, Kit Prescott, and extreme right, Frank Evans*

were one or two people who should never have been invited! When occasionally our openheartedness was allied with gullibility, it led us astray. But he helped us to learn a bit more worldly wisdom, and the phase did not last long.

In January 1935 he addressed a large assembly in the Winter Gardens at Malvern on his commitment as a landowner to stewardship of the land. In 1936 he accepted with my mother an invitation from Frank Buchman to attend the first North American Assembly of the Oxford Group in Stockbridge, Massachusetts. Rozi and I also went. On the *S.S. Europa* on the way over we were busy packing and licking envelopes for posting on arrival in New York. My father took a full part in doing this sort of donkey work. At the Assembly he heard Frank Buchman in action in his own country, and would often go out of a meeting chuckling at something Frank had said. He certainly took to him. Later, in I think about May 1938, he was a speaker at a memorable meeting in Whitbourne school, where local people spoke of their change. About 120 came. 'The Captain' spoke sensitively and genuinely to the men of his generation, and was well

Men with varied commitments to agriculture who met at Whitbourne in August 1936. They included a sausage manufacturer and a land agent – they also included Edward Hill, N.R. (Tandy) Wigan and David Bowerman. Years later David visited us again when he was President of the Horticultural Marketing Council

received. The main speaker was Tod Sloan of East London, a watchmaker and former agitator, whom some of us had got to know.

My brother John went into the Burma Frontier Service. He left home in November 1935, and never came back. He was on reconnaissance deep into Siam (present-day Thailand), when the Japanese broke through into Burma. He found his way alone, on foot, to the Chinese 93rd Division on the border of Burma and Siam. From there he raised guerillas from within Burma known as the 'Lahu Levies', and led them on forays into Japanese-held territory. He was killed on one of these forays. John's political superior officer wrote afterwards to my parents speaking highly of his guts, and saying he had marked him out for an important position if he had survived. I was always glad that John and I with our two younger brothers Robin and Pat had had a hilarious few days together fishing in Wales, only weeks before he left for Burma. Our cook Clara announced that she thought he was the only one in the family with any sense! My father also confided to a friend that he would have loved a job like John's if he hadn't felt bound to take on the family affairs at home.

As for me, the 1930s were a time of revolutionary change. My forays short and long into other parts of Britain, Europe and the United States taught me something about how a person's personal life can affect national issues. I felt at one with my team mates and that I was sharing in the fellowship of the pioneers.

While the momentum was at its height I fell in love with Erica Conner. Erica was the daughter of Col. William Conner R.E., an Irish Protestant who, after retirement, had gone back to live in his family home in Co. Cork and married Maye Leakey, his English wife, one of a large and enterprising family. The Irish 'troubles' caught up with their lovely countryside – and extremely happy life – in 1922, when Erica was eleven, and they had to leave Ireland hurriedly with the neighbours' homes burning all round. They came to Malvern, and after her father's death, her mother moved to Twyning with Erica and her three brothers. The Evanses and Conners had begun to know one another during the period leading up to the Malvern House Party.

It was three or four months after this that I proposed to her. She was quite unprepared for it and she refused me firmly. Knowing one another socially was one thing, but this was different! I wanted her, and quickly. I had no experience of sex, no previous girl-friends, and rather looked on courtship as a quaint and over-elaborate routine. So, bang! I swallowed the rebuff, and tried to carry on 'giving' to

John at Oxford, 1933

John on 'Blackbird' a few days before he sailed for Burma

people. At Rheinfelden in Switzerland, in the midst of a wonderful time of national recovery there, I suddenly had the thought – it seemed from God – 'Never fear. You will marry Erica some day.' The thought faded, and still I carried on for more than a year, gradually becoming more and more self-centred, like a hollow drum. Then one day a trusted friend and colleague walked into my room and said: 'Edward, Edward, let God do it. I think you've been trying too hard. You ought to go home and have a break.' I went, feeling genuine relief. I also felt a sense of failure, of course.

My parents welcomed me back and asked no questions. For a time I was haunted by doubts and fears. I felt like a watch with the mainspring gone. My mother said it was the 'dark night of the soul', and I must persevere through it. One Sunday morning just as she was going to church I asked her if we could have a talk. She at once cancelled church and stayed back to talk to me. We had a conversation which went something like this:

She: 'What is it?'
I: 'It's my nerves.'
'It's not nerves, it's sin.'
'What can I do?'
'Make a fresh start, and ask God to give you the strength for it.'
'I've tried doing that, and it does not work. I am afraid of trying again and nothing happening.'
'Well, that's what faith means. You take a step in faith. You cannot be sure it will work. You have to see.'
'All right,' and we knelt and I gave my life to God afresh and asked Him to bless and guide me in whatever way He chose.

God used that cutting-through remark by my mother. I felt refreshed, whole again, and healed. During the next days and weeks at home I had several thoughts which gave me insight. One of them concerned my relationship with my brother John. John by now was already in Burma. I wrote him a letter of apology for having closed my heart to him after he had rejected my effort to change him. I said it showed me that basically I was nice to people as long as they did what I wanted. Actually I had always been a sort of boss in my relationship with him, and he must have found it difficult to take, and I hoped he could forgive me. What I should have done was to continue to give him companionship after my change, sharing news, hopes, etc., without any demand for him to see things as I did. I was not wrong to stop trying to change him, I was wrong to cut off all interest in him. That was the gist.

It was an opportunity to consider in depth the implications of my father's change. I kept remembering that word in the Bible somewhere: 'Look to the rock whence ye were hewn.' It was a fresh thought. For the first time, I actually wanted to help my father maintain the estate. I learned how to lay a hedge, including 'pleaching', from one of the tenants, and selecting the long shoots so that they could cover the thin places, which to cut out and which to leave. I learned to milk a cow on our own farm. I started shooting again, and hunting with zest. I went regularly with Pa on his rounds of the estate men on their never-ending work of farmhouse and cottage repairs. Not easy occasions these, sometimes. Pa would get from the men details of what materials they wanted or needed and write them down in his notebook to order. But there was not much small talk and sometimes longish silences.

During the earlier months of this time, I did join Gwen and Rozi and about two hundred others for the last post-house party training time to be held at Oxford before the war (1937). At this training time, three young American women spoke together from the platform about love. They were Elisabeth, perhaps twenty-five, very attractive and unmarried; Jean, twenty-eight or so, also attractive and unmarried; and Nan, who was married and round about thirty. I cannot remember their exact words, but the impression they left with me was:

(1) If you have real love for a man, it will make you love other people more, not less;
(2) True love is all giving and no demand;
(3) One of our jobs with people is to make them 'marriageable', i.e. living a quality of life whereby the Holy Spirit can enable you to love without demand.

I was intrigued and delighted by this.

It was Nan's husband Garrett who helped me over the question of whether to fight in any war. For us British, with Hitler in power in Germany, this was becoming a live issue. I was asking Garrett what he felt about it. He said 'Do you love your country?' I said 'Yes,' and I meant it. He said 'Well, why not fight for her?' He made no great issue of it, just left the thought with me. Americans in those days were better known for isolationism than for any liking for war.

One evening during this time I went to see Frank Buchman. I had a recurrence of the love-bug. Frank said 'How are you?'

'Not very well, Frank. I've got a pain here,' I said, putting my hand over my heart, 'Do you think it's indigestion?'

'No, I think it's love!' said Frank.

After we had talked for a bit I said to him, 'However do you manage to keep so serene and cheerful with hundreds of people like all of us here, including me, on your hands all the time?' He said, 'Oh, I just never think of myself.' It was time then to go into the evening meeting, so we walked into the meeting together, and I sat at the back. Frank went to the platform and said 'Where's Ivan?' Ivan Menzies, the Gilbert and Sullivan opera star, said, 'Here, Frank.'

Frank, who was completely tone-deaf, asked 'What's that song about "Faint heart never won fair lady"?' And he got Ivan to lead the whole crowd in singing it for the start of the meeting.

I came to love America, through Frank and Garrett and other Americans who came and gave us British of their best during those pre-war years.

Back at home, I got Pa to tell me the story of how he led his company over the top against the Germans at Bazentin-le-Petit on the Somme. They were held up by heavy machine-gun fire. Pa worked his way to the front, and was in the act of waving the men forward again when he was hit in the shoulder, the bullet just missing his lung. His reaction, after all those years, was: 'We could have done it. The men were great, the officers were great.' His simple faith in the army moved me. 'We did not hate the Germans,' he said. 'We were doing a job.' Later on I was talking to Adams about how difficult I would find it to have to stick a bayonet into someone. Adams was one of our estate men, who had been wounded at Loos, when a grenade hit him on the head and then exploded at his feet. He looked at me and said with great conviction, 'It's him or you, Mr Edward. It's him or you.'

CHAPTER III
Into industry

How was it that I came to make the transition from full-time work with the Oxford Group to a job in industry? The starting point for me was recognising that the future of Whitbourne depended on what happened to the vinegar works. In fact it had been borne in on me during the last four years with the Oxford Group that industry was to any nation what the engine-room was to a ship. It was where the wheels went round and affected where we all got to. Yet our class did not expect to go into industry, and were not aware of it as a major factor shaping our way of life. So, first I took an eight-week 'Pitman's Intensive Business Course' in London – the only eight weeks I can remember during which I wore a stiff white collar every day. Then I accepted an invitation to 'go through' the office at the vinegar works in Worcester. This finished after a week or two with a letter from the managing director regretting that there was no permanent job there for me at present. He added: 'May I say that the army is some good preparation for business, and the Territorial Army has replaced the old Militia!' I decided to ignore this advice, and keep trying to get a foot-in-the-door start in industry. My father encouraged me, in a rare outburst at breakfast one morning. 'Get a job. Any job!', I remember him saying. So I went job hunting in industry.

My friend Raymond Williams, head of a corn merchant's business in Bromyard, took me on his rounds visiting customers as a fill-in. I came near to accepting a job from some little-known firm selling chocolate coverture on commission only to sweet factories. The sales director of H.J. Heinz Co. asked me if I thought I could transfer my enthusiasm for the Oxford Group to selling Heinz's 57 varieties of canned food. It was a good question, of the 'when did you leave off beating your wife?' category, and I cannot remember exactly how, or if, I answered it. I felt sure he seriously considered giving me a job. But he did not quite do so, the reason given being that there was always a chance that at some time in the future I might have a part in the direction of Hill, Evans and Co. Ltd. and, Heinz being a leading customer of theirs, there might be problems.

Somewhere during these goings on, Angus Lamond, a colleague of mine in Moral Re-Armament who knew me well, remarked to me: 'You want to watch out about making success your aim. You gave up all prospects of success when you left University. Then you tried to be a successful Oxford Group man, and that failed. The danger

George Richards, Sales Director of Swallow Raincoats Ltd. Courtesy of Sally Bullock, his daughter

now is that you will try to be a successful businessman.' Meanwhile another colleague, George Richards of Birmingham, who with his wife Kathleen had become a friend of our family, was also watching my efforts with sympathy and understanding. In the end he offered me a job at Swallow Raincoats Ltd., Birmingham, the successful family firm of which he was sales director. I accepted. The weekly wage was to be £3. I was elated at the prospect. This was November 1938.

'The Swallow', as we called it, was a family firm, but with a difference. Its then chairman, C.M. Witt, was a little cock robin of a man, who had started as a barrow boy selling men's clothes in the street. He boasted of having had no education and worked his way up by his own efforts. His son, a well-dressed modern type, E.C. Witt, was managing director, in charge of production and finance. They were known as Mr Witt and Mr Chris. The third director, in charge of sales, was my friend George Richards. He was known as George, and was thought to have become a lot more human and easy to talk to since his encounter with the Oxford Group. Chris Witt and George between them ran the show, with old man Witt coming along now and then.

The general sales policy of the company was what you might call thrusting. The aim was to get a network of retailers all over the country who would stock no raincoats but Swallow Raincoats. There were three main types of raincoat on offer: The 'Slip-on', which we sold for 14/- and the retailers for 21/-, the 'Beatall' for 30/- and 42/-, and a more expensive one at 40/- and 63/-. The Slip-on was easily the most popular. But of course great efforts were made to cover every possible requirement of the retailers, including a fair number of coats for outsize customers etc. which we would make to measure. These were called the 'red specials', and Swallow undertook to deliver them by post direct to retailers within seven to ten days of receipt of an order.

George put me in charge of the 'red specials'. There were plenty of complaints from retailers that the seven to ten day undertaking was not being honoured, and I had to see that the specials moved steadily through the factory with no hold-ups. I could go anywhere and enlist the help of any departmental head in this. So, armed with a list of every red special order, I pursued them systematically through the works.

I remember the first time I went to see Hilda, the red-headed Black Country girl in charge of the band of about forty skilled women who made the specials. She had a huge pile of coats beside her, all coming off the assembly line, and there, right at the bottom of the pile, was a big splash of red labels – my specials! Hilda explained to me that there was a natural bias against doing the specials promptly because the girls were on piece-work and could work more quickly and therefore make more money on the stock sizes. However, she obviously decided to get them flowing, and they began to flow from then on.

Sparks flew, to start with, with some of the men. It started with a bit of a row with Tom, in charge of the cutting room. I walked straight up to him and started asking his help on some question to do with the work. He just exploded. What business had I to come upsetting things in his department? Was I some military man, or something? I had realised my first appearance might have been a bit sudden, so I said:

'Look here, I did rather march up to you, but I'll tell you why I do sometimes do that. It's because I'm shy.'

'You shy?'

'Yes.'

All I can say is Tom's heat gave way to warmth. He expanded on the work of the cutting room. From that moment on, and on all my subsequent visits, I had nothing but help from him.

With Jack, the 'Passer', whose job was to check personally every coat out of the factory into the despatch department, my conversations were more low key. But they were substantial. He started by telling me that he had seen plenty of my sort come and go, and they usually lasted about a couple of months, etc. I would say I was only interested in the red specials getting off on time. After a bit we got on quite well together.

But there was a price to pay. We got on so well that I was soon personally ferrying loads of 'specials' over my shoulder to the packing room for despatch that same day. Jack had passed them. It still remained for them to be packed in boxes and put in the post. The packer was a former sergeant-major of the Guards with handlebar moustaches and a wooden leg. He only had the specials to handle, but he took a dislike to my brisk appearances with piles of coats, sometimes late in the afternoon, and made it plain with the most ripe and rare language directed at me, listened to also by the two or three boys or girls in the small packing room with him. I stood this for about a week, and then one evening I decided to risk drastic action. As soon as he opened up, I shouted: 'Shut up! If you can't shut up and keep quiet, I'll push your head through this wall!' He relaxed immediately, and said: 'I never knew it was that important to you.' I invited him out for a drink round the corner. We had Ansells bitter. Very good too.

So we all finished up good friends. And the 'red specials' hit the target for the Easter holiday. For the first time ever, not one was left. George Richards was delighted. And I think the salesmen (we had twelve covering the country) were helped.

When I came back to the Swallow after my annual fortnight's holiday, I was astonished to find myself greeted by all sorts of people all over the factory, and pumped with questions about what I had been doing. I seemed to have become quite popular. Harold Price, the despatch manager, became a particular friend of mine. A Birmingham man about my own age, he was in charge of the despatch clerks who had to keep the shelves stocked with coats and make up the orders as they came in. (I spent the whole of my first day at the Swallow folding coats.) Harold turned out to be a skilled and keen angler, and I invited him over to Whitbourne to fish our lake. He took me to Villa Park and I got my first taste of professional football, seeing Aston Villa play Arsenal.

The Oxford Group, meanwhile, had given birth to Moral Re-Armament, and a campaign to launch it was gaining considerable public attention in 1938–39. In 1939 British industry sent a message of support to MRA in Washington D.C. to be read into the Congressional Record. Harold Price and I led the signatories from the Swallow and all the men in the factory signed. I was hauled over the coals by George Richards for this, but could truthfully tell him that I had not wasted one minute of the Company's time. All my canvassing had been done in the lunch break or one of the other breaks.

How do you sum up the value of my time at the Swallow? People were kind. It was hard work, but I enjoyed it, and friendships made there have lasted right up to the present day. Till very recently Harold Price still came over to fish. In 1980 he brought with him other old Swallow men – Jack Bagnall, George Stubbs, Norman Caldecott – and we reminisced together about the days of the Swallow (now long since taken over by Aquascutum) forty years before.

I remain ever grateful to George Richards that he had the flexibility and imagination to take me on there. He said to me: 'I have known adversity. Now you are experiencing adversity for the first time. I am going to give you a job which no one before you has been able to do, and I am sure you will do it.' It did a lot for me that I did not let him down.

The Swallow seems now to have been an interlude. But it did give me a feel of the 'nuts and bolts' of industry, which had up to then been lacking.

CHAPTER IV
World War II

WAR WAS DECLARED against Hitler's Germany on 1 September 1939, the day after the invasion of Poland. But for me, and I think for most British people, the key time when we decided to go to war was in April 1939, when Hitler marched into Czechoslovakia without warning. This time he had no pretext of going to help the Sudeten-Germans, which he had used at the time of the Munich agreement six months before, and the Munich appeasement policy was finally discredited. Hitler was a naked aggressor and had to be stopped. Chamberlain's government introduced conscription, supported by the Labour Party. In many British hearts and minds, I think, a key was turned, and though things went on outwardly as before there was a resolve building up.

When war actually came in September, it was almost a relief.

Being on the Officers' Special Reserve, I volunteered and was sent to the first OCTU (Officers Cadets' Training Unit) run by the Guards at Sandhurst. There I got much amusement from experiencing the efforts of the N.C.O.s to knock some discipline and military zeal into us. One sergeant in the Grenadiers was telling us how he had retired from the army, and rejoined again because he was so fed up with civilian life. Someone asked him: 'Why did you dislike it in civvy street, Staff?' His reply was: 'I didn't like the way nobody cut about, Sir.' They got us 'cutting about' at Sandhurst all right. I was fascinated by a lecture on the internal combustion engine given by a transport sergeant to our class of predominantly Eton and Winchester Officer Cadets. They were all people who drove a car, probably a fast car, at home; but when it came to plugs, carburettors, compression etc., they were all as helpless as babes. The look on the instructor's face as it swept over him in waves what he had to contend with was delightful. Amusement, exasperation, the struggle for courtesy, determination to be clearer, followed by disbelief, etc! Having had a classical education myself, I was fully in sympathy with the class. I have always found mechanical types baffle you with words, and rattle on until you've lost the thread of what they are trying to explain.

I did feel vaguely then that a mechanical aptitude was something often lacking in the officer class. I feel it even more now, with hindsight. It applied not only to tanks and other armoured vehicles, but to rifles and Bren guns as well. Ammunition was scarce, it is true, but when I finally went into action in March 1941, I had only fired five rounds from a pistol, two or three bursts with live ammunition from a Bren gun, and a dozen or so rounds from a rifle. I was certainly not at home with my .38 pistol, the only weapon an officer carried.

From Sandhurst, I went in April 1940 to Norton Barracks, Worcester, as a Second Lieutenant, and then in August was sent to join the First Battalion of the Worcestershire Regiment at Port Sudan.

At Worcester, still the home of the County Regiment which is amalgamated with the Sherwood Foresters, I found a large and companionable crowd of subalterns, new like myself, plus I don't know how many hundreds of civilian conscripts being turned into soldiers. There was a sprinkling of regular officers and N.C.O.s to give the training.

One day in early June, one thousand men marched in through the main gate and onto the square at Norton Barracks. They were survivors of Dunkirk. They carried no weapons and their faces looked drawn but cheerful in a restrained sort of way. We looked at them with awe, curiosity, and an attempt at friendly welcome. We knew that Dunkirk was both a disaster and a deliverance. We new soldiers were not called upon to play any part in sorting them out. We understood that 329,000 others were being sorted out at depots all over the country.

We listened on the radio to Winston Churchill's immortal speech, 'We shall fight them on the beaches' etc. with solemnity. We felt proud to be British, and that God was reserving us for some big job. When France fell, there was a sense, like it or not, of relief. We felt: 'Ah! Now we are alone. Nothing can beat us now if we are all willing to stand together.' It was something sensed rather than talked about. Amateurish perhaps; romantic, certainly. But I think many who remember 1940 will vouch for the truth of it. At that time America was not yet in the war. Russia was allied to Germany, and the Communist Party was putting out propaganda against the war.

Then came the miracle of the Battle of Britain. We heard it over the radio on a liner somewhere on the ocean en route for the Cape. We were part of a convoy of fifteen thousand troops, escorted by two cruisers and seven destroyers. It was an astonishing victory,

victory against all the odds. When we docked at Cape Town, every single one of those fifteen thousand men was caught up into a tremendous round of parties, dances, sight seeing, being entertained in homes, etc. The South Africans were unforgettably generous hosts. 'It is not difficult to be proud of Britain at this time,' one remarked. I was slapped on the back in a main street of Cape Town, and it turned out to be a Rhodes Scholar contemporary of mine from Corpus, Oxford. He took me to a café and introduced me to his girl friend and we had a good chatter.

It was heady stuff, that first introduction to Africa. I think most of the officers on that convoy felt as if we were being given a splendid world tour at government expense. It was my first experience of the tropics, feeling the night air growing warmer and warmer, seeing unending shoals of flying fish, and enjoying the company of our particular lot of subalterns from the Rifle Brigade, K.R.R.C. (Kings Royal Rifle Corps), Essex and Royal Sussex. I did not conceal my connection with Moral Re-Armament. One chap in the Royal Sussex asked me to speak about MRA to his draft of about twenty soldiers. I did this, but I think they found it a bit mystifying.

The whole convoy went on to Suez. Most of us then snaked into Cairo on a long troop train.

In Cairo, we Worcestershire and Essex were put in a hotel for two days to await a train south to our units. Two of the Essex men and I found ourselves with nothing to do one evening, so I said 'Let's go to a dance'. I discovered the name of a well-known night club, and the others came along. We sat down at tables and I selected the best looking girl I could see in the room and asked her for a dance. We had several dances and a drink together. In the end I went back and joined the others, who expressed themselves highly disapprovingly, saying: 'Here you were talking about Moral Re-Armament, and then you go and behave like a he-goat.' I almost forgot this incident, as we travelled next day, but not quite.

I and 'Hutch', a fellow officer, arrived at Port Sudan on the Red Sea on a September afternoon in 1940. 'Hutch' was Second Lieutenant Hutchison, a married man of about my age who worked for Sovereign Pencils, and had been in the Territorials. We both felt honoured to have been posted to one of our regiment's two line battalions. We knew we were green, but we expected some sort of a welcome. We thus felt somewhat dashed (at least I did) when a tall figure with a moustache loomed up and simply said, looking through us,

'Where's your luggage?'

We found the luggage, boarded the transport and were driven the short distance to a hutted camp on the sea shore about a mile outside Port Sudan. This was where we were to live for the next three months.

It was hot, 110° in the shade. Work finished at about 11 a.m., with a short period from about four to five in the afternoon. I learnt that we were a 'detachment' of the battalion. I never made out exactly where the others were, I think at Gebeit. But Battalion H.Q. under Lieutenant Colonel Lawrence was nearby in Port Sudan. The mood in the Officers' Mess was a bit subdued because we had lost a subaltern the week before, killed while on reconnaissance at Gedaref across the frontier with Eritrea.

The battalion had done duty in Palestine putting down an Arab revolt against British rule, and had come to the Sudan straight from there. They were one of just three British battalions in the Sudan standing guard against the Italian armies in Ethiopia and Eritrea under the Duke of Aosta. Regularly about twice a week a group of Savoia bombers would fly up over the sea from the south, do a left turn just beyond Port Sudan and fly back over the harbour pranging shipping and installations. We watched them as the sun glinted on them on the way up, and we watched our own Gladiators leave the aerodrome and spiral up to intercept them. Sometimes two Gladiators, sometimes only one. Usually the Italians lost a bomber. On one dreadful occasion we lost both Gladiators. We never asked what damage was caused, but it was not great. I was deeply respectful of the pilots who flew those Gladiators; they were very manoeuvrable biplanes but a lot slower than the enemy bombers, and had to attack them from the underneath, timing themselves on a near collision course. Later, over Keren, I saw one Gladiator shoot down two Italian fighters in a close-range dog fight.

I found commanding a platoon of thirty regular soldiers in barracks, in the tropics, a task quite beyond me. The troops were properly browned off. Owing to the heat we did no demanding work and the attitude to any parade seemed to me casual. The small talk between us new officers demonstrated two main lines of thought on how to handle men: one was 'You've got to be a father to your men.' The second, more prevalent: 'You've got to make your men fear you more than they'll fear the enemy.' I heartily disagreed with both, but I was hard put to it to find a middle way. Now and again it seemed to be coming, as when I was ordered to march my men into Port Sudan and give them a swim in the local swimming pool. We had a splendid time ducking one another for ten minutes, during which I brought off a few satisfactory rugby tackles from underneath on one or two insubordinate characters. Unfortunately I got the most excruciating earache after this and could not swim there again. And I rather made matters worse by putting one of my N.C.O.s on a charge, for being badly turned out on parade. He appeared before the adjutant in the orderly room, was heard briefly, and the case was dismissed. Everyone in the hearing of course kept a perfectly straight face, but one of my friends among the newly arrived subalterns said later on, 'Your trouble is you've got this habit of putting your best N.C.O.s on a charge.' Weeks later at our Regimental Christmas concert another of them put on a skit about a corporal with dirty bootlaces!

What did we talk about in the mess? At first it seemed a rather strange world – homes, wives, if any, and families were seldom talked about. The progress of the war and related matters of a serious nature, never. I cannot remember that any of us straight out from England were asked what it was like there now. From about 11.30 a.m. till 2 p.m. and again from 6.30 p.m. onwards till after dinner we were usually all together. I came to enjoy the company, including the eccentricities of our Detachment Commander (who had met us at the station). He had a habit of inviting outside guests to dinner and then going to sleep on them before the meal was over, leaving us juniors to keep the party going. I made a decision to do my best to entertain his guests or anyone else's who came to the mess, however long they stayed and however much they drank.

On Christmas Eve I was suddenly ordered out to guard the aerodrome with my platoon, the RAF being off duty. We had no instructions how to do this, or what we were guarding it against. We pitched our tents in what seemed a good place behind some Blenheim bombers. A party of RAF ground staff then turned up and told us we would be in the way of the slipstream if the Blenheims had to fly. We pitched them again somewhere else. The truck with our food and drink got stuck in the marshy ground on the way to the aerodrome. Night fell and a deputation of three men arrived at my tent. Two of them said the third was taken ill and they must get him back to the camp – I said 'Can you get through?' They said 'Yes,' so I said 'I'll come with you and see if I can rustle up some food.' We arrived at the camp to find the Christmas Eve celebrations in full swing. I tried this person and that, but it became evident that we would have to wait for the morning and we drove back empty-handed. We were very hungry on Christmas morning. At last Christmas dinner of sorts arrived – I forget what – and with it our cheerful and gracious Second in Command, Major Jock Knight. He parked himself outside one of the tents with some food and drinks handy, and also for some reason a shooting stick, and seemed delighted to be able to greet each of us. About our predicament, he said nothing at all. We moved back to the camp on, I think, Boxing Day.

Things were meanwhile working up to an invasion of Italian East Africa, in which we would participate. Slowly the inexorable cogs of the Middle East Army machine were turning. Every unit was to send two or three officers to be trained as Field Works Officers in Cairo, and I was one of the pair from our battalion. Off we went, half tickled at the chance of having a look at Cairo, and half scared that we might miss some real fighting. We were there for a month – it was my first real meeting with Australian, New Zealand and Indian army officers and a really enjoyable time. At the end of it we were all given a report, as at school. Mine said 'Practical work fair' and 'Fit to be a Field Works Officer.' 'Some hope' was my reaction. I did not think there was any danger of my becoming a Field Works Officer.

CHAPTER V
Keren

WHEN WE GOT back to the battalion it was at Barentu, deep inside Ethiopia. The whole spirit and bearing of the men had been transformed. There were smiles and cheerfulness all round. They had successfully driven the Italians out of Barentu, beating off an armoured car counter-attack with small-arms fire, and were awaiting another move. Philip Graves-Morris, my Company Commander, had won the M.C., but my batman, Dai Davis from the Rhondda, had sadly been killed in a skirmish earlier.

We moved to an encampment near Tessenei in a forest of spreading palm-like trees where we were invisible from the air. Our next move was to be the hundred miles or so by truck to the bottom side of the escarpment leading to Keren.

Keren was undoubtedly one of the major battles in the Ethiopian Campaign, which ended in the defeat and surrender of the Italian East African army of 250,000 men in June 1941. We approached to a point about three miles away from where the town was hidden by the various jagged features of the escarpment. The road wound its way between heights up the Keren gorge. There was no way through for tanks or any transport except this road, and the Italian engineers had done a good job of blocking it. They controlled the heights on either side of the road and their artillery had the range of the road itself. The key task for us, therefore, was to attack the heights on either side of the road. We had two divisions to do this: the Fourth Indian Division, who had already attacked and made some ground on the left, and the Fifth Indian Division (including the Worcestershires) who were to attack the right. Each brigade had two Indian and one British battalion. We also had a regiment of the Royal Artillery, with 25-pounder guns.

Our numbers on paper should have been about twenty-five thousand men, but I guess they were a fair bit less. The Worcesters, with a paper strength of six hundred, could only muster four hundred men at the start of the battle. My platoon should have been thirty strong, but was twenty. This was due not only to casualties but to illness, and especially what were called 'desert sores' – painful and debilitating, as I am sure our M.O. could testify. (I can too, because I had one on my foot under the bootlace.) It was common to see a proportion of active men with bandages over their knees or elbows, to keep the flies and jagged rocks off these things.

At 7.00 a.m. on Saturday 15 March 1941, our guns opened up on targets in front of the Fourth Division, attacking the hills to our left front. We happened to be sitting awaiting orders about a hundred yards in front of them. This was the first surprise we got – the effect on our eardrums. I seem to remember we all tried to relax our facial muscles, with furtive glances at each other. We waited a bit while the sun climbed and then got the order to move forward, in open order with gaps of a hundred yards between platoons. We halted every hour under a Tabaldi tree (we called every tree a Tabaldi tree). On our second halt I stopped, and my platoon to a man did likewise, under a tree. The unmistakeable voice of P.S.M. Knox came floating from behind us, 'Oh, give us a tree!' and I saw what he meant – there was another a reasonable distance ahead for us, but nothing behind for them. We restarted ourselves immediately and took root (temporarily) under the more forward tree. The main theme of Keren – exhaustion, and the effort of putting one foot in front of the other – was becoming apparent.

We fetched up that afternoon under a rocky outcrop that looked to provide cover from enemy shell fire and waited again. There was some very desultory shell fire and at about 4 p.m. 'Dolly' Cooper, the Quartermaster, arrived with a truck carrying tea and, I think, sausages for all – a real treat. I was sitting chatting with Philip, the Company Commander, shortly after this, having left my equipment on the ground in front of my platoon, when a solitary shell landed only a few feet from my equipment and burst backwards, spattering my men with bits of shrapnel and rock. I saw a row of bleeding faces and arms in a state of shock. There were some Indian Medical Service troops cowering nearby, and I shouted at them 'Can't you do something?' Not that I knew what to do myself. Our truck drove up and nine men climbed on board and were taken back as casualties. My haversack had several holes in it.

In the later afternoon we had good news. Fort Dologorodoc, our main objective on the right of the advance, had been captured. We were to pass through it and capture Mount Falestoh, a peak behind and to the right of Dologorodoc overlooking Keren. We set off after dark in dead silence, in single file by platoons. The enemy sent over quite a few shells this time – they must have guessed what was up. I learnt to listen for the shells and gauge where they were going to fall – beyond us (a moan), short (a whistle) or right at us (a screech). Once, early on, I made the mistake of faltering and the platoon all went down in response. Anyway there were no more casualties, we crossed the road and got into dead ground for the climb to Dologorodoc. We were always in single file, following a wire laid by the Signals. When we got to 'the Pimple', a conical hillock like an enormous anthill, we were astonished to find ourselves stepping over the bodies of sleeping Maharattas, who had captured the hill in fierce fighting a few hours before. It was a long climb – the whole march up to Dologorodoc took us about six hours. Towards the end we were told to sit still and let the 6/13th Frontier Force move through us. They did so within a few feet of us, looking as fresh as men from the Khyber can look in those conditions. George Bharat Singh, with whom I had shared a room in Cairo on the Field Works course, exchanged greetings with me as he passed.

It must have been after midnight when we were allocated pieces of ground to occupy for the night on the outer perimeter of Fort Dologorodoc, on the north side – I don't know if anyone slept, my bit of ground was not level enough. At 4 a.m. we were on the move.

'We are now going to attack,' Philip said.

I remember saying 'Attack, we cannot!'

Philip replied, 'You're going to.'

I said 'Right Sir' – or words to that effect. I am grateful that I felt able to say an outrageous thing like that to Philip, and grateful that when he ticked me off for it I felt reassurance as much as anything. So we set off to attack. But the attacking was actually done by A, B and C Companies – our Company D was to be in reserve. We moved along the side of the mountain face with peaks on our left for perhaps three hours. We heard the crackle of rifle and Bren gun fire coming from in front where the forward Companies were engaging the enemy. We heard afterwards that they made good progress until they stepped over the lip of the summit into intense machine-gun fire. On the approach along the side of the mountain, you could not know where to go except by following the man in front. The man in front of me happened to be carrying a Boyes anti-tank rifle. Suddenly he sat down and said to me with a beseeching look, 'Do you mind if I don't go on Sir?' My mouth worked, I tried to think of something useful to say and my eye caught the next man in front of us receding behind the boulders. I said 'We've got to get on' and I left him.

(Before the end of the year the Boyes Anti-Tank rifle was removed from the establishment of infantry battalions; it was found to be too heavy!)

We emerged into a flattish place with about a dozen Italian prisoners sitting down under guard, and began a long wait for news while the sun climbed. At about 10 a.m., news came through that the forward Companies had been held up – Philip Ray, O.C. B Company, had been killed and 'Dusty' Miller, acting O.C. C Company, had been badly wounded in the thigh. I was ordered to take my platoon forward – Philip himself with Company H.Q. had already gone, so had P.S.M.Knox. The way lay over a deep ravine, and up a steep boulder-strewn slope beyond it. As we approached the ravine a single African (enemy) soldier came charging down the opposite slope to meet us. At the bottom of the ravine – about twelve feet deep – he turned left and shot away down hill and out of sight. We crossed the ravine and began to climb. Almost immediately we began to lose men to an enemy, unseen but probably the most formidable we had to face in the Sudan and Eritrea – heat exhaustion. My platoon began to pack it in. I struggled on, accompanied by one blessed N.C.O. Now and then we waited and coaxed and cajoled the men on till they arrived at our stopping place and collapsed again. After a pause and some words of encouragement (all too short for them) we would go on with one or two less. We got to the top with four men. There was an open space and a gentle slope for about two hundred yards. At the top of it I was delighted to see some cheerful men from A Company (I believe), who said 'Don't go across there, Sir, you're in full view of the enemy.' 'To hell with that' I thought and plodded on, beginning to run and swerve about in case we were shot at – but nothing happened and in no time we arrived at a 'Sangar' containing the Company Commander, C.S.M. and P.S.M.Knox's platoon – just the people I wanted to see. Philip hailed me and said,

'Where are your platoon?'

'They're coming Sir,' and thank God they were.

'How many?' Philip demanded.

'Four.'

A 'Sangar' is a circular stone enclosure with dry stone walls all round about two to three foot high, which offers some all-round protection to infantry. Straight ahead of us was another wooded ravine, beyond it a bare saddleback reaching up to Mount Falestoh overlooking us from the middle distance. To the left front was an expanse of bare land with boulders, to the right, steeper slopes led down into the valley from which we had climbed. It occurs to me now that we may have been in a Sangar which our forward troops had captured in their advance; I presume that they were somewhere on that saddle.

Our party was under fire from somewhere. Several of P.S.M.Knox's platoon had been killed, and another was shot soon after we arrived. Philip ordered me to locate the enemy and engage him with Bren gun fire, so I crawled forward and scanned the position with field glasses. Not a thing was visible except a small cairn of stones sticking up about two hundred yards away on the left front. I thought that might be the place and ordered up the Bren gun (our only surviving one), but the Lance Corporal in charge reported it out of order. 'This is the end,' I thought, and started crawling back to have a look at it. I think I was crouching over the gun when something hit me hard in the behind. It felt like being kicked by a horse. My right leg swung loose, someone bound up the wound with a field dressing and I lay there feeling pretty done in. I think they got me into some safe-ish position. I remember Philip coming over and saying 'Edward, I'm sorry I gave you such a bloody job!' A little later Bobby Frith, the Commander of A company, turned up alone for consultation with Philip and our C.S.M. They obviously devised a plan of action and disappeared, apparently on a reconnaissance forward. After an interval of two or three minutes the C.S.M. scrambled back, white-faced, followed by Philip with a machine gun gash across his back – Bobby Frith, who was leading, was killed. We now had all our Company Commanders put out of action. Men continued to be hit occasionally – orders came from Battalion H.Q. that we were to wait for cover of darkness and withdraw back to Dologorodoc – the attempt to capture Falestoh had failed.

We had about six hours to wait for nightfall. Discussions went on round me in an undertone. I took no part in the various arrangements for the evacuation of our position. I was told two medical orderlies would help me down to the M.O. They asked me to see if I could walk down the mountain side. I could, between the two orderlies, putting only one foot to the ground.

The doctor, who knew me, said 'That's splendid, you've been hit in the best possible place – OK you can walk back!' Knowing the doctor, I did not argue. We set off, as before, for some distance along a road. We were quite alone, the three of us. The orderlies said 'Can you manage it, Sir?' 'Yes, if you don't mind stopping now and then so that I can have a sleep.' Then came quite an important moment;

we arrived at a turning where we had to leave the road and go up a narrow zig-zag path perhaps four to five hundred yards uphill to the fort. This path was being shelled by the enemy, not heavily, but constantly and very accurately – we could see the flash of every shell-burst as they played up and down it in the moonlight, always landing within the zig-zag. We knew that every burst sent a hefty amount of rock splinters flying about in addition to pieces of shrapnel.

We had a good look at it and agreed it would be impracticable to try to avoid the shells by going round them to right or left; it was far too rough. I felt God was wanting to guide us through it and that I should do it deliberately without hurrying, always lying down for a rest if possible somewhere near where a shell had just burst. Anyway we had two or three rests in those four or five hundred yards (you are safe lying down except for a direct hit). We were dusted up once or twice, but never hit and never had to take sudden evasive action. Arriving safely at the fort, I felt a sense of inner peace, even exhilaration. As for the two orderlies, they were magnificent – I never knew their names. One of them put his haversack under my head as they put me on a stretcher; I only hope he recovered it.

The first quarter of an hour I spent in the fort lying on the stretcher at the bottom of a concrete trench crammed with troops, all in among their feet as they waited to repel an Italian counter-attack. The Italian barrage was heavy and continuous, and practically every shell hit the concrete wall of the trench or the ground immediately behind; but the trench was impervious to shelling and only one man, judging from the shouts I heard, was wounded. Just before this I had met 'Bull' Sergeant, one of my friends from the Port Sudan Officers' Mess. I could tell from Bull's face that Bn H.Q., to which he was attached, had taken a pretty fair pounding. I found afterwards that they had used the captured enemy H.Q., which was on the south side and completely covered by the enemy guns. Bull told me that Mickey Kerans, one of his best friends, had been killed, and I wondered how the H.Q. managed to get any messages to us at all.

We wounded spent that night on the northern slope of Dologorodoc; We were taken in the morning on stretchers down the mountain side to the road, and then in transport to the Casualty Clearing Station. At the C.C.S., to my great surprise, I was asked if I would like a beer. I accepted, wondering if it would come flowing out of me somewhere lower down in my body. It didn't! I have an idea I was given it to reassure me that things weren't too bad after all – it did that anyway. Then more transport to rail head, then overnight to

Khartoum, then river steamer to hospital at Wadi Seidna on the outskirts of Khartoum.

In hospital we learnt of the capture of Keren, one week later. Our troops had stayed in Fort Dologorodoc and helped to beat back eight Italian counter-attacks; then the Italians had been taken by surprise by an attack by Fourth Division through a disused railway tunnel. Suddenly the heights were ours and the road was cleared. The pursuit continued, with the capture of Asmara and Massawa, and little major check until Amba Alagi, deep into Abyssinia (Ethiopia). Our battalion had lost a third of its fighting strength at Keren. Units of Fourth Division on the left had borne the brunt of the fighting. In the next bed to me was an officer of the Cameron Highlanders, whose body was peppered with wounds received from the Italians' light red hand grenades, thrown with the advantage of height from the feature they were defending.

At first it looked as if I would soon be OK; Philip, who was in the same ward, said emphatically, 'You will get back to the Battalion as quick as you can.' But when I started to walk, the right foot still flapped. The doctor explained I had a 'dropped foot' due to the bullet having damaged my sciatic nerve. I said 'How long will it take me to recover?' 'You may never recover,' he said. And so it was.

I spent six months in hospitals in the Middle East having electric treatment to try and bring back the leg. Finally I was graded bottom grade, unfit for active service, and sent back to England, where I arrived in July 1942, fifteen months after the battle of Keren.

CHAPTER VI
Behind the lines

THOSE FIFTEEN MONTHS were basically a matter of waiting for the army to shunt me round Africa from one hospital to another. It was a long time and, for me, a difficult one. The only military duty I performed during the whole of the fifteen months, apart from reporting for medical treatment, was one occasion when I was called to sit as a member of a Court of Enquiry to determine the circumstances under which a soldier had lost an eye from the cork of a ginger beer bottle.

It started well, when I was lucky enough to be farmed out to stay in the 'bachelor' home of two members of the Sudan Political Service in Khartoum. They were George Bredin and K.D.D. 'Bill' Henderson. They put me to occupy somebody's desk at their H.Q., and had papers brought to me by assiduous Sudanese orderlies. (I think they stopped short of having me sign anything vital.) The orderlies and I treated each other with grave correctness, just a hint of amusement sometimes showing through. The only thing of substance I remember was a shower of letters from junior officers of the service applying for indefinite leave to join the armed forces, all of which had received appropriate replies refusing their request and saying that it was all the more important in a war for them to stay where they were.

On my birthday, 26 April, George and Bill took me out to dinner in a hotel. In the middle of dinner a waiter came up carrying a tray on which lay two cloth officers' stars, with a note which said 'Pip! Pip!' I had been promoted from Second Lieutenant to Lieutenant the day before. I remember also a game of bridge with Bishop Gwynne and a lady from Northern Ireland, who remembered the Oxford Group's visit there in 1934. She said: 'You said then you had wanted to go to the Sudan, and now here you are.' There was also a dinner one evening with Dick Roseveare (R.V.H. Roseveare), whom I had known as headmaster at Cheltenham in succession to Hardy.

I said goodbye to George and Bill feeling quite good, and was sent from Khartoum to another military hospital at Gebeit, where I expected treatment for my leg. Someone drove me there in military transport and left me at the door. A nurse opened the door, and looked at me in some surprise. 'Damn!' she said. 'All right. Come in.' I went in and stayed for about a month. No treatment there. Apparently the only place with the right equipment was in Cairo.

At Gebeit one day I found my bed surrounded by about eight off-duty R.A.M.C. orderlies, one of whom had been a scout at Queens College Oxford during our house-party there in 1936. I asked them all how they had got into the R.A.M.C. To my astonishment, all had previous experience that was nothing to do with medicine. One was an engineer, and so on. They said, 'Well, we got called up and gave our particulars and this was where we were sent.' They seemed quite happy about it. I suppose the army just happened to need medical orderlies at the time.

Also at Gebeit we heard Winston Churchill on the radio speaking about the German invasion of Russia. It was one of the amazing transformations of the war. On one day, 21 June, the Germans were allies of the Russians. The next day they attacked them on a broad front and did not stop until they had nearly reached Moscow. Churchill moved our whole thinking about Russia in that speech. We had to get used to embracing the Russians as allies, and we did get used to it. We genuinely admired their resistance to the colossal onslaught. As to the Germans, I remember Churchill's words: 'Their air force, bearing the scars of many a recent British whipping, has now turned on their allies . . . etc.' He cracked the 'whipping' out like a lash.

Churchill's oratory was many-sided. Some today might object to such words. But Churchill had seen British cities bombed. Perhaps the most recent 'whipping' the Germans had received had been the discovery of how to 'see in the dark' by our night fighters. Thirty-three bombers were surprised and shot down over Britain one night, and the major air raids were stopped dead in their tracks. Churchill dared to say things which Englishmen felt but could not quite express. 'Let us so conduct ourselves that if the British Empire and Commonwealth were to last for a thousand years, people would still say "This was their finest hour".'

I certainly enjoyed the fellowship that came my way from members of the various Commonwealth forces during those hospital months. There was 'Bud' from Canada, with his memories of being invited out to tennis somewhere in England with Miss so and so – 'You know, bud, one of those typical English beauties with feet like flat-bottomed barges.' There was Buster of the H.L.I., a tea planter from

Ceylon, who had damaged an eye in a booby-trap outside Asmara. There was also Pat from South Africa. He told me how the Ossewabrandwag (the extreme right-wing movement of that time) had roared through the streets of some town in the Transvaal in trucks wielding long steel poles which cleared all the blacks off the pavements. By this time I was in Cairo, and Mrs Smuts, 'Ouma' (Granny) to the South Africans, came to visit the ward. She looked small and rather frail, but shrewd – no flies on her! She had an appropriate word for each of us. When she got to my bed, she said:

'And where are you from?'

I said 'England.'

'England. Oh, you ought to come and live in South Africa after the war.' It felt like a royal invitation.

Pat and I once nearly came to blows. He was enlarging on how the whites in South Africa needed to keep the blacks in their place. I said: 'Oh, so you're really a Nazi then?' There was a slight stirring of interest in the ward, but the moment passed. I remember Van Niekerk of Vereeniging also. He had a metal plate in his head from an accident sustained while despatch riding in the Western Desert. And I remember one day in November 1941 when our first wounded poured into hospital from the battle of Sidi Rezegh. A Brigadier, only hours after arriving, described to some of us the turmoil and confusion which ensued when his tank unit went into laager for the night and woke up at dawn to find that a German tank Commander had chosen to do the same a few yards away. They woke up and went into action against each other in the same instant.

Most of the above incidents happened in Cairo, where I spent six of the fifteen months, June to December 1941. I was in the Fifteenth (Scottish) Hospital, Agousa, which became almost like a second home. I had electrical treatment to stimulate the muscles in my leg back into working use. First it was crutches to get about, then, to keep my foot up, a spring attached to a leather thong round my calf at one end and the toe of my boot at the other. Massage and electrical treatment were administered by Sergeant Bell of the R.A.M.C., who came from Yorkshire. We were in a ward for the less serious cases, and I was allowed out to the Gezira Club for as many afternoons as I liked. My brother Robin turned up from England, and we had enjoyable chats about home, the world situation and his likely postings. Cairo was the centre of the whole Middle East Force, covering from Egypt to Lybia, Palestine, south to Addis Ababa, and even Kenya. Admiral Sir Edward (Ted) Cochrane, Commodore of

Convoys, whom I knew slightly, very decently made a point of having a cup of tea with me in between two of his exacting and dangerous journeys across the Atlantic. Whatever we talked about, it was not about the war – not his war, anyway, nor mine. It helped me that he should have bothered to get together.

My sister Gwen sent me copy of Peter Howard's new book, *Innocent Men*. It was a journalistic scoop by Howard, who had gone through the records and accounts of the Oxford Group at their H.Q. in London. His honesty and directness were a breath of fresh air and sanity. Also at this time came a letter from my brother John in Burma – in China actually, with the Chinese 93rd Division – describing how he had just won the three-legged race at a fête, tied to an opium smuggler whom he had been trying to catch while he was in the Burma Frontier Service. John replied to my letter of apology from Whitbourne mentioned earlier. 'I got your letter, and re-read it several times,' he wrote. 'It was a wonderful letter. You need not have apologised. I am really the one who should have done that. For envy, I mean. I always envied you at school for the way you went straight for what you wanted, while I led a more careful life, and kept out of trouble . . .' Both these letters, from Gwen and John, picked me up tremendously.

It also helped when six or eight of us were moved to the end of a wing in the hospital, where there was a view over the city, with palm trees and glimpses of people in the streets. A New Zealand baritone called Eric (I think) Simpson used to teach us a few simple choruses which we bellowed out with gusto on occasions. Quintin Hogg (now Lord Hailsham) turned up one day in the next bed to me, having picked up a bad inflammation of the ear while with the Rifle Brigade in the Western Desert. We had mutual memories of a far to the right body in Oxford called the 'English Mistery'. 'They talked lovely,' said Quintin. An open-hearted but slightly shell-shocked padre who had been through Crete kept us amused. He did not mention it, but we gathered he had held together thousands of troops in their march across the mountains to reach the navy who were to evacuate them.

Buster and I went to a tea dance at a well-known 'dive'. He danced, and brought his partner back to our table for a chat afterwards. Taking her at her word, I accepted an invitation to visit her 'any time', and turned up one day at her home. She was obviously annoyed, and introduced me to her husband who was less than cordial. Not the way to carry on, apparently. I soon excused myself and left. Buster said: 'I told you, didn't I.' He had refused to come with me, saying that I would get into all sorts of trouble.

In December the Japanese bombed Pearl Harbor, and the war with Japan was on. As we stood listening to the announcement over the radio there was an American Liaison Officer standing next to me. His face worked, as he stood transfixed. We all received the news in silence. It was too big to digest.

It was in December also that I received my marching orders to proceed to Mombasa, and to go and stay in Kenya for three months with my uncle, who was a doctor, and aunt, who was a nurse. I had in the meantime become friendly with a girl from South Africa who worked as a secretary at Middle East H.Q. in Cairo. I was beginning to wonder whether she could be the girl I should marry. I asked her out a couple of nights before I was due to leave, and proposed to her. To still the voice inside me which was advising caution, I drank a couple of whiskies first. She was fond of me, but could not say yes at once. She and I had first met during the campaign of the Oxford Group in Switzerland in 1935. During our talks in Cairo she had asked me: 'Teddy, how much have you kept of your experience then with the Oxford Group?' And I had replied: 'All of it.' Now, after a short talk in a taxi for privacy, we said goodbye on the steps of the hotel. The dream faded. I heard later she had married a businessman in Johannesburg. She was a nice girl but I am very glad she did not say yes decisively.

I set off for Mombasa in a crowded hospital ship, and we celebrated Christmas aboard, with all lights blazing.

My uncle Wilfred Brierley, who was to meet me in Mombasa, was the youngest of my mother's brothers and my godfather. My earliest memory of him is of a tall figure giving me a hand to jump a yew hedge at Whitbourne Hall. He would then have been on leave from the trenches in World War I, in which he served as a medical officer attached to an Indian battalion. He and his brother Charles, both in the I.M.S. (Indian Medical Service), were at one stage, while stationed in Bareilly, known as the 'Bareilly brothers', notorious for their escapades. These included getting themselves flown under a railway bridge to see if it was wide enough to take the aeroplane. When my mother wrote and told the various Brierley brothers about her change through the Oxford Group, they replied that the Group might be good for her, because she had 'never lived' before. They, the implication was, had lived, and therefore did not need it!

While still in the I.M.S., Wilfred had bought a plot of land in

Kenya, and become one of the early Kenya settlers. He was a coffee planter. By now he had become a senior and respected member of the settler community. I was warmly welcomed by him and his wife Norah, who was an even more senior Kenya settler than he was, and introduced to their friends from among that fascinating and mercurial crowd. Wilfred told me tales of Lord Delamere, the father figure of the White Highlands. He lent me a book, *Lord Delamere and the Making of Kenya*, which gave a sympathetic picture of this Cheshire landowner who had seen the potential of the land in Kenya and poured in his capital, and in the end the whole of the capital invested in his English estate, to start a farming revolution in the White Highlands of Kenya.

Great battles were going on between the Russians and Germans. Wilfred used to say: 'I hope they kill as many of each other as possible.' He felt the world would be a better place if peopled by Anglo-Saxons in as many key positions as possible. He and Norah took me twice to a fishing camp on the Matthioia River below Mount Kenya – two red letter events for me. I caught a brown trout of 3¾ lbs. I was putting them back at 1½ lbs, because we could only keep three in any one day.

They sent me to stay with friends: Cartwright at Naivasha, James Butterfield at Kericho, and the Head of Government Posts and Telegraphs in Nairobi.

I admired the neat plumbago hedges and beautifully kept gardens of the settlers. I became very much aware at that time of the difference between the British relationship with the African population in Kenya, and in a West African country like, say, Nigeria, where there were no British settlers. I believe it is true to say that a good part of the early British settlements in Kenya, which were all supposedly on unused land, were in fact on land which had been occupied by certain African tribes such as the Kikuyu, but had been vacated by them for a spell of years to enable the land to recover. The concept of staying permanently on one piece of land and looking after it, by manuring it etc., was on the whole a British, or European, concept. At any rate the almost universal opinion among settlers seemed to be that to get the best out of the land you needed the British. They were trying to train African leadership on their farms, but with limited success.

Relationships between master and man were, however, friendly enough. I remember seeing James Butterfield, finding some of his staff standing around chatting, going up behind one of them and doing the knee-trick on him. The fellow turned round to see who it was, and seeing who he burst into delighted and uproarious laughter. It was James's way, I supposed, of telling them to get a move on. James, as an older man, took a lively interest in my ideas on life. After one conversation, I remember him saying: 'I've enjoyed our talk and your heart's in the right place, but you have got some unworkable ideas.'

While in Nairobi, I accepted an invitation to stay for a week with Dr Gerald Anderson, one of the best known physicians in Kenya, who was also well known for his pioneering work with the Oxford Group. His wife Caroline was crippled, I think with arthritis, in constant pain and most of the time in a wheel-chair. They had a steady stream of people coming through their home for consultations. Gerald was busy with a fellow doctor lobbying M.P.s on some issue which they both felt was vital for the legislature. Their family, sons and daughters, were I think all away on war service. While with them, I suddenly went down with my first attack of malaria. Gerald ordered blanket upon blanket to be piled up on me till I had stopped shivering, and explained that I would start to sweat and then everything would be OK. And so it was. But it was a bit alarming while it lasted.

Before leaving Nairobi I carried out a personal 'raid' on Second Echelon H.Q. of Middle East Forces, which managed the movements of all odd military personnel like myself, with the object of getting them to find my papers and tell me what the prospects were of getting home to England. To my astonishment they found the papers, and told me that I was on the list to leave – I forget how soon – but I would be informed shortly. I came away satisfied, and quite impressed. No one seemed at all put out by my visit, though I thought myself it was rather a bold and 'unregimental' thing to do.

As I said goodbye to Wilfred and Norah and thanked them for looking after me, one thing emerged pretty clearly, or as clearly as anything could to me in my muddled state of mind and heart. Namely, that if during the weeks in Kenya I had been living by those standards of honesty, purity, unselfishness and love, I might have been able to give back to them something really worthwhile. But I wasn't. So I didn't.

The next move was from Mombasa to Durban. At Durban, I was shocked at the sight of hundreds of magnificent Zulu men in the prime of life running with rickshaws carrying people from place to place. 'What about Isandlwana? And Rorke's Drift?' I thought. But there was no sign on the part of these African men of anything other than pride and pleasure in their work. The only other thing I remember about Durban was being sent to hospital for a check-up on my leg, and there contracting malaria again just before we were due to sail. The nurse at first thought I was malingering because I didn't want to go on, but she soon changed her mind. I think I was nevertheless sent on to Cape Town on the next ship, which had medical facilities. I know that I lay in a wooden bunk in the hold sweating it off and was looked after by a medical orderly named Tom Valentine, who was in the Oxford Group. I appreciated his goodness and understanding, and he soon got me over it.

Next stop Cape Town, where we had been received so wonderfully in 1940. But this time – about June 1942 – there was an anxious feeling in the air. However, I caught up with one or two friends. My army companions included an N.C.O. called Jim who was being invalided home from the Far East. One afternoon he and I went and had a game of golf. Neither of us was any good at the game, and it was fun to see him scratching up the turf and cursing. But we fell in with an army parade, where the troops were to be addressed by General Smuts, and that was interesting. Smuts praised them to the skies for the first ten minutes, then for the second ten he shook them over the pit, with the urgency of the war situation, finishing with a clear challenge to tighten up their act. I admired his performance enormously, and Jim did too.

The final leg of the journey home was on the S.S. *New Holland*, one of those few fast unarmed merchantmen which carried passengers. She was unescorted all the way, relying on her speed to avoid submarines: a German surface raider was said to be at large in the Atlantic somewhere. The company on board was rather a gloomy one, consisting largely of refugees from the Japanese, mainly Dutch from South East Asia, and some twenty or so unattached British like myself. The talk was mainly about recent disasters in the war. The Japanese had incomprehensibly marched into Singapore on its undefended land side, and received the surrender of the Commander-in-Chief and some hundreds of thousands of British troops. They had also bombed and sunk two of our best battleships, the *Prince of Wales* and the *Repulse*, off Malaya. It was a staggering blow. They could go where they liked in South East Asia. But for a couple of stunning victories by the American navy and carrier-borne air force we might have lost the war there and then.

So our mood was solemn. Some outspoken comments by a Dutch

officer seemed to have a ring of truth about them. He said: 'The trouble with the British is you have no good senior officers. From Company Commanders downwards, the regimentals, fine. But at the top, no one any good.' The force of this view was perhaps driven home by a shell-shocked brigadier who appeared to follow me around. He would say 'Ah! Is that you, Oldwhistle? Let me see, have I organised you today, yet?' He would then give me some orders and pass on murmuring 'Now I must find so and so and organise him.'

One morning somewhere in the South Atlantic the ship's captain warned us that another ship of unknown nationality had been contacted. He sent all of us unattached officers and men down to the hold. It felt awfully lonely down there below the water line. There was a distant boom followed by a nearer blast – obviously a shell landing near by. Was this to be the end, after all? But after a few minutes it was announced that the ship was one of ours, just checking on who we were.

We arrived in Liverpool without further incident. Somewhere by the docks there were roses in bloom. I was issued with a railway warrant to Worcester. It was July 1942.

CHAPTER VII
H.Q. Western Command

My father met me at the station. He was just the same, but we seemed strangers. Half way home in the car, he suddenly said: 'There's not much to eat you know, Edward.' My introduction to rationing. We sat on a bench in the hall at home, and I spilled out to my parents what a shambles Keren had been. The Birmingham boys evacuated to Whitbourne for the duration of the war clustered round and said 'Give us a war story, Mr Edward.' I declined. Instead I tried to pick up some threads of my previous life. George Baker, who had become the gardener, said 'Well, you must take it easy for a bit and get away from all the pother.' Adams's comment about me was 'It's taken twenty years off his life!'

Gwen and Rozi were in London, and at some early stage after getting home I went up and met them and other old friends. Kit Prescott was in hospital for some minor thing, so I went and visited him. He kept saying 'God has sent you back to us.' He was bubbling over with pleasure.

During those first few weeks while I was waiting for the War Office to give me my next posting, I fought and won a battle within myself to start again having regular quiet times in the morning. I knew that regular quiet times were the 'air' element in a person's spiritual growth. Listening to God is the important part of prayer. If you neglect it, you are going to cut yourself off from a lot of chances of receiving God's grace. This is especially so when, as in my case, you have proved it by experience and then allowed it to lapse.

At any rate the devil made constant attacks on me to stop me from starting quiet times again. I remember well one walk down the Fulham Road and back by Victoria to Berkeley Square trying to clear away the black mood which had descended on me. I also remember sitting up in bed and punching at the devil whom I pictured as having difficulty in keeping his hands off me. What he was perhaps trying to say to me was: 'You've been in situations where you could not have regular quiet times. Thousands, millions of people are in that position. You know that for real men of action quiet times are just

Staff Captain, Western Command, 1943

not practical. Now that you are back among people who are used to having them, you want to start them again. Is it not just for the sake of a quiet life?'

This was not true, but it appealed to my pride. It was this very pride, the pride of attempting to be the self-sufficient man, which gave the devil this chance with me. I had taken back my life, having promised it to God. Now I wanted to give it back again to Him wholeheartedly. I needed God, I wanted Him. I did not want to be any sort of man except a man who belonged to Him.

Seeing this, I decided to start again.

Somewhere about this time I had a letter from a friend, Edward Hill, who was a major in the Welsh Regiment, and a D.A.Q.M.G. at H.Q. Western Command, Chester. He said they were in urgent need of a Staff Captain there and he thought the job might suit me, and would I let him ask for me to be asked for? I accepted this. Then I had a letter from the War Office saying that I was posted to some unit for forgotten soldiers in Montrose. I duly got on a train one evening in London straight from a showing of MRA's excellent play *Giant Otherfellow*, to travel to Montrose. It was a pretty bleak prospect there. They obviously did not know what to do with me. But the very next morning a telegram arrived from the War Office ordering me to report immediately to Western Command in Chester.

Western Command covered the whole of Wales, Cumberland, Lancashire and a large slice of the Midlands from Cheshire and Staffordshire down to Worcestershire. It was commanded by a full General, with a Major-General in command of Administration. There were about 120 officers employed, from full Colonel down to Captain. I became Staff Captain Q (Quartering). The particular section in which I worked consisted to start with of six men: Colonel Fraser, the A.Q.M.G. (Assistant Quartermaster General), who had a room to himself; Lieutenant-Colonel Francis and Major Edward Hill, both D.A.Q.M.G.'s, and myself, Staff Captain, in an adjoining room; and two civilian clerks, Mr Watkinson and Mr Kirk, in a third room across the passage, who were responsible for all the typing and looked after the files. There were also two A.T.S. woman secretaries.

Very roughly, the job of 'quartering' consisted of finding accommodation for all military personnel in the area. One of the chief ways of doing this was by requisitioning any building, public or private, which was empty or could be vacated. The officers responsible on the ground for serving the requisition notices were called Quartering Commandants, with the rank of Lieutenant-Colonel. They were usually professionals such as Chartered Surveyors serving in the army for the duration of the war, and they ran their own offices and staff dotted about the country. They must between them have overcome thousands of awkward problems which never got up to us at H.Q.

I felt that this time I had been put firmly in the position of 'Staff', as contrasted with that of soldiers engaged in the action. We were Civil Service-type soldiers. I recalled Philip Guedalla's remarks in his book on Lord Palmerston: 'Life at the War Office proceeded in a decorous administrative confusion.' Life with us was certainly decorous. But it was hard work, and increasingly involved long hours, especially as we had to accommodate upwards of a million American troops as well as our own.

If I had been underemployed in those fifteen months in Africa, I certainly made up for it in the next thirty months in Chester.

In easy reach of Chester, near Tarporley, was Tirley Garth, the only centre belonging to Moral Re-Armament in Britain that was located in the countryside. Its owner, Miss Irene Prestwich, had given it to MRA just before war broke out. Now she remained there as hostess with a skeleton staff. Six volunteer land girls were taken on, under the head gardener, to grow vegetables and fruit for market in the extensive gardens. A group of elderly and middle-aged women did a host of household jobs. There were very few men there, sometimes I think only the Secretary-Treasurer, whom I had known in Oxford days. The women, and not least the land girls, steadily built it up into a centre where people in reserved occupations, such as teaching, industry, engineering etc., could come for weekends, together with such services men as were in range. On my first visit there I was met by a Scottish landowner named Charles Burns, who drove me from the station in splendid style in a pony and trap. Irene asked me to come when I could, and I very often did.

However, in spite of the fact that I knew and liked many of the people there, I felt a bit like a fish out of water with them for a while. Tirley was a close-knit community, of disciplined and committed people. They did not seem to me to relax much. But I did get perspective from their idea that we had two wars to fight: the war of arms, and the war of ideas. Both had to be fought, but you had to distinguish between them. Victory in the war of arms would not automatically bring victory in the war of ideas. The war of ideas, which was concerned with what idea should run the world after the war, could and should be fought now. This interested me.

One particular weekend at Tirley remains in my memory. It must have been, I think, Christmas 1943. We had had news of the death of my brother John in April. The Germans had finally been driven out of Africa with the capture of 350,000 prisoners. Britain was filling up with Americans. At Western Command I had been working, weekends included, for about twenty days on the trot. I came to Tirley, feeling like a drink and a dance. We had a Christmas tree with candles and we sang carols round it. The carols included Christina

Rossetti's 'In the bleak mid-winter,' with its last line, 'What I can I give Him, give my heart.' I went up to my room, knelt by my bed, and gave Jesus my heart. I felt His presence in the room. It was indescribable. Wholly reassuring. A load of hardness and cynicism slipped quietly away from me. The steady thought came 'Every day counts,' and 'It all depends on you.'

A little later, perhaps next day, or two or three days later, I had the clear thought: 'Let God choose your friends.' I had been introduced to the Reverend Alan Blencowe, a fairly elderly bachelor clergyman who was rector of a parish on the outskirts of Chester. Now for some weeks I went off to visit him after work on my bicycle, simply to exchange thoughts which had come in our quiet times. He became a friend, and introduced me to his churchwarden, an executive in Shotton Steelworks nearby, who in turn invited me to visit whenever possible.

One day, during a particularly busy period, I had the clear thought in my quiet time 'Look out for so and so this morning.' In the canteen, between eating lunch and going back to work, I found myself sitting next to 'So and So', and we talked. I forget what we talked about, but it may have been *Battle Together for Britain*, a handbook which was about to be published by Moral Re-Armament. In the middle of our talk, the man on the other side of my friend suddenly put down his paper and leaned across and said 'Do you mind if I listen?' This was Lieutenant-Colonel B.G. Robbins, Officer in command of Technical Training, whom I knew slightly but had never had any real conversation with. So we talked on, and Robbins asked if we could meet again. We did, several times.

Robby was fascinated with the idea that he might try having a quiet time at the start of the day. When he did so, he became a changed man. Before, he had given the impression of being somewhat worried, his brow often puckered with problems both technical and other. Now he became cheerful, and the lines on his face seemed to vanish, or alter, he was always bursting out with corny jokes and comments on life. It did not come easily. We had little in common. But I grew to be more and more at home with him. Our friendship matured noticeably during a game of golf we played together one afternoon. Where, or even how, we played, I have no idea. But it injected a bit of fresh air into us both.

Robby was a convinced Christian already, and a respected figure in his church and profession – for many years after the war he was to be Secretary of the Institution of Mechanical Engineers. His conviction about the importance of what he was learning through MRA steadily increased as he continued with his daily quiet times. In May 1944 he joined me in giving a buffet supper at the Grosvenor Hotel for officers of Western Command and their ladies to meet the Tirley Garth family. It happened that my sister Rozi had joined the strength at Tirley some weeks earlier, so she came along too. There were about seventy guests all told. Robby spoke with cheerful conviction. Angela Knatchbull from Tirley sang a song composed by herself called 'Even a worm can turn'. *Battle Together for Britain* was allied to a revue which had gone the round of the United States called 'You can defend America,' and the Tirley chorus gave a spirited rendering of this. It included the refrain:

'We're the arm behind the Army,
We're the V. behind the Navy,
We're the force behind the Air force,
We're the breeze behind the red and white and blue!'

Colonel Francis was ceremonially presented by the Tirley visitors with the first copy of *Battle Together for Britain*, and made a suitably gracious reply. The news went round Western Command H.Q. that it was a good party, and so it was.

Encouraged by this, Robby and I got an appointment with the Commanding General, and he and I and another officer duly turned up. We found that the General had got the M.G.A. (Major-General in charge of Administration) along as well. Robby opened for us. After a bit the General said: 'I have had the impression that Moral Re-Armament are not very keen on fighting.' I stepped forward smartly and said 'I think you might get a different impression, Sir, if you would read this,' and I took out of my tunic pocket a copy of *Fighters Ever* by Peter Howard, and handed it to him. The M.G.A. stifled a broad grin at this piece of brass. The general remained courteous and non-committal, but he took the book.

The M.G.A. had indirectly taken a hand in our efforts to strengthen our growing team at Western Command. Another officer, a younger married man, had announced his desire to work with us, saying that we were 'cutting ice', whereas according to him the officers' christian organisation, to which he belonged, was not. He had a number of pin-ups in his room. The M.G.A. on a tour of inspection happened to come in and see them and took exception to them. So down they had to come. This officer had his wife and young family, of school age and under, living in lodgings near Chester, and one weekend he invited me over. What stands out in my memory is that his lodgings were so tiny that he insisted that he bring me my breakfast in bed, because if I went anywhere outside the bedroom I should only be in the way.

He became one of those who met for several weeks regularly in a room provided by Bishop Tubbs (formerly of Rangoon), who was then Dean of Chester Cathedral and who took an interest in what we were doing. There we had a study group, based on *Battle Together for Britain*. Alan Blencowe's churchwarden also came.

Lieutenant-Colonel Francis, my immediate boss, was a study in deliberation and precision. He always went to the same place in the canteen, with the same newspaper. If someone rang up and said: 'I want to speak to G (Ops),' he would invariably reply: 'I don't see why you shouldn't. Their number is 123456,' and put the receiver down. His career had been in the Indian Army, from which he had retired as a battalion commander before the war. He had come back to serve in any capacity and had been given the job of D.A.Q.M.G. He had excelled in shooting with a pistol. He would say that he always tried to find something that every one of his soldiers was really good at. He used to hang up the office key on a nail outside the door when we went out for lunch, so that whichever of us arrived back first could let ourselves in with it. I could never fathom the security thinking behind this habit!

It was a real entertainment to see Francis deal with the various U.S. Liaison Officers who came in, urgently wanting to know where their engineers could live while prospecting for a site, or how they could bypass some regulation which prevented them starting immediately on building accommodation for this or that unit. Francis would stand up and put the tips of his fingers together and deliver them a lecture on how Britain was already full, was only a minute island compared to U.S.A. and they had to be patient while people either made way for them or found them land to build on. He would then listen carefully to what they had to say. As often as not, the interview finished with him giving his personal opinion that they might as well jump the gun and do what they had to do straight away. These meetings usually broke up amid laughter, and the visitors would go away thinking this 'Limey' was a bit of a card. In fact they sometimes seemed to be coming in mainly for the entertainment.

Rather different was our top boss in the room next door, Colonel Fraser. He gave the impression of never relaxing, and you never went in to him unless you had something crisp and clear-cut to say. If something politically controversial arose within the Command, he would say: 'We mustn't let those six hundred wasters at Westminster get hold of this.' I wrote a report at one stage, using mainly material supplied by the Quartering commandants, on how the problems of accommodating U.S. troops were being overcome, which apparently was thought sufficiently well of to be sent up to the Army Council for information. I remember that on the initiative of Edward Hill, who had seen much more of Fraser than Colonel Francis, I was appointed to organise a medium-sized dinner party for him on his retirement in the Grosvenor Hotel, and he said how much he appreciated it. It had been really 'matey'.

One noteworthy effort at Command H.Q. to cement relations with the Americans was a dinner party for a large number of senior officers from both armies to meet one another. It was a sit-down dinner with named places. There was a certain amount of awkwardness to begin with, but then a British officer took out of his pocket a piece of paper supplied by his liaison officer listing 'subjects of conversation' to try out with his next door neighbour. The subjects were: baseball, handball, netball and volleyball. This caused pleasure all round. Very soon most of the other officers, on both sides, were pulling out their 'subjects', and the party never looked back.

I think that by a blend of systematic thoroughness and having people on the ground with plenty of horse sense, permitting occasionally extreme flexibility, the army did succeed in taking on the American influx with a minimum of fuss.

It was the time of the first post-war general election, at which the British people, having given everything through 6 years of war under a Coalition Government, and having won total victory, decided that they could not stand another peace-time Tory government. They voted the Tories out, even Churchill out, and Labour in by a thumping majority. I remember being taken by surprise at a public meeting during the campaign when my neighbour (a stranger) turned to me and said 'I think those landowners have got a lot to answer for. We ought to get rid of them!'

When my time came for 'demob', I drew a sports jacket and grey flannel trousers, and headed for Whitbourne. The decorous years of 'civilised' army life were over, and soon seemed to slip away. But what I had learnt in those years about teamwork and God's guiding hand and His amazing generosity has never left me. There was a unique quality about the teamwork I found with Brian Robbins.

CHAPTER VIII
Erica

IT WAS TYPICAL of Brian that he should say to me thoughtfully one day, not long before we both left Chester: 'Hm. How old are you? Thirty-five? I think you ought seriously to consider getting married. I suggest the year after next.' I was amused at his suggesting the time, while apparently leaving the choice of wife up to me.

Brian knew nothing about Erica. She had spent practically the whole of the war in India. She had then made it to the United States in the Swedish vessel *Gripsholm* and after nearly a year there arrived in London with 150 other MRA full-time workers in April 1946. I was in London at the time. We met for a few moments at a crowded tea reception. And that was all.

That summer I left Whitbourne and travelled to the first ever Moral Re-Armament conference at Caux, Switzerland. It was nine years since I had attended my last Oxford Group house-party at Oxford. I sat in the train from Knightwick station as it puffed along towards Worcester, feeling that a chapter had ended and a new one was beginning.

It was just a month after my sister Gwen's wedding to Francis Goulding, a wonderful event at which a huge number of guests filled every seat in Whitbourne church, and in the house and lawn afterwards. Uncle Percy (the then Lord Somers) gave the toast. Pa said a few well-chosen words, finishing up with 'and I hope . . . I hope . . . (child's cry from somewhere) . . . Quite!' All the women wore ridiculous small hats with flowers, in an invasion of the village from London. One of our farm men said to me: 'I'll find one to suit you out of that lot.' Frank Buchman was a guest. I met him at the station at Worcester and just as I was negotiating the corner into Broad Street, he asked me: 'When are you planning to have *your* marriage?'

So there was a certain expectation building up in me. But it did not happen at Caux that year. Most of my memories of that time are of struggling to look after the practical needs of the six hundred or so delegates. I joined a cooks' shift under Hilda Collison (now Hilda

Grimshaw), a W.R.N.S. officer of senior rank who must have needed all her gifts of organisation to get her inexperienced team of six to turn out decent meals. But it happened somehow. I was not alone, I think, in never having cooked before anywhere! There was a Swedish pastor, a young man of some standing in theological circles at home. He was no cook either. We fairly soon enjoyed it and looked forward to being together. The equipment in the hotel was very basic – just adequate for the job. I remember once – it may not have been part of the cooks' shift but an extra – grinding up cheese in a grinder, which for some reason was well above my head, for $3\frac{1}{2}$ hours.

There was also the 'economat', or storeroom, through which all food – meat and vegetables, milk, butter and cheese as well as shelf stores like biscuits – came. The ordering was in the hands of two delightful and determined Swiss ladies, Monique Neher and Frieda

A conversation at Gwen's wedding between (l to r) the Archdeacon of Worcester, Tom Wilson, Mrs Winifred Wilson, Frank Buchman and John Wood from the U.S.A.

Nef, assisted by six or so executive types, to wit: Leo Exton (hotelier), Stuart Sanderson (textile manufacturer), Thorvald Pedersen (confectioner), Farrar Vickers (oil man), Alfred Nielsen (timber grower), and myself (ex-soldier cum budding estate manager). The two women were fully stretched running the show in the local dialect, which the men could not understand. Seldom have I seen so much ability crowded into one room with so little chance to deploy itself. We ended up, I think, after some hilarious and some exasperated moments, by ourselves doing a certain amount of fetching and carrying the heavier crates, and leaving the admin. to the women. It was a chance for three Englishmen, a Scotsman, a Norwegian and a Dane to compare notes with one another. Personally, at the end I was still pretty much at sea as regards the work, but warm friends with all my fellow-workers.

Caux was a miraculous development in the work of Moral Re-Armament, which we owed to the vision and sheer courage of the Swiss, many of whom sank their personal capital to buy it, and many hundreds of whom came to get it ready to take the conference in time. Caux has existed ever since with a paid staff of maintenance workers only. All the work of the conferences, such as cooking, washing up, flower arranging, laying and serving tables for meals, is done by the members of the conferences themselves.

During that first year I had wondered for a short time whether to try seriously to enter Parliament. I felt at one with the considerable body of Conservatives, led by R.A.Butler, who were in favour of a National Health Service. After the Conservative defeat in the election, Butler, assisted by Cuthbert Alport, was successfully building up the Conservative Political Centre. I joined the C.P.C. and spoke once or twice to captive audiences in London and Birmingham. In London, my speech coincided with an electricity failure. It was a cold night, and of course food rationing was still on. I was listened to with attention until I said something like 'Thank God in Britain we've still got our freedom.' The audience exploded in laughter. In Birmingham they tried me out on most of the West Midlands party top brass, and I think found me wanting. I did get a letter from Roger Conant offering to give me an introduction to Stanley Baldwin, but I did not accept.

Meanwhile, however, I got to know our own Member of Parliament, A.E. Baldwin. Archer Baldwin was a refreshing figure. Earlier, I had met him out hunting with the Clifton-on-Teme, and later watched him ride his own horse in point-to-points. A gunner officer in World

War I, he became head of a leading Herefordshire firm of auctioneers, estate agents and valuers. He was also a keen farmer, and much respected in the neighbourhood. As he said himself, he knew nothing much about politics, but he thought he would have a go for the North Herefordshire seat, and he won it by six hundred votes from his Liberal opponent. I went to his first public meeting in Bromyard, and there and then, in the street, offered the agent my subscription. During his speech, a young heckler on a bicycle shouted something insulting. Without hesitation Archer confronted him and suggested they settle their differences with their fists. The heckler moved on rapidly.

Archer became a firm friend and counsellor to me. He was a strong Christian, believing that the best hope for Britain lay in a village-based, church-based renaissance. My interest in becoming an M.P. myself had evaporated somewhat by the time I went to Caux. I was realising that working with the likes of Archer Baldwin might be closer to what God intended.

A theme at Caux was that Moral Re-Armament was meant to give democracy's inspired ideology to the world. In common with many men and women of MRA who had been through the war, I tried to see where my particular part in this lay. The thought that emerged was that I should make England my sector of this world enterprise. I had only the vaguest notion still of how the British Commonwealth and Empire was started. I had not heard of the Statute of Westminster, whereby the original Dominions got their freedom from Britain. I studied a bit, and began to be captured by the idea of a British Commonwealth of free countries – countries into which Britain had put all she could in the way of training for government, only to free them to govern themselves.

In this I was lucky to find a kindred spirit in London. Hugh Elliott had been my contemporary at Oxford, joined the Colonial Service, and had served three or four stints in Nigeria, during the course of which I received one or two letters from him. Now here he was in London, seconded for a spell to the Colonial Office, and disposed to help in my Empire studies.

Hugh represented the West African school of thought among British colonialists of the time. He had not much faith in the contribution of settlers in Africa, believing that the whole purpose of government was to make the Africans free for self-government. He and I gave a talk one morning on the British Empire in the World to a group of Americans – not the most receptive of audiences then (or perhaps now, for that matter). As soon as Hugh stopped speaking one of those listening, a young teenage girl, said: 'Well, so this matter of giving the colonies back to the people might be the greatest thing you have ever done?'

I tried a little later to give the idea to the girls of Westonbirt School assembled for their Empire Day service in chapel on 24 May. I was received politely, though I did not feel much of what I said had gone in. The whole event was a bit intimidating, including lunch after chapel with the Headmistress and prefects. The invitation had come on the initiative of the Arts Mistress, who knew me slightly. Four years later she married Hugh Elliott!

In London that spring and early summer I felt that now the time had come to open proceedings again with Erica. What I did not know was that a great deal was going on in Erica. She had long held thoughts of another man. She had a clear and decisive thought one morning 'He is not for you' followed swiftly with 'Don't try to qualify this.' She accepted it and as she did so she began to find that Jesus was becoming her greatest friend.

Meanwhile the thing was how to proceed? I prayed about it and consulted one or two trusted friends, in particular Bremer Hofmeyr. He said 'you may have to court Erica.' I asked her to meet me in a small sitting room near where we were both working. She came in and sat down opposite me.

I said; 'I just want to tell you that I do love you very much. I want you to know that, and also I do not want any reply yes or no or anything at all. I just wanted to tell you that.'

'Is that all?'

'Yes.'

'Thank you very much.'

After a few minutes she left.

The next day she sought me out and said; 'I think we should get to know one another.'

I invited her to a Conservative exhibition and took her out to tea at the Coq d'Or. She remembers she was wearing a new blue dress and hoped she looked good in it. I thought she looked delightful, though I had not noticed the dress.

Neither of us can remember anything about the exhibition. I was also aware that she had kept me waiting forty minutes for our date. She had not seemed to notice anything and I was too overcome by relief that she had turned up to mention it. By the time we said goodbye after our tea at the Coq d'Or, I was walking on air.

She left soon after this for Switzerland, to help at the summer conference at Caux. She and Döe Howard had to partner two of the Indian Davis Cup team in an exhibition tennis match during their visit. Long after, Erica told me she had suddenly heard my laugh (a rather unmistakeable one) on the terrace below the big hall not knowing I had come over, and she realised that she was deeply sure.

My father came with me to Caux that summer. We spent almost all the time together. I remember a merry meeting with some West Indians. I also remember the two of us going into the Victoria Hotel, Glion, one day and having a delicious beefsteak meal. It made a change from rationing. I was waiting for the moment to propose to Erica. Pa burst out at one stage: 'Damn it, man. It's not a game of chess!'

At last it happened. We arranged to foregather one evening. During the afternoon Erica broke not one, but two strings of beads! That evening we were seeing off some special friends who were leaving for the States. With about a hundred others we surged out onto the road in the dark. We waved them off and found ourselves walking together. The others went in and we strolled on towards the little Maria Hotel where, with Bremer's collusion I had booked a sitting room. I put my arm round her as I led her up the steps to our room looking over the lake. 'There's so much I want to tell you about' she said. We talked for perhaps an hour. I then went down on both knees and asked her to marry me, and she gave me the long delayed, the unimaginable 'Yes,' which filled my heart.

I brought Erica over to Pa's room to tell him our news. Fully clothed he was patiently sitting on his bed swinging his feet. As she threw her arms round his neck he said with his roguish smile: 'Well you've been a long time making up your mind.'

We were married at Caux on 4 October 1947. It was the last week of the conference. Frank Buchman's card to us said: 'To a happy couple, in the steps of St Francis, on his day.'

To start the day, our whole family party met for a Holy Communion at the Anglican church a little way up the hill. Both my parents were there, and my brothers, sisters, cousins, uncles and aunts. (Both Erica's parents had died, her father when she was sixteen and her mother not long before the war.) Her elder brother Richard, a regular army Lieutenant-Colonel, gave her away, and he also became a sort of marshal of the family party, making a point of getting to know everyone and helping them to know their way round at Caux. It was the first time she and her brothers had been under the same roof for seven years. An older couple, Lionel Jardine of the Indian Civil Service and his wife Marjorie, who had both looked after Erica and worked closely with her during her time in India, 'stood in' as parents during the civil ceremony the day before in Glion.

All clothes were still firmly on coupons but somehow our five bridesmaids looked lovely, and Erica's wedding dress almost knew its way up to the altar on its own.

The marriage itself was in the great hall of Mountain House, Caux. It was taken by John Tyndale-Biscoe, chaplain to the Bishop of Rangoon, at whose own marriage Erica had been a bridesmaid, and by Hallen Viney, another Anglican clergyman friend of ours. Frank Buchman gave the blessing. It was he who had asked Erica if she would like to be married at Caux.

The reception included everyone left at the conference. Hundreds of people crowed into the downstairs dining-room for the reception. The majority of them were Germans, a vast number of whom had come to Caux, following the first German delegation the year before. As Erica and I walked in through the door, Loudon Hamilton got the whole party to give us three cheers. Erica insists that they also sang 'For they are jolly good fellows.' Anyway we are at one in remembering the wave of love which came across to us in an utterly spontaneous way. Many of our families spoke, there was a sword-dance from Scotland and a love-song from Sweden. A lot of our 'guests' must have had little idea who we were. But for the Germans one thing which contributed to their feeling at home was that practically all the music chosen for the occasion happened to be German. Of those who did know us, quite a few were, I think, still gasping with astonishment that this lively, attractive and popular Irish girl should have fallen (at last) for me!

We left Mountain House for our honeymoon under an impromptu archway of crossed swords, rustled up from somewhere by Hugh Elliott. I had asked him to be my best man, and he had detached himself from the Colonial Office and flown over for the weekend.

After an idyllic week in the chalet of some Swiss friends, we boarded an Italian liner from Naples to New York. Frank Buchman had invited us to be part of the European contingent of an international group which was to introduce post-war Europe to America. There must have been about two hundred of us who mustered in New York, nearly half of us actively engaged in putting on a new musical revue called *The Good Road*, which had its genesis in Caux. Erica and I did not take part in this, except in handing out invitations,

Erica and myself, shortly after announcing our engagement at Caux, 1947

etc. While the shows were on, we often sat quietly backstage praying, while our friends sang, acted, changed scenes, prompted, rested in between appearances, and so on. On occasions we handed out our wedding cake backstage. Frank kept introducing us as a 'honeymoon couple' long after what I had thought of as our honeymoon was over! As a matter of fact, that period of living and working as just two members of a very varied team definitely helped to speed up our acceptance of having some newly-married corners rubbed off.

We put on *The Good Road* in New York and Washington, before moving to Richmond, Virginia. In Washington we had the privilege of hearing General George Marshall personally deliver a speech containing the substance of what became known as the 'Marshall Plan' to the Foreign Affairs Committee of the Senate of the United States. He spoke conversationally, as far as I could see without notes. The Marshall Plan is sometimes referred to today by politicians, such as M. Harmel, the Belgian Foreign Minister, President Mitterand of France, and African political leaders. They say, for instance, that we should have a Marshall Plan for Africa, and Europe should be on the giving end of it. Well, the original Marshall Plan was financed entirely by the United States, and Europe was on the receiving end of it. Its purpose was to bring Europe back from the dead, in economic terms – especially France, Britain, Belgium, Holland, Luxembourg, Germany and Italy – the countries most devastated by the war. The money was all given as grants, or interest-free loans, and was not repayable. But the conditions were stringent: European countries had to pull up their socks, along carefully defined economic lines. If they would not agree to this, no plan. To many members of Congress on Capitol Hill in Washington, the Europeans who accompanied *The Good Road* offered the first chance to assess whether they were justified in investing such a vast sum in Europe's future. Could it pull its socks up, or would the money go down the drain? *The Good Road* gave them some reassurance.

From Richmond, the party moved on to California. The main body, including the show, travelled through the southern states by coach, while Erica and I were privileged to travel with a small party of mainly British ex-servicemen and their wives across Canada. We addressed meetings, businessmen's lunches, etc., in Montreal, Ottawa, Toronto, Winnipeg and Calgary. These were laid on in advance by our Canadian hosts in each city. Brigadier 'Rab' Beaman of the Canadian army travelled with us with his wife Nancy, as did Paul and Elizabeth Nanton from Winnipeg. I do not remember much about our speeches, except that they were all warmly received. But I do have lasting and pleasant memories of the company of our small party on the train, in which Erica and I were two of the junior members. They included Lieutenant-General André Lesaffre of Belgium, who had commanded a crack division of their army against the Germans in 1940: his division had stood and fought the Germans for nearly a week. He was a cheerful and merry soul, who now approached the task of trying to give a faith to Canadians with a military directness and few words. At times the demands of little adjustments in plans, dashes to catch trains etc., became too much for him, and he would exclaim under his breath: 'J'en ai ma claque.' (A young airman who joined us from his home in the Mid-West asked: 'Who is this guy Johnny McClack you are all talking about?') Also in the party were Admiral Sir Edward Cochrane, Major-General George Channer, and Colonel Malise Hore-Ruthven of the Black Watch. Malise and I thought we would go for a moonlight stroll in Toronto one evening. Paul warned us we'd find it too cold, but still we went. We strode out from the hotel. When we had gone about ten yards we both put our hands (gloved) up to our ears, looked at one another and turned round and went in again. Earmuffs it was, from then on.

We met up with the main body again in Los Angeles. I think it was in the same year, 1948, that the Communist Party made L.A. their centre of operations for America. MRA acquired premises at 833 South Flower Street, known as 'The Club'. They were quite large, with a patio on the first floor and a meeting-hall, though nothing like as large as Caux. Erica and I lodged with a couple off Verdugo Boulevard. We all set to to make 'The Club' ready for guests. I seem to remember spending some time scraping floors with a razor blade.

In April, we flew home and opened our wedding presents.

In July, Erica gave birth to our first child, Edward William, in Hereford General Hospital.

During the next two years, 1948 to 1950 – the years which led up to our final move to Whitbourne to take on the estate – we lived and worked mainly in Birmingham. Our first home was a flat on the third floor of the big vicarage of St George's, Edgbaston. The flat had just been vacated by Harry Wickham, who had become West Midlands Area Organiser for the Labour Party. Our host, the Reverend Basil Farncombe, vicar of St George's, and his wife Jennie were already our friends. Jennie gave Erica invaluable training in how to run a home in post-war England. Basil was wonderful company. In addition to his Edgbaston parish, he had taken on the coalfields of the Midlands, and would regale us with stories of miracles which resulted from his sometimes terrifying adventures.

In that vicarage I remember meeting with most of the shop stewards' committee of a well-known brewery. They were reeling from the impact of the return from Caux of their brewery manager. This man's reputation as a tough negotiator on wages and conditions was such that he was held responsible for the workers' representative who dealt with him having gone down with stomach ulcers. He came back from Caux a changed man – a humble man, who asked forgiveness for his overbearing ways, and suggested they all make a fresh start together. Those shop stewards were having a sweepstake on how long the change would last. Most of them gave it about a week, but it was permanent. That brewery manager became a regular attender at St George's church, and later a churchwarden.

He was one of a group of people in management who arose as a result of the visit to Birmingham of *The Forgotten Factor*, a phenomenon in the British coalfields and factories of the immediate post-war era. This was a play written by Alan Thornhill, formerly chaplain of Hertford College, Oxford, about the family of the head of a company and of his chief Trade Union negotiator, and it dealt with a strike situation and its solution. It played through the winter of 1946–47 in London. Hugh Gaitskell was the new Minister of Fuel and Power, and he came to see it. His comment was: 'You are pressing the button that can make the coal industry work.' Many miners' delegations came to see it that winter, and the following summer and onwards, it spread to the coalfields.

In Birmingham, we were to measure the legacy of *The Forgotten Factor*, and the impact of Moral Re-Armament, at first hand over a longer period. This was made possible for Erica and me by the selfless way in which a Birmingham girl, daughter of a prominent businessman, came into our home to look after our baby boy. She could share all home duties with Erica, and she often freed her to come out and visit with me. She became like one of our family.

One day Erica and I were invited out to tea (the evening meal) with Bert and Gwen Allen. I had heard quite a bit about Bert, and had heard him speak at meetings, but had never met him socially. He was the convener of shop stewards at Reynolds Tubes, part of the Tubes Investment Group. He was also a member of the District Committee of the A.E.U. (Amalgamated Engineering Union). Before he joined

Reynolds Tubes, he had been a London taxi driver, and a waiter in the dining car on the G.W.R. I had not seen Gwen at all. But I knew that Bert had astounded her after his first meeting with MRA, by getting home when she was out and having a cup of tea ready for her on her return. They probably knew that we were landowners from the country. Bert was fairly adept at making friends with all sorts of people, but I sensed that even he was not quite sure how to treat us.

At any rate they laid on a beautifully prepared meal, and we talked. Gwen told us she had got fed up once with the way Bert was taking no notice of her. He was away for a bit, so before he came back she decided to dye her hair and appear to him as another woman on the station platform when she went to meet him. On the platform he walked right past her without recognising her, and she was delighted to be able to introduce herself. 'That was the sort of way I had to take him down,' she said. Bert told us how when he was elected to the A.E.U. District Committee, he went to his first committee meeting not knowing the ropes at all. The chairs were set on two sides with a gangway down the middle. Someone said to him:

'Which side are you going to sit on?'

'Why? What difference does it make?' asked Bert,

'Oh, Communists on the left, all others on the right.'

Bert seized hold of a chair, placed it firmly in the gangway in the middle, and sat down on it.

In the factory, his leadership of the shop stewards had been a stormy one. Strikes were two a penny. April was thought to be a good month for strikes: 'Come on. The daffodils are out. All out!' Bert used to say was his philosophy. Suddenly he perceived that there was something in the words of the trade unionist in *The Forgotten Factor*, 'What matters is not who's right, but what's right.' When next called upon to put the claim of the shop stewards for a wage increase to the managing director, he said he now wanted to negotiate what was right for the firm. He came away with more money than his membership could have asked for. They never had another strike at Reynolds Tubes as long as Bert was there, which was thirty years.

In the District Committee of the A.E.U., where he sat in the gangway, he was responsible for a further and much more important development. It was a particular ploy of the Communist Party at that time to try to use the Trade Union movement to influence foreign policy – always against the official Labour Party policy of Ernest Bevin, the Foreign Secretary. Bert found out that the Communists on the committee were having a planning meeting before every

Bert Allen (foreground) fishing in the pool at Whitbourne with Sid Cresswell, Divisional Organiser of the Amalgamated Engineering Union (A.E.U.). Looking on, father and myself

Jim Leask (r) in conference with Tom Oswald M.P. from Edinburgh, and Purshottam Trikumdas from India (centre)

committee meeting to decide how to get their way at the main meeting. He therefore started an unofficial Labour planning meeting before every committee, to get *their* way. It was the first time the Communists had been stood up to in this way, and it gave enormous heart to the Labour boys. The discovery of this real rift between Labour and the Communists was definitely a part of my education as a Conservative.

It was a great day at Whitbourne when, with the help of Archer Baldwin, I was able to arrange a supper party there to bring this home to some of our Conservative friends. Archer had plenty of friends across the floor in the House of Commons, as well as on his own side. He got one of the most right wing of the Conservative M.P.s to come to that supper, a fellow whom he had described to me as being 'his own worst enemy.' The Birmingham party included, as well as Bert and Gwen Allen, Jim and Lucy Leask and another shop steward from an engineering company whose name was John. Jim Leask was the Area Trades Group Secretary of the Transport and General Workers Union, and quite an up and coming man in the Labour Party hierarchy. John was a Scotsman, a raw character if ever there was one, accustomed to getting his way with his fists, but now a changed man.

Archer's friend came in late when we had already started supper, and was about to sit down without acknowledging either of my parents who were at each end of the table. Archer had to nudge him into doing this, explaining that it was not a club. Bert, Jim and John all spoke briefly after supper about the war of ideas in industry, and the difference Moral Re-Armament had made. Afterwards in conversation, our M.P. friend made some remark to the effect that a politician could not play any part in this because he could not take sides. Lucy Leask exploded in anger. She came up and shook her fists at him – not in his face, because she could not reach that high, but somewhere about his chest – and said: 'How dare you say a thing like that? We're looking to you for something better!' It is my most vivid memory of the evening.

Jim and Lucy became good friends, and my mother took on their son, Graham, once for a visit so as to free the parents to go to an important conference together. Lucy had taken the little chap to the Natural History Museum to condition him for the horned heads of East African animals which he would see arrayed round the hall on his arrival at Whitbourne. His main preoccupation then was to dash round the back passages to see if he could find their bodies and tails.

Also, one Sunday afternoon a colleague and I concreted the whole of their garden path for them at Smethwick while they were out. This went down well. The said colleague, whose name was Stan, later married John's daughter.

Of John, I must record another word. I have said he was a raw character, but he was also a real gentleman. You could read it all in the face of his wife: the hurts she had received, and then the gradual dawning of gratitude and hope, and finally – after he changed – something like security. I do not know how he changed originally. But I do remember very well how he came to find a belief in Christ a little later. He had been invited to go over to Germany as a spokesman for MRA. After he came back, he told some of us that for some time after meeting MRA, he had put right some things he had done wrong, and had gone around proclaiming the ideology to answer Communism, but there was still inside him a dryness and a deadness. Someone, I think on the boat going over, had asked him: 'Have you ever given your life to Jesus Christ as a personal Saviour? Someone who loves you? And asked His forgiveness for your sins?' John knelt down and did that. I remember his words as he described it. 'It was as if the whole world came green again.'

'The ideology to answer Communism' or 'Democracy's inspired ideology'; this was how I saw Moral Re-Armament. But I never saw it, nor was it ever, an ideology *against* Communism.

The Communist Chairman of Shop Stewards at Dunlops started to become different, and to take an interest in Moral Re-Armament. Erica and I used to go and visit him and his wife, a teacher, in their home. They had young children and we thought them a very nice couple. Then Frank, the husband, was sent away on another job by the company to South America. The Communist Party promptly sent a lodger to come and live with the wife Cicely and family. One evening a colleague named Bill and I went down expecting to meet him. Bill had his knife into the man for coming to separate Cicely from Frank. On the way there, in the street, he told me so, and there and then surrendered his sin of hatred to God and asked forgiveness for it. The Communist tried to goad us by abuse of America, but he could not get us to react there. He then talked about the British upper classes. I said I was one of those and we could change, and I had changed. Billy said how he had hated the chap's guts until a few moments before and was sorry for the hatred. We were onto the subject of changing human nature.

It was an effort on the part of both of us, but it was not enough.

Cicely rejoined the Communist Party and stopped having us in her home. The couple separated. Frank was last heard of still in South America. Cicely and the children we lost touch with.

Another member of the shop stewards' committee who stuck with us was a contrasting character; quiet, steady and solid. And there was also the works manager, who was genuinely impressed by the influence of Frank and the others on the work force. This man was one of those who showed round a Japanese delegation who came to Caux and to Britain in 1950, an event I was privileged to be in on. They were the first delegation of comparable rank to visit Britain for seventy years.

In 1949 Erica and I accompanied a delegation of Birmingham management to Caux, and they met there a quartet of Americans who were invited back to help us develop the work in the Midlands for the ensuing year. They were Bill and Katrine Stubbs, Gene Bedford and Jack Currie.

One other important event has to be reported during our time in Birmingham. In October 1950 our second son, Christopher Frank, was born in Marston Green Hospital. I took him to visit his grandad in his room at Whitbourne – or rather William did, struggling in with the carry-cot, and announcing: 'Here's my baby.'

PART II
DOWN TO BUSINESS

I am the land of their fathers,
In me the virtue stays.
I will bring back my children
after certain days.

Under their feet in the grasses
my clinging magic runs.
They shall return as strangers;
They shall remain as sons.

        from *The Recall*, by Rudyard Kipling

CHAPTER IX

Gathering up the reins

PART TWO OF this account now begins. I intend it to be the story of the Whitbourne Estate from 1950 to 1980, the year in which I retired and William (Bill), our elder son, took over. But it may not work out that way. I had better follow the same method as I have for Part One, and write down events as they happened with a minimum of comment. The one comment I would like to make now is the extraordinary accuracy of God's guidance in the matter of my engagement and marriage to Erica. 'Extraordinary accuracy' is how it appears to me as a human, anyway.

One of my main 'fresh starts' in life was in 1950 when I was just over forty years old. It was at 45 Berkeley Square, the London home at that time of Moral Re-Armament, and we were renewing our commitment and especially our financial commitment to the work. Something happened, or was said, or brought together existing thoughts I had already had, which made me leave the meeting with the clear determination to play my proper part in getting our family's financial affairs in order. It meant that from then on I was to live and work at Whitbourne.

My father was then seventy-six. I knew he needed practical help in running the estate and home farm. Now I realised I could at least try to suggest ways in which death duties might be avoided as well. I had spoken about this with Archer Baldwin, and he had said to me: 'Well, I don't know what you ought to do, but do something for your dear old Dad.' So we did something. My father had to live seven years before his various dispositions could take effect. He lived seven years and three weeks. I remember him as he lay in bed chortling at having 'done in the tax man'.

My father did all his work and letter writing at a big desk with a huge bookcase above it in what was known as the Writing Room. Opposite him, from 1950 until his death in 1958, I worked at a smaller desk. Between us was a vast window, single-sash, looking out onto the terrace and the Italian Garden. The only occasion I remember him giving me any advice on how to run the estate was when I was wondering whether to appoint a forestry adviser, and he said: 'I think you'll have to stand on your own feet, Edward.' He was a bit deaf, especially when we were discussing some of the trickier problems. So I learned to speak up. Now that I am slightly deaf, and sometimes cannot hear what people say because they seem to me to mumble, I remember those years with Pa. He was marvellous, the way he gave me my head and did not interfere.

His advice on forestry, coupled with the fact that he had given me no forestry training himself, freed me to take it on from scratch. I started off with our biggest wood, Willey Hill, which was about fifty acres of mainly semi-mature oak. Of course I knew every corner of Willey Hill already from shooting. Now I began to get to know the wood from the point of view of the trees growing in it. I remember quartering the wood systematically to and fro, making rough notes of the girth and height of the trees, their density, and the extent of competition between their crowns.

I did the equivalent in all our other woods. It took some days. From this it emerged that most of our oak woods needed thinning.

This was a concept new to me at the time. It meant you had to go into the wood with a hacker and a pot of paint, select each tree that needed to come out, number it clearly in white paint so that the buyer could see the number from the previous tree, make a note of the estimated height and girth, and calculate the total cubic footage of the tree and so of the parcel you were about to offer. These sales of 'big thinnings' appealed to me enormously because they seemed to be pure gain. They made quite a fair amount of money – say 2s 6d a cubic foot in those days. For 250 trees averaging 30 cubic feet that's £1,000. This improved the wood by assisting the growth of the trees that were left. As I saw it, they actually added to the capital value of the wood.

How did I learn about the measurement of trees? It was Adams, my father's right hand man on the estate between the wars, now in later age become our head gardener, whom I consulted. He said: 'I've got this book of "Hoppus" timber measurements. I cannot find any use for it now. You have it.' So I had my Hoppus tables. The 'timber inch', in fact four ordinary inches, became the norm by which I judged the girth of all trees. I had a tape, I think thirty-six timber inches long, with a large hook at one end. Small trees you simply embraced with the tape and read the girth. With larger trees you stuck the hook in at chest height, and holding the tape aloft scrambled knees up over the brambles until you got round to the hook again.

There was no handy device for measuring the height of a tree, but I developed a simple rule of thumb procedure for calculating height. I got reasonably certain of where the twelve foot mark came (twice my own height). I would then stand well back from the tree and reckon how many more similar lengths there were before the first major branch or fork. That was the timber height. The rest was tops.

After satisfying myself that I could get it near enough right, I asked a local forestry consultant if he would mind coming over and giving me an 'exam' on the ground. He did so willingly, and we spent an amusing afternoon, at the end of which I passed the test to his satisfaction, and gave him a small fee – very small, I think, taking into account the security he gave me by his endorsement of my skills.

Gathering up the reins, you might call this process in those early years.

Reins had also to be gathered up in that other main department of estate management, namely the tenanted land. Here I found I had to plunge deep into the feudal system. 'Know your place' was the watchword; or rather, perhaps it was a prerequisite for human well-being and happiness. The nature of my place as estate manager was conveyed to me by a kind of benign telepathy, enhanced by the fact that I was also in the eyes of the tenants the owner, or prospective owner – the young squire.

It so happened that the nearest other young squire in the neighbourhood, Miles Bellville of Tedstone Court, came home to take on his estate at about this time, and he introduced me to an important new factor in estate management – one which most landowners of my father's generation had seemed to be largely unaware of. It appeared that a Herefordshire landowner called Richard Verdin was putting forward the proposition that landowning was a business. It could and should pay its way. And in particular, agricultural rents ought to go up. Miles and I went to a crowded meeting in the Winter Gardens in Malvern, at which Verdin spoke and developed this theme.

This was in the Britain of the early 50s, with a Labour government in power. The price of agricultural land was about £20 per acre. The price to the farmer of what he produced was fixed one year in advance by government. It could not vary from the previous year by more than three per cent, up or down. I never remember it varying upwards! So all in all, such a clarion call to landowners created quite a stir. Miles was a member of the Country Landowners Association (C.L.A.), who had organised the Malvern meeting. He had a C.L.A. man out to do his accounts for him, I remember.

GATHERING UP THE REINS

Edward, Erica, William and Christopher 1951

Adams: in his later years he took charge of the gardens. With William Evans

Anyway, I pondered on all this, and it became evident that our rents at Whitbourne would have to go up. I decided to go and have a talk with Ernie, the tenant who in that previous era before the war had taught me how to lay a hedge. What was his opinion? He said at once: 'Yes. The rents ought to go up. But not by much.' And that was how it was. I raised the rents from about £2 to about £2 15s per acre. But first I visited every tenant personally and told them what I was going to suggest. Until this was done, no one had any written notice of a rise in their rent.

As far as I remember, all this happened without the advice of an agent. But this did not mean that I did not from time to time take their advice. The first I consulted was John Kent, a partner in the local firm of Bentley, Hobbs & Mytton. He came over and valued all our properties on the estate. There was one cottage which I was not sure whether I owned or not. He smiled and said 'It can happen.' He also valued our woods. I remember him pausing in Longfield Coppice, a twenty-acre wood full of beautiful straight mature oak. He said: 'If you want to make some money now, here's where it is.' He would come to lunch with us, refusing a drink if I remember right and often bringing a bar of chocolate for each of the children. His off-the-cuff remark over a cup of tea in the kitchen I have always remembered. It was: 'H'm. The estate's all right – The farm's all right. But the house may be a problem to you.' John Kent sadly died when still a young man. But one of his partners, Ted Rayer, is still with us and still able to offer helpful advice, having lived through a revolution in land values in a countryside still populated by many of the hundreds of families he knows by name.

On the farm, it was a matter of gathering up the reins and holding the horse as steady as I could until Pat arrived. Pat had taken an agricultural degree at Cambridge, and then after a period with the Ministry of Agriculture had joined Peter Howard's staff at Hill Farm, Suffolk. There was an understanding between us that he would come when the time was right; meanwhile I was to get going without him.

The farm workers that I can remember at that time were Denis, Percy and old Tom. It needed only two of them at any one time to work our sixty-six acres, and they did so by well ordered routine with what seemed to me the minimum of intervention by my father. He, as I said before, ran the farm at a loss.

I asked the men where they thought I could help, and they suggested I go to the markets and learn to buy cattle. I remember vividly the first two bullocks I bought. One was quite a nice

Hereford/Shorthorn cross with a strawberry roan touch about him. The other was also Hereford/Shorthorn but browner and a bit heavy in the shoulder and light at the back end. They weighed 5 cwt and cost £25 each. I got a carrier to take them home for me; I was worried sick that they had some incurable disease or that the carrier would not turn up with them, or if he did the men would not be impressed. What Denis did say when he saw them was: 'Yes. I think they'll grow into some money.'

So I became the cattle buyer. Otherwise it was mainly a matter of fitting in. Scattering flea-beetle dust on the roots, weeding, and of course threshing. Once I helped Denis to plant a two-acre field of kale with an old drill which you operated by hand, one pulling and the other pushing, up and down the rows. We finished that in two hours before breakfast. That was a breakfast I earned. Afterwards I was introduced to a beautiful tool called a seed-barrow. It was twelve feet wide, and quite light to handle for one man.

This seed-barrow planted our first ley on the farm, and it was a beauty. The seeds mixture was devised by Pat and he properly went to town on it. There was ryegrass, meadow fescue, all the grasses practically except, I think, cocksfoot; red clover and white clover, and a sprinkling of herbs. The particular twelve-acre field in which it was sown had grown a succession of corn crops with narrow strips of potatoes and mangolds. The grass crop came up so well it caught the eye of the local W.A.E.C. (War Agricultural Executive Committee), who graded the farm up a notch to Grade A, I think largely on the strength of it.

Pat and I had agreed that the right farming system for us was to be a system of long four or five year leys – 'taking the plough round the farm', as it was called. This was first propounded by Sir Richard Stapledon, whose book *The Land: Now and Tomorrow*, published in the 1930s, is still an agricultural classic. Today, in fact, it holds its ground interestingly as a means of improving the fertility of the land organically. Even now any land on which we grow corn is 'rested' by a break of a year or more after three years of corn.

Organic farming – that is, farming without chemicals altogether – never seemed quite a practicable proposition to us. There was a book very much in vogue at the time by Newman Turner, a Somerset dairy farmer, who obtained spectacular results in curing contagious abortion in his herd, and other things. I tried one or two of its recommended practices on our farm. For instance, I borrowed someone's subsoiler and tried it on one of our fields, but our tractor was not powerful enough. I also invested about £200 in some hay tripods, in the hope that we would get beautiful fresh hay with the wind blowing underneath to dry it. We did, the first year, from the record grass ley which I have mentioned above, and we found it useful for a few more years, especially with lucerne. But in the end it turned out too costly in labour.

Having no ready capital to invest, we fell back on a more orthodox style of lowland stock raising, and 'finishing' if possible. The fresh thing was the constant renewal of the land by the rotation of crops – grass, basically, and corn. However, there is still one ten-acre field known as 'the Park' which has never been ploughed. Its natural mixture of grasses and clovers have achieved balance and remained unaltered for at least the whole of this century. Thousands of acres in Britain, especially in the East Midlands, are still like this. So this field and a few other permanent pastures, smaller and on steeper ground, remained outside our rotation policy.

Fortune sometimes smiled on our efforts to avoid extravagant expenditure. The first car-trailer I ever bought cost just £6. There it was, laid out in a field at a farm dispersal sale and I got it! But I had spent time going to at least two or three other sales before I did get it. We bought our first threshing 'tack' – a big complicated machine operated by eight men – for just £47. On this occasion Denis came with me. On the way home, one of the wheels came off. We were totally unprepared for this, but by lucky chance he found a spare wheel with timber spokes and iron rim tucked away inside it somewhere, put it on, and away we went again. That threshing machine served us for a number of years. Then we felt the old 'Aunt Sally' haymaker was a bit out of date, and we had better get a stationery baler, so we saw one advertised at a local sale and Pat went along to bid for it. The bidding went up steadily till there were only two in it. The other bidder suddenly realised he was bidding against Pat, whom he knew, and very decently stopped! Pat got that baler for £36.

During this period the tenant of Crumplebury Farm, John Orgee, suddenly gave notice and moved to a bigger farm not far away vacated by a member of his family. This was a stroke of luck. Or was it a provision by Him up there? Crumplebury Farm marched with ours on the north side for the whole of its length. John Orgee was quite a young man, good, we had thought, for another twenty years of tenancy, and we had not expected to get possession of that farm for a long time. (There was no way a landlord could evict a tenant, other than by death or non-payment of rent or a conviction for bad husbandry.) Anyway, he left of his own accord, and that gave us 130 acres instead of 66. In those days it made the difference between a non-viable small farm and a viable one.

Now we really did need Pat to come and take on the farm, and he came. At first, neither of us found it easy to work together. Pat was eleven years younger than me, and I sometimes told him off in a patronising elder-brotherly sort of way. Pat was apt to say nothing and retreat into his shell. I noticed one day a deep gash in the neck of one of our boars. Questioned about it, Pat said that another boar had broken in to him and done it. He was sorry, but he had not told me because he was afraid of what my reaction would be. It made me think.

Blackleg in the cattle was another problem which sometimes caused tension between us. But it culminated one morning when Pat burst in on me uncharacteristically in the writing-room looking wild-eyed and blurted out that we had just lost three of our best bullocks from blackleg. This time we were more united in our grief. Blackleg was an elusive thing which could apparently strike anywhere. Very soon after this the vets came out with a vaccine against it, and from then on all beasts that came onto our farm were inoculated against blackleg as a regular routine. What I learnt from this incident was that Pat cared about the animals as much as I did – perhaps more, because my 'care' was largely about the money we were losing.

To my great surprise, Pat, having read the last paragraph, has told me that those bullocks died not from blackleg, but from another potential killer called bloat. Certainly we did lose cattle through blackleg, and it did cease to be a problem when the vaccine against it came in. But bloat was another problem, and it still is, especially if you put cattle suddenly onto a pasture of grass rich in clover soon after rain. Their sides swell out and they can die. So if, forty years later, our memories are at odds, you'd better take Pat's story as the right one, because he was there and I was not! My comments about what I learnt from it are still very valid!

On the other side of the coin, I had to swallow my pride and ask for Pat's help when I got stuck with the tractor on top of the silage clamp which I was compressing. He drove the tractor nonchalantly down over the edge, a thing which I had not liked to risk.

I also made a serious error one day over some sheep. Pat asked me to accompany some store lambs he wanted to sell to market, and see the sale through. I liked going to the market and said I wouldn't mind having a go, but I had no eye for lambs or their value, and was not very confident. I went, and the lambs came into the ring and failed to reach the reserve price, so I withdrew them. Then I panicked rather, not wanting to spend money on a carrier to take them home again. I entered them a second time at the end of the sale, and they made 10s a head less than the £4 odd which had been offered first time round; but I let them go. I drove home, seething with anger at myself and others at the market who I felt (unreasonably) had conned me. For some reason, I had occasion to call on the way back on the rector of Whitbourne, and I told him about it. He laughed and said: 'It's very good for you, Edward.'

I think the rector was right there. And Pat was also right in saying that I over-reacted when things went wrong, and had a tendency to treat every setback as if it was a ghastly tragedy. An experienced stock farmer whom we were showing round once remarked: 'Where there's live 'uns there's dead 'uns.'

We were always having to press on to make ends meet, and there was not a lot of time to spare. We kept pigs, to start with, in several small pigscots and sheds scattered about the farm, some of them in the fold-yard next to the big Pool. One day in summer two sows walked unconcernedly in through the open kitchen door at Whitbourne Hall, obviously expecting to find something in one of the buckets under the sink. They had taken advantage of low water in the Pool to skirt round the outer edge of the iron railings which enclosed it, and so made their way up the drive and into the house. No harm done, and we rather liked the way they seemed to feel they belonged.

Next winter, however, the Pool froze over, and it snowed onto the ice. This time three sows walked out onto a lovely wide expanse of snow with eighteen feet of water underneath it. They were heavy sows, two of them, at least, in pig. They fell through the ice. It was a shock, and quite a loss. I don't remember recriminations or reactions, other than genuine sadness. And even that did not last long. It just seemed that nature had won this round in the battle. I happened to be at a party in London a few days after the event, and I told some senior army officer about this. He was appalled, and could not get over the awful tragedy that had overtaken us. I liked his sympathetic understanding of the countryside, but felt he had over-reacted a bit!

We did not see those sows till it thawed in the second half of February, and they were washed up on a westerly breeze into the shallow end of the Pool. Pat put on his bathing dress and waded in up to his waist and pulled them out before they could decompose.

So I learned, through our adventures on the farm.

I have left out an important element in the 'chemistry' of running an estate. It concerns the relationship between landlord and tenant, and it is still relevant I think today. It was one thing to raise the rents, however cautiously. But what were we to do for the tenants in return? The landlord was responsible for the maintenance of all buildings on a tenant's farm. This included the farmhouse, and all the outbuildings. It also applied to cottages, whether occupied by farmworkers or anyone else. That we were familiar with. But he also had to supply such capital improvements on the farm, or new buildings, as he deemed necessary or desirable in the interests of the farm. I am not quoting from our agreement, but that is a rough interpretation of it.

So I set out to become not only a maintaining but also an 'improving' landlord.

At that time, as now, all our tenants (except one) kept beef cattle. They were usually Herefords crossed with Shorthorns or Friesians. Herefords were bred originally for their hardihood. They have gone all over the world, especially the United States and Canada, because they can winter out, and our Hereford cross beef cattle had usually been wintered out. You did not need a building for that; or perhaps you had an open cowshed with a manger at the back and the hay tucked into a small loft above. But on the whole one could see that the system was on the way out: suitable perhaps for the horse and cart age but not for tractors ploughing through muddy gateways and making deep ruts. It was expensive in labour. The cattle themselves also 'poached' the ground, making it that much harder to prepare a seedbed in the spring. Perhaps most decisive of all, the pressure was on for more food to be produced, and you could certainly carry more cattle if they were housed under cover near the farmstead, and you did not have to drive across fields to get to them in the November to April period, when the grass is usually better left undisturbed.

So the first new building I put up was a covered yard for cattle for the tenant of Woodhall Farm. It was a matter of inviting tenders, and taking as low a price as you could get. It was the first of several, spread over the years. The Ministry of Agriculture gave you a grant of about thirty per cent of the capital cost, and you charged the tenant an agreed interest on your outlay. To get the grant, you had to show that you expected the tenant to produce such and such a percentage more as a result of having the building. Tenants always thought they would produce more. They did not seem to mind the interest.

A point was that to be able to do this effectively I had to make an appraisal of sorts of the present and possible future performance of every farm on the estate. The best way of doing this seemed to me to be to get to know the tenants one by one, and as far as possible to use letters only to confirm what had already been agreed verbally. We gradually improved the estate, just as fast as the money from rents and timber sales permitted. We had to carry the wages of about four men (forestry and maintenance) full time. (I did not pay myself any salary from the estate at this stage.)

'Farm-gate diplomacy' became a part of my way of life. It is a type of diplomacy which only functions fully when the participants move around on foot. In those years, I usually walked everywhere. You would meet someone, and stand and 'cover the country' in conversation about local affairs, starting with the weather, moving on to the health of one another's families, the size and shape of the fields, crops, market prices and so on. Finally, if there was some piece of information you really needed, you might or might not ask for it straight out. If there was something the other man wanted from you, he would often come out with it too. Sometimes this was the only way you could find out that someone's outhouse roof leaked, or the chimney smoked when the wind was in the wrong quarter, or one of the dozens of other things that make for inefficient living for which we had to thrash out solutions. Letters of complaint were very very rare. Letters of any sort were exceptional.

One major new step we took at this time in the development of the estate concerned water: water both for people, and for animals. Up to then, water for people had come from wells of varying depths, in farmhouse or cottage gardens, or sometimes across a field as far as a hundred yards from the dwelling. Keeping people's water pumps going was one of the constant maintenance jobs. Nobody complained. Well water was usually beautiful to drink, and for all we knew pure. The most generous natural spring of all those on the estate rose on New House Farm, and had been piped and carried by gravity to Whitbourne Hall, a distance of about 2 miles. This supply to the Hall only took a fraction of the water available at the spring, however, the remainder being diverted into a channel which carried it down into a tributary of Whitbourne Brook. So here was the northern third of the estate, about five hundred acres, without water practically except for the wells, and there was all that water going unused from the spring at New House Farm. Could we use this water to give a drinking trough to every field on those five hundred acres, and a tap of running water to every kitchen sink in the area?

It was the County Land Agent, Mr Sturgess, who gave me the right answer: a Hydram, commonly known as a 'ram'.

I had only heard of one ram, which had been installed by a neighbour, and had been a failure. I now learnt for the first time that the word stood for Hydram. Rams were only supplied by one firm in Lancashire. The price seemed remarkably low, given what they were supposed to be able to do. Stories came to light of rams going on pumping water for months, even years, without any supervision. So we got out a plan and installed a ram. We piped the surplus water from the spring to a concrete chamber thirty feet lower down the slope, in which we housed the ram. The ram pumped one tenth by volume of the water it received up a $1\frac{1}{2}$ inch galvanised pipe to a reservoir some six hundred yards away, and about 150 feet higher up. From there the water could be piped by gravity along $\frac{3}{4}$ inch pipes to all the required drinking troughs and kitchen sinks.

The ram is still working today.

The only crisis we have had was in the drought of 1976. Then the water in the spring fell so low that it could not produce enough pressure to drive the pump in the ram. An emergency meeting of all the interested parties was held in the house of one of the tenants, at which I was quite understandably 'put on the spot'. The estate had to find a powerful pump with a petrol-driven engine which could pump the water from the holding tank above the ram up to the reservoir. The son of the tenant volunteered to operate it on everyone's behalf. He did this, morning and evening, for several weeks, and it made a din louder than a chainsaw. You could not miss it if you were up that way, as I often seemed to be. But it was a relief.

During those years of 'gathering up the reins', as I said before, I paid myself no salary from the estate. So what was I living on?

This brings me to the astonishing and I think unique arrangement which we came to as a family when my father's affairs were reshuffled to provide for the estate's future. The law of primogeniture, whereby the father leaves his property to his eldest son, and the other children get a token hand-out, was well entrenched in my father's dispositions for the future. I was the eldest son, and he was going to leave me the whole estate plus enough money to live on while I ran it. But he was caught by the 'death duty trap'; meaning that on his death I would have had to pay such huge sums to the Inland Revenue that the estate would have ceased to exist (in those days the whole of the landed estate, including every farm and cottage and Whitbourne Hall, was valued at a mere £120,000).

We got the best possible advice on this from our solicitors, a well-known London firm. The principal partner concerned came up to Whitbourne and spent a night with us, with his assistant who was to do the work. Both became our friends. The partner, Alan, said: 'We were a bit doubtful at first whether the scheme could work. But now we've been up and met your family, including your father and his grandchildren, we think there is something permanent here. The estate definitely seems to us to have a future.'

The scheme they worked out for us has stood the test of time. The parts of it that were to do with the structure of the estate are still in place. First, my father transferred to all his children, with immediate effect, the whole of the landed estate, in four separate parts: part A, which included Whitbourne Hall, to me absolutely; part B, in trust for my children, part C into a joint ownership of all the brothers and sisters in equal shares, and part D into a discretionary-type trust in favour of the same brothers and sisters and their heirs. Next he gave three quarters of his shares in the Hill Evans and Co. to my brothers and sisters in equal parts, instead of leaving most of them to me. My brothers and sisters all then felt that since they were free to do as they liked with the resulting extra income, they would hand it over it to me as a voluntary gift year by year. And this they did for many years. That was how my family and I were enabled to live and to look after Whitbourne Hall.

So here was I, a bachelor for thirty-seven years, now turned into a family man, responsible not only for my own family, but also to my brothers and sisters for the management of the estate of which they were all five joint owners.

Gwen and her husband Francis were away most of the time in London, Scandinavia, Italy and Iran. Rozi was largely based in Paris. Mary had worked in industry during the war, becoming a shop steward at the Rover works in Solihull. In 1954 she married Ronald Mann at Whitbourne: Ron had made an adventurous escape from a German P.O.W. hospital in Italy during the war and had recently

Our parents on their Golden Wedding day, 1955. Behind (l–r) Ronald and Mary Mann, Robin, Erica, Pat, Rozi, Edward

The Captain with Christopher

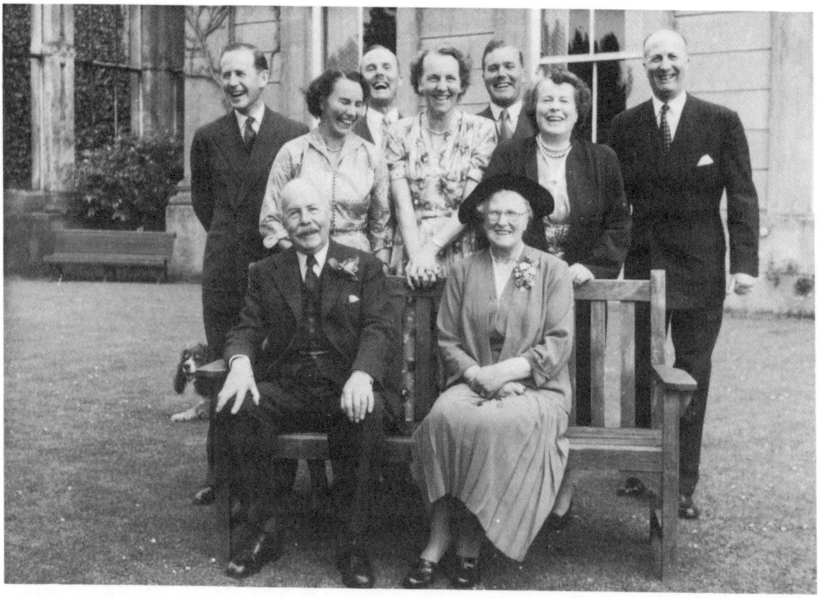

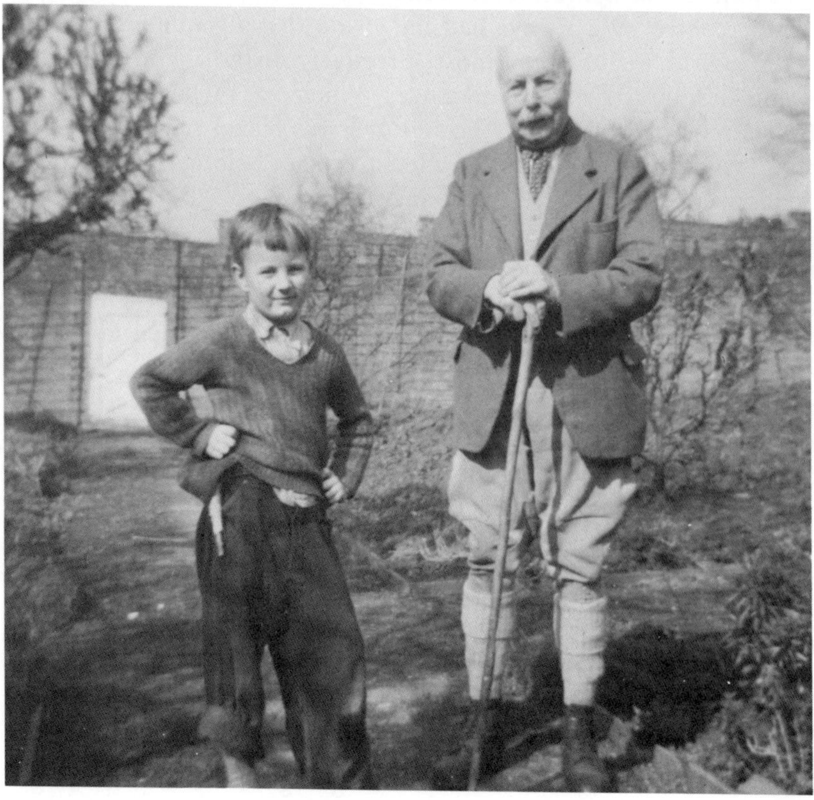

returned to Italy as one of the pioneers of Moral Re-Armament there. The wedding was enlivened by the presence of some of his Italian friends. He and Mary then spent some years in South America before 'settling', if that is the word, in London. Robin had distinguished himself in the war by leading his platoon of the Green Howards through a minefield to capture an enemy outpost, for which he got the M.C. Later he married a French girl, introducing a new and good element into the family.

None of them had any money to spare, and this is an understatement. And they were not in any way obliged to send me anything. Thank heaven I never doubted that their cheques would roll up on time!

The fact is, they all felt not only that it was 'God's money', but that they were making it available (they hoped) for God's purposes. Many of the girls who came to help in our home went back to their countries with a renewed faith. According to one good friend from overseas who came to stay, and saw something of what went on, Whitbourne was a mixture of 'a home, a business and an ideological training centre'. We always had the vision that a genuine revolution in the world might stem most effectively from a home like my parents' home, and a family like ours, which was then largely written off as a relic of a past era. Another overseas friend remarked to me: 'H'm. You cannot do that if you feel the place belongs to you'. Both friends were incidentally Canadians.

The way Whitbourne Hall was run in that post-war era was nothing short of revolutionary. Up to 1939, my mother had employed a cook, a kitchen maid, two parlour maids, and two house maids, all living in. There was also 'Nursie', now retired, who died in 1939.

By the time Erica and I got there in 1950 with our two boys and the girl who was looking after them, there was no regular paid domestic staff at all. The one exception was the cook, who was new, and she left quite soon. From then on, the place was practically staffed by a succession of girls from Scandinavia, Germany, and many other countries, none of whom fitted in the very least into any English 'feudal' system! All needed some training in housework, and Erica with my mother tried to give it to them. At the same time they were usually looking to us to give them some social life, and some wider picture of what we were aiming to do, while teaching them to speak English as well.

At some early stage in this my mother handed over the keys of the store room to Erica, and said 'Now I am going to let you take charge.'

From then on, she and my father retired to the writing room to have their evening meal together. My father used to wheel the supper trolley across the hall to the writing room, usually whistling as he went to deter collisions. The hall was a great place for indoor games, including cricket and a form of hide-and-seek called 'tallywags'. Someone could generally play the piano, and we had concerts and skits. It was often good fun, but could be exhausting. One Christmas after a wonderful day Erica and I had staggered up to bed before we remembered that we had forgotten to give each other our Christmas presents. Another time some understanding friends snatched us away to their country cottage in Essex for a week's holiday. They insisted on bringing us breakfast in bed every morning. Life flowed back into our limbs and peace into our spirits, so that we returned with zest to the fray.

The house in the meanwhile contained, by invitation, two permanent residents, Clare Gillibrand and Mrs Short.

Clare was an aunt of Erica's, her mother's sister. She had married 'Gilly', a housemaster at Bromsgrove. He died about now, and she was left a widow, with family grown up and away. She accepted our invitation to come and live with us at Whitbourne Hall. She gave a lot with the girls, and her skills in housekeeping, gained while feeding sixty boys as the housemaster's wife, were fully used. She was also a countrywoman, and a good sport – once referred to by Adams as a 'knockabout woman'. Her youngest daughter Sheila was married at Whitbourne to Dr David Sturdy, a cousin of mine. We introduced her to our builders, Smith & Sons of Worcester, and they converted our big old nursery into a flat for her. When Clare left after some years, to make a home with her own daughter, she bequeathed to us the boat which the boys of Wendron House, Bromsgrove, presented to Gilly and her on their retirement. The boat, named *Wendrona*, was built at Pershore. We still have it on the lake.

The other lady, Mrs Short, had arrived on the estate as tenant of a small cottage in a remote valley far from the road, on the other side of Sapey Brook. She too had lost her husband, but she had a young family of four girls. My parents used to take their coal to the cottage by horse and cart as far as the footbridge over the brook, and then by hand up to the cottage. The time came when she could not manage any longer, and my mother took her in and gave her some rooms in the former servants' quarters at Whitbourne Hall.

She walked with a limp, but she could scrub, and she became our scrubber-in-chief – the kitchen first, then the marble staircase into the hall, even I think the vast hall floor itself, before electric power and an industrial cleaner were brought to bear. She loved my mother, whom she thought an 'angel in disguise'. My mother taught her to listen as well as pray. Her sure touch with God, and her honesty when she fell short and had to change again, were an object lesson to all of us. She sometimes had words of ripe wisdom for our girls in the house.

The daughters were a lively and attractive lot. The eldest, Betty, was wooed and won by Werner, a former Prisoner of War from East Germany, who later came to work for us on the forestry. After some years he got a job in industry and they left, but they remained friends with us till Werner's death not long ago, and Betty still keeps in touch. The other girls were all happily married before Mrs Short died.

My mother, I might mention, housed up to sixty boy and girl evacuees in our home during the war – all I think from Birmingham. They used to come back regularly and visit us. The last visit was after Erica and I had moved into Dial House.

This is the barest outline sketch of how it was during those four or five years in which I was 'gathering up the reins'. At the end of that time Pat was firmly in the saddle as our farm manager. We could see the beginnings of income from timber sales. and we could also see the prospect of a gradual rise in farm rents, plus with any luck a corresponding rise in living standards, and in production on the tenanted farms.

Two things happened in 1955 which opened out this situation further: I took on an assistant manager on the estate, and we realised the unheard-of sum for us of £9,200 on a first thinning, including some specimen trees, of the oak in Longfield Coppice.

CHAPTER X
The Vanishing Island

IT WAS QUITE an eventful end to the year 1955. The man we were looking for as assistant manager on the estate had to be able to free me to an extent from the mounting office work, and the buying of outside supplies and materials. It would be an advantage if he had some practical skills as well. Above all, he needed to be good with people. And it would be a real help if he could share our basic aims, not only on the estate but also outside it.

It so happened that one of Pat's former colleagues at Hill Farm, David Morcom, was looking for some job like this. I made him an offer, and he came and joined the strength. During the waiting period he got married, and he and Diana his wife came straight to us from their honeymoon. Pat came back up to the Hall to live with us and the Morcoms took over Crumplebury.

In January 1956 Erica and I embarked on a new adventure. Peter Howard had written a musical play called *The Vanishing Island*. Initiated by the Foreign Minister of Denmark, and led by Peter himself, a world mission of some 250 people was assembled to take this play to the world. It travelled through America, Asia and Africa. Early in 1956 it reached Europe, where Erica and I were invited to join it.

Erica and I joined *The Vanishing Island* in Paris in January. We were to stay with it for two months. Erica left the care of our two boys, now both at the village school, to the family under my parents with Clare Gillibrand. I left the estate to the newly arrived assistant manager David, able to draw on the experience of the staff as required, and of Pat. We both regarded it as a protracted 'holiday' from home affairs, and as a time of fresh perspective for ourselves. After five years of intensive rooting into the feudal system at home, the quality of teamwork and initiative required to work our way into a position of being of some use in that international group was quite a challenge.

The Vanishing Island is the story of two countries, a prosperous constitutional monarchy (the island of Eiluph'mei) and an impoverished totalitarian state (Weiheitiu). Unwilling to share their wealth with their less fortunate neighbour, the people of Eiluph'mei instead send a delegation, led by their prime minister, to change Weiheitiu and make it 'more like us'. Odioso, however, the stern dictator of Weiheitiu, is disgusted by their selfishness, and casts a spell which causes their island to disappear. The situation is resolved by the king of Eiluph'mei, who lays aside his crown and humbly suggests a better plan for both countries, a plan of sharing and forgiveness. The island reappears and wins Weiheitiu and Odioso to a new destiny.

That play was prophetic. It was also very amusing, and very moving. I never tired of seeing it, and learning from the reactions of different audiences.

Peter Howard's daughter Anne travelled with us. She later became Anne Wolrige-Gordon. In her book about her father, *Peter Howard: Life and Letters*, she writes of *The Vanishing Island*: 'This world mission marked a turning point in MRA's history. It cut across old concepts, and dealt publicly with national issues.' It was impossible to see *The Vanishing Island* without equating the island itself, in a symbolical way, with Britain.

I think it was in Dortmund that I was asked to join the chorus of businessmen. The opening words went:

We wish we had time to reply,
But out diaries are full, flowing over.
If you ask what we're doing, or why,
We are keeping the country in clover.

It was fun. We were always well received, how far as a comic turn I am not sure.

In the Ruhr one of my chief memories is of acting as a steward with the job of marshalling the huge crowds that tried to get into the hall. We had to have one or two overflow meetings. There were no tickets, and as far as I remember no charge for admission. Once or twice we stewards had to hold hands and form a human barrier to stop a dangerous number of people getting in.

After the show we would usually stand in the foyer and try to be on the alert to meet interested people who had seen the show. A man came up to me one evening and we got into conversation. He pressed me to come and stay with him and tell him more. Next morning we were due to move on to another city, but I felt it would be useful for someone to stay behind and try to go a bit deeper with the people in Dortmund, and I said this at our get-together in the morning. Peter

Howard said he thought that if I felt like that it would be a good idea for Erica and me to stay with this chap we had met. So we did.

Our host – let us call him Ernst – worked in industry. His wife had a maid of Czecho-Slovak origin working for her in the kitchen. The Ernsts were pleasant and hospitable. They compared *The Vanishing Island* with *Mother Courage* by Bertold Brecht. They talked a lot about the effect in the Ruhr of MRA on some of the big steelworks. They told us that there were 45,000 East German 'spies' in West Germany at the moment. Once Erica and I happened to be in the kitchen talking to the maid when the Ernsts were not there, and she inexplicably burst into tears. We said nothing, realising that there was something tragic in the not too far distant past. But we had become a little wary of the Ernsts themselves, who asked us a lot of leading questions about what the 'strategy' of MRA was in various parts of the world. We mostly did not know, and were able to tell them this. But we were not sure whether they were trying to find out for some sort of intelligence agency. Later I voiced this doubt with one or two of our German colleagues, who had met the Ernsts at a social evening to which we invited them. After some thought and discussion their verdict was that Ernst was probably an 'agent'.

So we disengaged politely, and moved on. The next stop was Berlin.

Berlin ist radioaktif;
Es strahlt in alle Welt.

Berliners had kept control of their own municipal affairs, by their own efforts, and the initiative of men like former Mayor Neumann. The allies – the U.S.A., Britain and France – had supported them by the Berlin airlift, when the Soviets completely blocked all land traffic between Berlin and the West. As a result, we could be sure of a warm welcome. And we got it. This was a year or two before the Berlin Wall was completed. Trains could still run between East and West Berlin, and people from East as well as West Berlin flocked to the show. They interrupted Howard's opening remarks several times with applause. At the climax of the play, when someone declares: 'Together we from East and West can dare to build a world for all men everywhere,' a great roar (or was it a sigh?) came up from the audience.

Within a very few years the Berlin Wall was completed. All contact between East and West was barred. Now, still in our lifetime and against all the odds, the Wall has come down again. It is a safe guess that bits of it will have been taken as souvenirs by some of the sons and daughters of those *Vanishing Island* audiences in 1956.

We left Germany to come home and tidy up some end of the financial year business. But before we left we met with a section of our group including Peter Howard at a house in the Ruhr for a weekend of quiet reflection. There we sought to renew our commitment to Jesus Christ and the Holy Spirit, the true source of the ideology for democracy that we were promoting. Peter showed care for every individual, including Erica and myself. He said some words of understanding about the sacrificial qualities needed to live a life like St Francis's in the setting of a country landowner. They brought tears to my eyes. A colleague noticed the tears, and said to me after the meeting in a very awed way: 'What, you? Crying?'

We tidied up the business at home. David Morcom had written to me while I was in the Ruhr reporting the spectacular price received for timber in Longfield. £6,000 of it went into the farm as capital for expansion. £1,000 went to Moral Re-Armament in France. £1,000 went to Moral Re-Armament in Africa. By the end of May, Erica and I found ourselves again in support of *The Vanishing Island*, this time in London.

We lived in a house with about a dozen people, including an Egyptian businessman and his wife, and an Arab nationalist from a Mediterranean country. We felt at home there, and tried to make it a home for everyone else. One evening the Arab felt a bit too much at home and made a pass at one of the British girls on the stairs. She was upset and angry. He retired to his room, hurt and ashamed. When I realised what had happened, the thought struck me at once that I had the same evening looked with desire on a girl in the street. I felt I should go and tell this to the Arab. We were quite good friends, so I knocked on his door, and told him. He brightened up tremendously. We knelt down and prayed, he in Arabic and I in English. We asked to be forgiven and thanked God for the chance of a fresh start.

I don't think there was any particular sequel to this. It seemed to be all in the day's work. But the incident was memorable.

Shortly after this we were invited to Coventry, to help prepare the ground for the visit of the mission to that city. I found myself working closely with Leslie Fox, a chartered accountant of some distinction, who had resigned from his position in a well-known firm to take on the whole work of Moral Re-Armament in the world.

Leslie was a dignified and well organised man, and I enjoyed working with him. But as the pressure mounted with the approaching arrival of two hundred-odd people in the city to put on the show, the moments when we could consult together became fewer and fewer.

At last, on the day itself, it was 'Mr Fox, please, on the telephone,' and Leslie striding imperturbably to and fro to take the calls about bookings, tickets, hospitality, what have you, while I could only look on helplessly. Punctually in the afternoon the cast and others arrived, and filed cheerfully into the foyer. They found me and Erica as the only ones to welcome them. I did not know where any of them were staying. I only knew there was a buffet tea being prepared somewhere in the building. With practised eyes they took in the situation, and relaxed. And I thoroughly enjoyed myself, solemnly shaking hands with all and sundry, most of them after all by then my comrades in arms.

One evening Erica and I were invited out to dinner in the country about fifteen miles out of Coventry with some friends. It was an enjoyable evening of about eight guests, among whom happened to be the chairman of the company who owned our hotel. The next morning, back at the hotel, we found that the suite of rooms there which we had booked for the Omukama of Bunyoro, Uganda, who was coming to join the MRA World Mission that night, had been allotted instead to some members of an industrial conference. The management regretted this change of plan, but would do their best for the Omukama somewhere else. The Omukama was in fact the King of Bunyoro, one of the four regions into which the country of Uganda was then subdivided.

It seemed obvious to us that this was not the way to welcome an African king to a British city. I rang up my friend and fellow-guest of the night before, and explained the situation simply to him. He saw the point immediately and rang the hotel. The Omukama got his suite of rooms.

The first night of *The Vanishing Island* in Coventry was a brilliant success, with two overflow meetings. The second night was almost a flop. On the third night there was an improvement and by the end of the week it was a full house again. Later on, we learnt the reason for this from a member of the Communist Party in Coventry who had joined our ranks. The Party, which at that time had a powerful organisation in Coventry centred on the Canley works of Standard Motors, had sensed on the first night that the message of the play was a threat to themselves, and had passed the word round through their membership to stop people going to the show. That they briefly almost succeeded in doing this was a tribute to their skill and dedication. It was also an illustration of the vulnerability and gullibility of the British public.

This ex-Communist colleague became well known as a spokesman for MRA across the world. He would often describe how each member of the Party was trained to enter a certain trade or profession, and then instructed to get a job in a certain city or factory, with the aim of fomenting the class war. His change began when he walked one afternoon into a church, and was met by a vicar sensitive to his needs, who led him to a personal experience of Christ.

From Coventry we invited members of the mission and cast to come to Whitbourne one afternoon. It was just sixty miles away. A busload came, and several cars. Erica and I drove home in time to receive them, with my parents. Among those who came was the King of Bunyoro. The king sat on the terrace, surrounded by a sort of informal garden-party. People were brought up and introduced to him from time to time. There were no speeches. I wondered then, and still wonder, what brought him to come and join the world mission. It seemed not to be the kind of thing one could ask him. He seemed quite content sitting there, and now and then I caught a gleam of a smile in his eye.

It was shortly after the Coventry episode that the mission's historic journey round the world came to an end. Many of the cast and accompanying team left for the summer conference at Caux.

Erica and I resumed life at Whitbourne. There was a difference in us after the months with *The Vanishing Island*. We saw the family of Moral Re-Armament in the world as a body of people for whom we were to take on responsibility for the rest of our lives. But we saw that this responsibility was not geographical. We were not necessarily to travel the world. Rather we were to seek to affect issues by the way we lived at the heart of the establishment in Britain. Perhaps we did not 'resume' life at Whitbourne. Let us say we entered on it afresh, knowing that our lives did not belong to us.

The coming of David and Diana Morcom to the estate was indispensable to all these absences of ours with *The Vanishing Island*. They were to stay with us for seven years, at the end of which time David felt he was ready for a job of more responsibility as manager of a National Trust estate in the south of England.

David lifted from me the constant to and fro-ing to Bromyard or Worcester for spare parts for machinery and building materials, which were necessary to keep our staff working efficiently. He was also a handyman himself, as our present converted henhouse with its large timber buttresses can testify. Perhaps the chief practical legacy he left me was a reorganised and rejuvenated estate office with a proper filing system, including printed wage packets to replace my practice of simply handing over cash with a piece of paper to the staff on Fridays. He had a dead-pan sense of humour all his own. He also had a strong artistic sense and a feeling for old buildings. He helped me over a period of transition. After he left I no longer thought there was room on the estate (or money) for another manager, but thought in terms rather of a reliable head forester and a reliable maintenance man with building skills.

Within a few months after our return from *The Vanishing Island* we lived through the disastrous episode over the Suez Canal, which led to the resignation of Sir Anthony Eden as Prime Minister. To the surprise of most of the nation, the new leader was not 'Rab' Butler, but Harold MacMillan. I well remember MacMillan's first appearance on TV as Prime Minister. He had to deal with a nation that had lost its nerve over the Suez affair. He kept on saying, 'Of course, we're a great nation.'

What happened over Suez was that the British had an agreement with President Nasser of Egypt to relinquish control of the Suez Canal and withdraw from Egypt sometime in 1957. Nasser jumped the gun and declared the Canal nationalised in summer 1956. It was a unilateral action, taken without warning. We protested angrily, but could do nothing about it immediately because our forces had been so thinned out we were militarily powerless. France and Britain collaborated to send task forces to strike at Egypt simultaneously. At the same time, Israel was keen to attack Egypt on land. We colluded with the Israelis so that Israeli and Franco-British forces could arrive at the Canal at the same time, which they did in November. The United States under President Eisenhower reacted with fury, and insisted that we hand over military control of the Canal to a United Nations force. Anthony Eden was compelled to agree to this and resigned as British Prime Minister.

I vividly remember the TV broadcast by Hugh Gaitskell, leader of the Labour Party, at the Suez time. He declared passionately that it was not Nasser, but we, the British, who were the aggressors. Frankly, I agreed with him. I happened to be with John Kent the next day, and he was rather shocked by my views. Certainly his view was shared by the majority of British people at the time. They wanted

Eden to go through with the invasion. Many believed the stories they read about Communist agents being dropped from the air into Israeli territory by the Russians. Ordinary people in Britain did not like Eden giving in to America. But I am convinced that we owe America a debt of gratitude for having stopped us from taking a wrong turning.

At least that is how our own family felt, and I telephoned our old friend Archer Baldwin, saying that we felt the action was immoral and wrong. He said he had just been talking to the Foreign Secretary, and we'd find it would soon blow over. He added that in his opinion Nasser was a 'nasty piece of work'. It was the first disagreement we had had on a matter of principle like that.

I felt deeply unhappy about this whole incident. To some extent I still feel it, as I am not sure that all the historians have fully got the point. Nasser, and Egypt, had no real difficulty in managing the Canal afterwards, as many people here had said they would. Nor did Mossadegh in Iran have difficulty in managing his oil without the Anglo-Iranian Oil Company. It was like the crunch of a great bone breaking in the back of the British Empire – the bone of British control. Macmillan sensed this, when he sought to pour oil on the wound, by repeatedly telling us: 'Of course, we are a great nation.' But, of course, this was not really the point. Or perhaps one needs to ask 'What is greatness?' The English can be tremendous self-deceivers. I recall a noble English politician who was reported as having said: 'In a sense the Suez Canal is really an essential part of England.' I wonder in what kind of sense?

CHAPTER XI
The Captain

MY FATHER DIED in April 1958. He had a stroke, and his mind was taken from him. He was eighty-four. But his spirit remained, and showed itself in the resistance he put up to the attentions of the male nurse whom we had to look after him. He could still recognise me, and I tried to persuade him that the chap was not an enemy. Two or three of us were standing round his bed with our mother when the end came.

I loved my father. I loved his inimitable roguish grin when his cousin Ermine caught him in the act of having a swig from a hunting flask round the corner from her front door. I loved it when now and then he would put on an act of non-cooperation with my mother – as he did once over what colour the new wall-paper in the library was to be. He had a little ditty on husband/wife relationships which he used to recite to us now and then:

'Be to their virtues ever kind;
Be to their faults a little blind.'

I remember seeing him sitting in his chair in the writing room, in complete silence, in a daze of sheer happiness at the news of Gwen's engagement to Francis Goulding. I remember the occasion on one of our parties for the staff when Pa sang a song for them and then suddenly finished it off with a piercing 'view-hallo' as given on the hunting field, drawing the cheers and laughter of the company.

Quite late in his life I had gone with him to give news of Moral Re-Armament to a very distinguished admiral who lived locally, and had noted the easy way in which he explained we had some good news, and wanted to be sure it got to leading people in the neighbourhood.

Again, when he came with me to see the timber merchant's men in action in our woods, extracting some big douglas fir – it was the first clear fall of timber I ever carried out, followed straight away by a re-planting. We were standing in the field at the bottom when the men came out with some timber, and one of them said, half joking, 'Would you like to come for a ride, Captain?' Pa said 'I wouldn't mind.' So they helped him up into the seat next to the driver, and the tracked vehicle set out across the brook and up the bank the other side. Pa came back with a quiet grin on his face, and looked at me as much as to say: 'They never offered that to you.'

As it happened this same firm of timber merchants later on made me an offer for some timber which I thought was too low. I wrote and suggested they increase it, and they wrote back saying I was a 'hard man, reaping where I had not sown', and gave me a bit of an increase. Hard man, or soft touch? Perhaps we hit the middle way.

Pa never missed a season's shooting. His last day pheasant shooting must have been in the January before he died. For his last two or three years we had a regular routine after shooting-lunch. I would drive Pa round by car to the top of a steep bank where the guns were to stand, while the other guns climbed the bank on foot. The other guns, all our personally invited quests, were an interesting mixed bag. Some of the more usual ones were a local doctor, a senior farm tenant, a retired naval and a retired army officer, the latter a Protestant from Northern Ireland. Myself and Pat, and Robin if at home, were always in the party. There were eight guns, and about fifteen beaters under our gamekeeper, Bob Jones. We had four major shooting days in each season, getting round all the coverts twice. In addition to the big days of course we would go out and shoot cocks or rabbits and pigeons and other vermin in the hedgerows and other rough places. This would be singly or in pairs, or in small family parties with Bob and one or two of the estate men. Particularly happy days were spent partridge shooting in September, driving the stubbles and roots, field by field, with just four guns and four beaters. These included days on the next door Harpley estate with my father's cousin Geoffrey Evans.

To us boys there was, and is, a magic about shooting. John and I as schoolboys would go out into the yard on a winter's morning. First we went into the stick house and each chose a suitable stick to beat with. Then we waited in a frenzy of impatience for the guns to arrive, one by one in their cars, and go in to join my father in the writing room. At last, at 10 o'clock or so, out they came. Then another short delay while the beaters emerged from the loghouse and those allocated to carry each gun's cartridge bag made themselves known to their guns. Meanwhile the dogs present would be frisking about whining with suppressed excitement. We felt exactly as they did. Then we were off, swinging away on foot to the first covert, perhaps half a mile away. We boys all joined the beaters till we were thought old enough to carry a gun – usually at the age of fourteen.

The shooting has now long since been let to a syndicate, and this to an extent contributes to the estate's financial viability. The coverts are shot not four days in the season but twelve, and the number of birds killed per season has gone up from about 200 to 2,000. The number of people who get enjoyment from it has increased somewhat as well. And the magic seems to persist. Robin at the age of seventy-three has just resumed the practice of joining the beaters. Besides his love of the sport, he values the chance to meet the various characters who come to beat, pretty well all of whom enjoy it as well.

Topographically, it is an outstanding shoot, though a small one. Maybe the present-day magic is largely due to the present gamekeeper being a Whitbourne man. And to good liason between him and the present shoot manager, who is a doctor in a local hospital. He and others of the present members of the syndicate are good friends of ours, and I know I will be welcome if I can manage to get to watch them in action on a shooting day.

My father's death was to me like the turning of a key in the lock of a huge door. The door opened easily, at a touch. It led me into a vast room, full of files demanding urgent attention. Somewhere at the other end of the room a window looked out onto God's own beautiful world. Or was it rather a man-made world, reminding one of the gardener's remark to the over-enthusiastic visitor: 'You should have seen what it was like when God had it to himself'?

There was a welter of things to do, and looking back on it I find it hard to write a coherent record, or to remember in what order things happened. This may be just as well. It means I shall have to write down some of my outstanding memories, as they occur to me.

One of the early things that happened was that I had a phone call from the Clerk to the Rural District Council of Bromyard, asking if I would stand for the council with a view to filling my father's shoes, he hoped, in due course as Chairman. I slept on this, and phoned him next day thanking him and declining. I had an instinct that my father was one thing, but I in the year 1958 was quite another. I was distinctly pleased when before very long a good friend of mine who was a tenant on the estate stood and was elected, and spent fruitful years in local government.

My idea was that if I was to take any wider responsibility it might be in a professional organisation like the C.L.A. I had become friends with the secretary of the Herefordshire Branch, Vernon Dent. After we had one or two talks at the Three Counties Show, he asked me over to talk on landlord/tenant subjects to a roomful of farmers in Ledbury. In the early stages of our acquaintanceship, he even survived becoming a victim of a high pressure sales campaign I was conducting with a book about MRA. Eventually, I owed it to him that he drew the attention of our County C.L.A. Committee to the desirability of co-opting me onto the committee, and when they did so at the A.G.M. I accepted with thanks.

Those pressing 'files' of things to do were very much with me. After water, there was electricity. Electricity had fairly recently been nationalised. We came under the Midlands Electricity Board (M.E.B), who planned to bring electricity to Whitbourne: how was it to come across our land, and where, and to whom? I had several discussions about this with M.E.B. officials. As I remember, they were unfailingly courteous and quick to answer any points I wanted to raise. One man came and spent a whole morning with me in the writing room, re-routing the main supply line across our farm. He had it coming across an environmentally unacceptable area (as I thought), and was persuaded to use another route which I had outlined. No 'high horse' at all about 'his' plan. I was impressed by this.

As time went on I found it typical of the whole of the Agricultural Civil Service that I had to deal with. There was NAAS. There was the Field Drainage Officer, another good cooperator. There was also the District Surveyor, a quite outstanding public servant, who led me through the intricacies of how to comply with the building bye-laws. I remember he saw a picture of our *Vanishing Island* businessmen's line-up in a pictorial magazine, and pointed it out to me, saying 'It was very bold of you to be so exposed.' Modernising those beautiful black and white half-timbered houses could be quite awkward, especially when the recognised way to take the upstairs 'stink pipe' through the roof lay through a solid 300-year-old oak beam. I think he found my capacity for asking questions a bit surprising but he met me generously with unofficial advice as well as professional knowhow, and we remained friends.

All the same, the time came when I was faced with the need to draw up specifications before inviting tenders for house modernisations and/or extensions. Here I was rather stumped. I decided to ask my cousin by marriage, Tony Peacock, if he would possibly consider drawing up the documents and supervising the work on some six houses which were next in line. Tony was a quantity surveyor, and an associate of a large building firm in the North of England with I think some 80 partners and 120 associates. To my delight he accepted, and took all that side off me for the duration of the job.

Somewhere in the earlyish 60s we emerged with the estate fully modernised. That is, all dwellings (with one exception, where the occupants said they would rather be left as they were) were modernised up to a certain standard. They all had a supply of running hot and cold water, with indoor sanitation including a bathroom. Cooking was by solid fuel stove. Water was heated either by a boiler behind the stove or by an independent boiler somewhere else in the house. Electricity and electric appliances came in a little later.

We still had to attend to roof leaks, draughty windows and doors, and some damp walls. Damp courses were unknown, of course, when the houses were built. I started installing them, and when you replaced earth floors with concrete they became even more necessary. We tried the injection method of damp courses for the first time in those years.

For all these many modernisations, we always got a capital grant of something like thirty per cent of the cost from the government. For living standard improvements of this kind – as against luxury or fancy fittings which were not deemed obligatory on the landlord, though the tenant might instal them with the landlord's agreement – I did not charge the tenants interest on my investment. I did, however charge them for farm improvements which were directly designed to increase production.

This was the sort of vista that I looked out on through that big door after the death of Pa. I don't know what exactly we did do during the first months. But I do know that as the summer holidays drew near we heard from our friends Lawson and Mary Wood of Aberdeen that two ladies who were friends of theirs had a cottage on the Dee and would love to lend it to us if we were looking for somewhere to fish. We were, and off we went, just Erica and me, William and Christopher. I longed to be alone with my family, and that longing was fulfilled. I was introduced to the *Beano*. I caught my first three salmon. It was such a rest. I am sure Pa understood. I think Lawson and Mary understood too, and it was that that prompted them to find the cottage for us.

In the spring of 1959 Robin was married in Paris to Claire Weiss. Erica and I had days off savouring the sights of Paris, partly with Claire and partly with her parents. Her father, Jacques Weiss, endeared himself to us at the St Cloud Golf Club, where they took us for lunch, by marching us across the fairway to urgent shouts of the French equivalent of 'fore!' on the way to the clubhouse. At the ceremony (Protestant) we joined in the French custom of a 'social' afterwards at the back of the church; and then at the reception I had the pleasure on behalf of the Evans clan of welcoming the Weisses into our family.

CHAPTER XII
Allies

PAT AND I were concerned to increase production on the farm. That was the thing to do if you wanted to survive.

We built up a herd of cows on the multiple suckling system. Each cow would carry with its own calf up to three others as well, followed by perhaps two more in the same lactation. We built up the herd from our own heifer calves. This was very similar to what many of our tenants were doing. We also started a flock of sheep. A few Cluns first, then a few Dorset Horn. After the cattle have helped themselves to what they want from a pasture, sheep can come in and enjoy grazing off what they leave, and this 'close shave' will normally benefit the next year's growth of grass. So sheep and cattle are to an extent complementary to each other.

Our first major investment on the farm was in a pig unit. It was meant to be, and for many years was, our only source of regular weekly all round the year income. To get the pig scheme off the ground we employed a young farmer friend named John Sainsbury, who was leaving his post as farm manager in Shropshire. John stayed with us to see this scheme through before he moved on to his next management job. He lived with us, and worked closely with Pat. Every single person employed on the estate was found some part in the work. Even the gamekeeper did a bit. It was quite an effort.

By the time the great day arrived for the 'opening', Geoffrey Ballard, the co-designer of the Piers/Ballard bacon house which we had incorporated, had arranged for Pat to be interviewed on BBC Television about the scheme, and had told a lot of people about his invention. A huge crowd of eager farmers came trooping down our drive. I thought the procession would never stop. I happened to be in the Whitbourne Hall gardens when they walked past. With me was our newly employed head gardener from Yorkshire, Charlie Greenwood. 'Ee,' he said, 'Look at all them poor farmers.'

We farmers could not win in those days with the general public, any more than we can now!

Charlie Greenwood was a delight. When I advertised the job of head gardener I had three possible candidates to choose from, all well named: Barrow, Orchard and Greenwood. I chose Greenwood for interview first. We sat on a bench on the terrace with Erica and Mrs Greenwood. I was trying to get from him where his real skills lay. There was a long silence, which was broken by Mrs Greenwood asking him: 'What are you thinking about now?' 'Chrysanthemums,' he said. We all burst out laughing.

We grew chrysanthemums, lettuce and tomatoes for the market. With chrysanthemums, we grew them under glass, we grew them under polythene frames, and we grew them in the open to be covered with polythene frames before the frosts.

During those years that we kept the gardens commercial – about ten years – I reckon we marketed just about one million lettuces. The average price to us was about 4d. – certainly well under 6d. that is, in today's terms $1\frac{1}{2}$–$2\frac{1}{2}$p.

The tomatoes were all under glass, such as it was. We put up one new plastic 'glasshouse' on the old tennis court, which produced a superb crop of tomatoes the first year, a less good one the second year, and after that early lettuce followed by chrysanthemums.

Charlie had two young men under him in the garden, Ron and Billy, both considerable characters in their own right. I had to employ two of them, just to keep the ornamental part of the garden looking decent and supply the house with vegetables. Why not, I reckoned, employ one more man and make probably a considerably smaller loss than I was doing already? Mind you, Charlie's opening wage as head gardener was just £10 a week. I thought that rather a lot.

A Yorkshireman is not the same as a Herefordshire man. But Ron and Billy appeared to find life under Charlie quite acceptable. Charlie would say to me 'We've got Ron wife and Billy wife to help us pack the lettuce this evening.' He was full of suggestions, full of optimism. When I was inclined to object to the cost of such and such a scheme, he would say 'It's the initial cost, Sir.' I shared his enthusiasm, because I wanted the garden under him to become commercially viable.

It was early in these operations that we had, in 1959, a telegram from Caux, asking us to come and participate in urgent consultations about the international situation. The telegram was signed by Lawson Wood, the Scot who had laid on for us last year's fishing holiday. It was unusual to be asked particularly like that, so we thought we should go.

It turned out to be the conference which, running concurrently

The fish of the day. In Scotland. Photo by Erica

with its counterpart in the United States, produced that most widely circulated of all Moral Re-Armament's publications, *Ideology and Co-existence*. Twenty-four million copies of the pocket-sized handbook of 31 pages were distributed round the world. I thought it was a great pamphlet. I still do. It certainly did a lot to alert the Western world to what the Communists at that time were trying to do. Here is a key passage: 'There are two ideologies bidding for the world today. One is Moral Re-Armament, which believes that God's mind should control the world through human nature that has been changed; the other is Communism, which believes that men's mind should control the world through human nature that has been exploited. One or the other must win . . .'

We came back from Caux with renewed determination to play our part, but feeling that our friends at home were on the whole fairly apathetic to such a stark and disturbing picture of the world, and that perhaps only shock treatment could really be of any use.

Charlie and Mary Greenwood with David

Mrs Gladys Jones, an expert cook, who stepped in to help in 1953 and kept on coming for 36 years

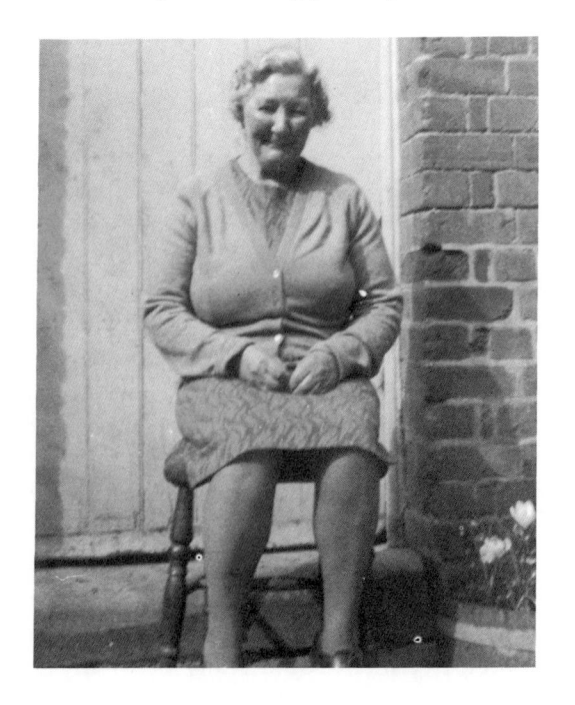

The first thing that happened back at home was that I went out into the garden and received shock treatment myself. The chrysanthemums were only half covered by their frames, and were lying around spoilt by recent rain and obviously not being properly looked after. When charged with this, Charlie Greenwood said: 'I thought you weren't interested, Sir, going away all this time.' I said: 'Not interested? This is what I employed you for. I wanted someone I could entrust the garden to whether my eyes were on him or not. Of course I'm interested.' 'Oh,' he said, 'Well, that's different.'

Different! From then on, I made up my mind to let Charlie (I had called him Greenwood up to then) know me as a man, and include him especially in my outside activities. I became a small example of the 'changed human nature' talked about in the pamphlet. Charlie became a true friend and ally. He never passed up any chances he got of coming up to the house in the evenings to see a film or hear a speaker, and more than once he would come to London with us at the week-end to meet a wider circle and see a play at the Westminster Theatre. His wife Mary often came with him, and they would bring others along as well. The garden under him began to look quite impressive. And we had many laughs as we learnt new tricks together. One new trick was growing mushrooms in the cellar at Whitbourne Hall. There was always great excitement when the time came to expect those tiny pin-pricks of brilliant whiteness in the black compost which heralded the arrival of the first mushroom. I would go down the cellar several times in a week to scrutinise the life-producing mass of compost hoping to see them. Erica often went too. And of course Charlie himself. One early morning on April the First we got there first and planted a few ping pong balls judiciously dug in for Charlie to find. He enjoyed that. So did we.

Sadly though, after five years or so Charlie's health began to break down, and in two or three more years he was gone. He left a gap, and I missed him. Mary stayed with us for some years. She played a key part with Erica in renovating the rich crimson curtains which still grace the drawing room at Whitbourne Hall. She has made her own home in Herefordshire, in Bromyard, so we keep in touch.

Then there was Alec, our neighbour, who farmed the land next to us. He had arrived on this farm before the war as a tenant of Oriel College, Oxford the owners, with just £60 and two cows. He had made good during the war years. One day he felled two or three trees belonging to us in a hedge which was our common boundary. I objected by letter. Next morning the phone went, and here was Alec objecting to my objection. He seemed to think I had no right to write as I did.

'What are you going to do?' he demanded: 'Going to law about it?'

'Good God, no,' I replied, 'I was just giving my opinion.'

'A bit shirty, wasn't it?'

'You should have seen it before I showed it to my wife. She got me to tone it down quite a bit.'

This got him roaring with laughter, and the row was over.

He and his wife came to tea with us a few days later, and we became friends. I think I always did business face to face on things like that, and not by letter, from then on. But it was an illustration of the enormous help I have always had from Erica as a confidential critic of some of my difficult letters!

Another incomer to the village was Fred, a greengrocer, and Lucy his wife who kept a shop for ladies underwear. Fred liked tennis and dancing and was a gregarious and public-spirited sort of chap. He got wind of our activities, and wrote a letter to the local paper saying that he could not see the necessity for all this Moral Re-Armament; it seemed to him that all we had to do was to keep the Ten Commandments and we would be all right.

On the strength of that letter, I went to see Fred. I apologised for having given him such an inadequate picture of MRA that he had felt able to write such a letter, and I outlined some of the world events I had seen at Caux. My approach was warmly received, and both Fred and Lucy became firm allies of Erica and myself, and friends of the family.

Fred played an important part in October 1960 when we had a dinner for some of the men who had fought against the British, and the white settlers of Kenya, in the Mau Mau rebellion. This was a memorable occasion for all of us. It came about like this.

During the Mau Mau uprising which arose among the Kikuyu tribe some two thousand African Christians were murdered and the full force of the white population, supported by many blacks and assisted by units of the British army, fought a war against the Mau Mau. The uprising was crushed and Jomo Kenyatta, a well-known African teacher, was held responsible and imprisoned for the duration. Many Mau Mau suspects were detained, the most violent of them at a camp at Athi river. The commandant of that camp was Colonel Alan Knight, a white settler. He and his staff had under their control about two thousand detainees. A moment came when, with the emergency still on, Alan Knight made a public declaration before all the detainees of his faith in a future for Kenya based on change by white and black people alike. It led to five hundred detainees renouncing the oaths by which they had bound themselves to kill the white man.

The emergency was lifted in 1959. Kenya sent a delegation to Caux in 1960, which included some of these former detainees from Athi River camp. They were planning to come to Britain in the autumn, and I took the opportunity of inviting them to come to Whitbourne.

Another important link between Whitbourne and Kenya was through Clare Gillibrand. Clare's brother, Gray Leakey, was a long-standing Kenya settler. During the early stages of the Mau Mau uprising, she accepted an invitation to spend a few weeks in Kenya with him. When she got home, she told us how tense the atmosphere was. Gray was deaf, and she had an arrangement with him, to alert him if anything untoward was afoot by throwing stones into the pool that he was fishing in the river. Months later the Mau Mau raided Gray Leakey's home and killed his wife. Gray himself they took and buried alive on Mt Kenya: they did this because their gods decreed that they must choose a 'good man from among the whites' for a human sacrifice.

When the ex-Mau Mau Africans arrived, we had also the most senior of Erica's Leakey aunts, Lilian Ridge, to meet them with Clare.

I did not have an easy ride inviting our friends and neighbours to meet the Africans. Miles Bellville refused point blank, as did one or two others. They probably represented a majority of people in Britain at that time, whose blood was still up against the people who had committed all those bestial crimes.

Miles was a person I had a lot of time for. He was a dare-devil, mischievous type with an original sense of humour. He is the only person I have known who has successfully introduced a flock of sheep into a ballroom floor during a dance (this was at Cambridge). He was also an Olympic Gold Medallist for Yachting (Berlin 1936), and twice decorated during the war, when he served with the Royal Marines. For some years he was Master and mainstay of our local hunt; I tended to follow his lead in the hunting field, and remember doing so once when he and I were the only two left in it at the end of a run.

So, one way and another, I was afraid for a bit that all our invitees would follow his lead in this matter, and decline. Luckily however, another Services man of comparable character and status, Jim Rice-Evans, had recently turned up in the neighbourhood, and he accepted. Jim was still serving, as a Colonel in the Royal Welsh Fusiliers. In the end we sat down about thirty-five for dinner.

During dinner a good bit of ice was broken, as people got to know our visitors up to a point. So when it was suggested after dinner that we should hear more fully from some of them, it was readily agreed. Two of those former Mau Mau men then spoke to that gathering of their former enemies. Their style was conversational and easy. They said, first, that they did not regret having fought for their country's freedom; but, secondly, they were sorry for the wrong methods they had employed to do it. They asked everyone to join them in building the future. They mentioned that Jomo Kenyatta was still in prison, and they wanted to go and see him and show him the African film *Freedom* (made by MRA in Nigeria four years previously) before he came out. When they had finished, up jumped Jim Rice-Evans, and declared: 'Well, if you say you are not sorry for having fought for your freedom, but are sorry for the way you did it, that's fair enough.' Fred Best said: 'All I can say is that if the leading people in Africa are like those who have spoken to us tonight, there would be no fear for black or white.' And he added: 'I would like to contribute £100 toward the cost of showing the film to Jomo Kenyatta.'

The Africans stayed the night with us afterwards. At breakfast they could be seen in long and earnest conversation with Clare and Lilian, sisters of the man they had so recently chosen to kill. Clare showed them the lionskin belonging to Gray which he had bequeathed to her

Guests from Kenya: Nahashon Ngare, P.C. Mulwa, Stanley Kinga, Paul Getata

and which now hung on the wall of the entrance hall to our house. Later it emerged that one of the four, Stanley Kinga, was a member of the committee which chose Gray Leakey as the white man who was to die.

Fred Best's £100 was added to the fund for showing *Freedom* to Kenyatta. When Kenyatta saw the film, he asked for it to be dubbed into Swahili in time for his release from detention. This was done, and after his release *Freedom* was shown to an estimated one million Kenyans during the weeks immediately preceding their first post-emergency general election.

Miles Bellville's boycott of the supper party did not affect his continuing interest in what MRA was doing. A short time later, he and I drove together to an evening meeting in Oxford, to hear the youngest Conservative M.P., Patrick Wolrige-Gordon, talk about his recent change. We were both enormously impressed by what he said, and the way he said it. Neither of us thought much of driving seventy miles and back in an evening in those days, if there was something we really wanted to go for.

CHAPTER XIII
Rozi's word

TOWARDS THE END of the year my sister Rozi came home from France. She was not well. I did not at first realise the gravity of her illness. She had had cancer in her system for some years; and now it was a brain tumour, and inoperable.

For some weeks she was in bed, steadily getting worse, looked after by a good friend of the family who was a trained nurse. Her speech went entirely in the end, but not her sense of fun. You could not visit her and be solemn. There was something in that room which I can best describe as holiness; it was not tinged with sadness.

Almost her last words to me were 'Launch out.' She had several shots at saying it, and I made several guesses at what she was trying to say. At last I got it: 'Launch out.' Rozi nodded, and sank back on the pillow with a look of relaxation and pleasure, knowing that she had got across to me. She died, appropriately, I thought, on Easter Sunday.

One of Rozi's friends, Baronesse de Watteville, wrote of her: 'Rozi fought so valiantly for France and the French, as if it had been her own country. We all loved her dearly, not only for her undaunted courage and straight fight, but for her delightful English sense of humour which nobody could resist, and we enjoyed daily.'

Rozi taught me a very great deal by being what she was, especially when we were all younger, in our twenties. She illustrated for me the Cross of Christ. First she was the pagan. Then she changed dramatically, and shared her enthusiasm generously, with an infectious gaiety. Then she was led into an altogether deeper experience, where self seemed cancelled out and Rozi's own experience seemed more like a small patch of a rich store of treasure, to be used as God directed. From then on her life was not her own. She lived at the Cross for others.

We launched out, with the assistance of friends in the Worcester, Malvern and Hereford areas, and of the media.

Miss Gray, the proprietor of the Scala Cinema, Worcester, allowed us to use her facilities for an invited showing of *The Crowning*

Experience on a Sunday afternoon in May. It was in the earlier days of the 'wide screen', which lent itself perfectly to this beautiful film starring Muriel Smith. We invited a distinguished cricketer, J.L. Guise, for the weekend, and he and I went to invite the Australian cricket XI on Sunday morning to the film on Sunday afternoon. Two of them, Brian Booth and Ian Mackenzie, came. The jam-packed tea reception in the foyer afterwards was not one of our smartest efforts as organisers. But Booth redeemed the situation by some appreciative remarks about the film, and urged people to carry forward its ideas.

We also invited our rector, the Rev Kenneth Fraser, to see the film. He preached about it in Whitbourne church, saying that he had been 'very moved – almost too moved.' Stan, our maintenance man, was another who praised the film. Another member of our staff said:

Rosalind

'Eighteen months ago people had heard vaguely about Moral Re-Armament, but no one knew what it was. Now everyone knows what it is. It is a great achievement.'

Perhaps the most ambitious 'launch out' of all was when we agreed to support the Westminster Memorial Trust in their showing of Peter Howard's play *The Diplomats* in the Malvern Festival Theatre. The play, with full West End cast, was to be produced there from 16 to 21 December 1963, prior to its opening at the Westminster Theatre in London after Christmas.

By now some lessons had been learnt, and, with the help of God and our friends the organisation appeared to run smoothly. First, we were able to assemble a first-rate team of helpers, including two trained secretaries. Also included was a long standing friend of the family, David Grimshaw, who did a great job as Field Officer and PR man. I think we managed to get most, if not all, of them living in at Whitbourne Hall. Then my brother-in-law, Francis, had the inspired idea that we needed a second telephone line at the Hall, and this was installed as a gift from him and Gwen. We could not have done without that. The legacy (Knightwick 418) lives on! An early encouragement to us as we set out to sell tickets on this week of all weeks just before Christmas was that Hilda Lettice, whom we had met at one of the *Crowning Experience* showings and who was now Mayor of Worcester, had asked if she could be patron of the Friday night performance.

It was very cold in those early days of December. It was essential that we send out our team of people, who were to go out and publicise the event for the daylight hours, warm and well fed and well briefed. So we met for an hour every morning in the writing room before breakfast. I got there early to make sure the fire was roaring by the time people came in. We felt warm. But it was nothing like the warmth that I felt towards that team. There was a common heart and mind; this was God's work, and our main purpose in meeting was to be with Him, and to listen to Him for His plan. And we reported realistically on the events of the day before. I remember giving repeated warnings not to sit back: 'At the present moment, as far as I can see, hardly anyone is certain to come!'

The Diplomats was a considerable success. The quality of the play itself did not escape Frank Greatwich, then editor of *Berrows Worcester Journal*. Frank had for years been an encouraging friend, sometimes rating MRA publications which I showed him higher than I did myself. Now he wrote of *The Diplomats*: 'The shade of Bernard

Shaw might have been seen about the Malvern Festival Theatre this week as a play, *The Diplomats* by Peter Howard, recalled something of the atmosphere of the Malvern Festival of the 1930s. . . . Peter Howard has a similar approach. He has produced a witty play as a vehicle for advancing the principles of Moral Re-Armament – mainly the 'absolute' of telling the truth. . . .'

The Worcester Clarion, the 'Worcester Church Newspaper', described the play as 'GREAT in the best sense of that word'. The total attendance for nine performances was 2,588.

It was during this period that a significant shift took place in the relations of the West with Soviet Russia. John F. Kennedy was President of the United States. He confronted a Soviet convoy with armed naval escort approaching Cuba by sea with a superior American naval force, and turned them back. He had flown over to Britain and convinced Harold Macmillan that they had good evidence that the Soviets were far advanced with plans to turn Cuba into a nuclear base from which to strike at the United States. Macmillan promised him Britain's support.

I remember the event, because on the very evening when the ships of the Soviets were approaching Cuba I happened to be at a meeting in Hereford, chaired by the Bishop, in the Town Hall. It was quite a big meeting. I was sitting near the back. Suddenly a crowd of young people near me shouted things like 'American Warmongers', and other things which sounded wide of the mark. I thought to myself 'We cannot let this go,' and on the spur of the moment shouted 'No! No! No!' The Bishop looked a little bemused, but succeeded in getting the meeting on course again. We might all have been at war on the side of the Americans by the next morning.

Next day, as it turned out, the battle of wills was won by the Americans. It was a turning point. The military threat from the Soviet Union, though not relaxed, nevertheless from then on never seemed quite so urgent.

In 1964 I became for one year High Sheriff of Herefordshire. I asked our rector, Kenneth Fraser, if he would be my chaplain, but he had to refuse for reasons undisclosed, which turned out to be that he was leaving. So I invited instead Hallen Viney, who had officiated at our wedding, and he accepted.

We set out with some gusto to enjoy the experience of attending Assizes three times in the year, and entertaining the judges concerned at Whitbourne. We appear to have succeeded, because the Under-Sheriff remarked at the end of the year: 'I always make a note of something special that strikes me about each Sheriff, and in your case it is how much you seemed to enjoy it.'

There were some interesting side duties, such as supervising the counting of the votes at the General Election of 1964, the year the Labour Party got back in after thirteen years of Conservative government; and afterwards announcing the results to the public assembled from the steps of the Shirehall.

Much the most testing experience of the year was having to respond to the toast of 'the Guests' at the Law Society's dinner in

High Sheriff of Herefordshire 1964

Hereford. I was terrified at the prospect of having to keep 130 keen legal minds in convivial mood entertained for (I was advised) not less than a quarter of an hour. I remember with shaking hands going through my notes again and again in my room in the Green Dragon Hotel, rehearsing what I had to say, jokes and all, and praying that in the event it would come out spontaneously. Luckily it did. All the same, I felt it was forced out of me. God honoured it, and helped me to get away with it. But it lacked somewhere the true freedom of the Spirit.

Certainly, in those years we cast our bread upon the waters, and God did honour it. But there were better ways yet to come.

CHAPTER XIV
A world aim for farmers

WHAT DO I mean by 'better ways yet to come'?

The years 1965 to 1980, when I retired and this account, such as it is, ceases, were marked by a pattern which was entirely unforeseen. We sold the vinegar works in Worcester in 1967. We sold three farms off the estate in 1974. We moved out of Whitbourne Hall in 1977, and sold it off the estate in 1980.

It hardly sounds like a growth industry, let alone a success story. Nevertheless I look back on those years with pleasure, mixed with some astonishment that everything came off.

The pleasure is partly due to the fact that we can still live surrounded by the natural beauty of the land in which I was born. There is also the feeling that even though I have relinquished control over some of it, it is still mine by virtue of the effort put in – rather like the Scotsman who sang 'when I've had a couple of drinks on a Saturday, Glasgow belongs to me.' But the real pleasure of those years is that Pat and I together, I believe, actually started to participate in something of significance to the world at large.

I have kept the first joint invitation card we sent to farmers in Europe in 1965. It was to a conference at Whitbourne, a visit to our co-operative, a visit to the Royal Agricultural Show, and a visit to London's Westminster Theatre. The headline we settled on was: A World Aim for Farmers. This was a challenge to all farmers, an expression of hope and of faith, and a commitment. It still is. The printed programme included this statement:

'We who send you this invitation represent men from every branch of agricultural industry. In an age of immense scientific progress, the biggest problems are no longer technical. We are convinced that the way ahead is through Moral Re-Armament. It is the key to that revolutionary growth in the spirit of man which alone can ensure that his technical abilities are used for the good of the whole world. We have decided to do two things:
1. To see that a hungry world is fed, and the contradictions of surplus and scarcity answered.

2. To create a farming profession of men and women who love their work, give of their best, and are determined to take on the moral rearmament of the world.

We would welcome your help in thinking this out, and planning for united action.'

   P.H.B.Evans
   W.A.Lang
   T.C.Harris
   N.R.Wigan

That weekend at Whitbourne a fellowship was born. Many friends and neighbours willingly gave hospitality. Eric Joseph, a professor at the University of Lausanne, stayed with Charlie and Mary James, our County Council roadman and his wife. The James's planted a lilac tree in their garden in honour of their guest. James Dickson, a chamberlain to the King of Sweden, stayed with Jack Harington, our County Court judge, and Lally his wife at Whitbourne Court. Lionel Pennefather of Northern Ireland entertained us after supper with sheepdog stories. Heinecke Werner, a German student, offered to push the crippled Jules Fiaux, ex-Secretary of the Agricultural Workers Union of Switzerland, round the Royal Show in a wheelchair, and Jules had something like a royal reception at various stands as he cheerfully drank everything in. We were driven to Oxford by a local contractor, Bill Morris, in his coach. Bill regaled us on the way with comments on the country as we passed through it. He was suitably thanked by a gentleman from Lillehammer, Norway, who composed a song for the occasion and had us all singing the words to him. In the party were three of the men who were to come with me to Africa the following year.

That weekend we dared to bite off more than we could chew. For me it was a significant step into unexplored territory.

I owed it all, personally, to one particular event in London some weeks earlier, which gave meaning to my participation in this farmers' conference, and which keyed it in to my life at Whitbourne. It was this event which was to me truly the generator of those 'better ways yet to come'.

A group of us were together to take counsel about the future of our work. Someone said: 'Hands up all those who feel that their job is an essential part of their revolutionary Christian commitment.' I thought 'Good question', and started to put up my hand. But it would not go up. It got stuck somewhere about the level of my shoulder. Nothing was said, and the meeting went on, but I could not forget the experience of my hand stopping half-way up. Of course it taught me that while I knew that my job ought to be an essential part of my commitment, in fact it was not. I asked myself: 'What, in God's mind, is a farmer for?'

Perhaps it is appropriate that I cannot remember any exact banner headline in which words presented themselves to me. But the thought was clear enough. It was that the true calling of farmers is to see that the world gets fed.

God only knew how this was to be done. The only farming I knew was our own farming in Western Europe. I started wondering whether our experience was in any way relevant to farming in the rest of the world. Why not make a start in Africa, where I had already some connections?

I started by inviting Ove Jensen. We were in a car travelling to meet a German farmers' leader in Schleswig near the Danish border. The thing I remember we brought back from this German was a reassuring and confident opinion that there would always be a place for the family farm in Germany. This was at a time when there was a great rumpus in Europe over what was known as the Mansholt Plan. Sicco Mansholt, an influential Dutch economist, was advocating

Our farmers' group on arrival in Khartoum in March 1966. (l–r) David Ogilvy, Edward, Lennart Sjoegren, Ove Jensen, with Peter Everington, a teacher from England whose knowledge of the Sudanese people and language was invaluable

that huge numbers of family farms in the European Community would have to go out of business in the interests of 'efficiency'.

I did not know Ove very well in those days. My heart leapt a bit in surprise when he seemed quite interested in coming to Africa. 'That's one of our team,' I thought. Ove is a substantial farmer at Edsvalla in central Sweden. He would tell us, in his (then) distinctly halting English, how he had once entertained a Soviet delegation on his farm. The Russians were deeply impressed by the milk yield of Ove's cows. They asked him what the secret was. He told them to ask his workmen. The workmen said: 'Well, you see, the boss changed, and started to treat us properly. So we changed and started to treat the cows properly!'

Lennart Sjoegren, an engineer who spoke excellent English and could interpret for Ove, also volunteered to come.

The fourth man was David Ogilvy from Scotland, a fellow farmer and landowner, who started us off with a visit to the ruling el Mahdi family in the Sudan, some of whom he had recently entertained in his own home.

We decided four was enough – few enough to get into one car if necessary.

Invitations came: to Kenya, from four white farmer settlers; to Rhodesia, from Captain Ridley Waymouth, R.N. (Rtd); to South Africa, from Bremer and Agnes Hofmeyr; and to Nigeria, from Hugh Elliott, who was at that time District Officer at Enugu, and responsible for carrying through a number of important agricultural development schemes.

Lennart was amused to see from the aeroplane that Khartoum is laid out in the form of a Union Jack. Later, in Kenya, when we were taken to the annual agricultural show at Eldoret, he was similarly amused at the British 'tea-party' atmosphere of the whole thing, with squads of white settlers competing with Africans at spearing coloured discs on horseback at full gallop, and such like. At Eldoret, incidentally, an African broke ranks from a group in the main ring and ran over and greeted us – none other than Stanley Kinga, who had been in the party at Whitbourne five years earlier.

Alan Knight took us to another very British garden party in Nairobi, which was addressed by Jomo Kenyatta, now President. An African came up to Alan, and they greeted one another like old friends. The fellow said: 'We are living in happier times now, aren't we?' He had been one of Alan's detainees at Athi River camp. His matter-of-fact remark, rather like someone saying 'The weather has improved at last' came I felt from a contented heart. I could see Alan was moved and heartened by it.

Early on we were introduced to a farm co-operative, and I found myself in the office having to explain our mission to a dozen or so African officials. Introducing our party, I told them that we had learnt lately that it was the job of farmers to co-operate with one another to feed the world, and we had come to see how they did it in Africa. I had thought they might think it was some neo-colonialist plot, or at least pretty good cheek on our part. But we were met with complete openness, and a flood of questions, such as did we think tomatoes would grow in such and such a soil, etc.

We were entertained to lunch in the round hut of a young smallholder and his wife, who appeared to have cooked one of their only four chickens for the occasion. He was newly settled on his own forty acres, and was just starting up in tea. He was dead keen, like any starter farmer at home would be.

We were also entertained to lunch in the pleasant and spacious farmhouse of Lord Delamere, son of the founder of the White Highlands. On hearing that he had 54,000 acres and that it was all divided up into paddocks of 1,000 acres each, I asked him if he used a post-hole digger. He smiled and replied 'I've got hundreds of post-hole diggers, and they are all very willing.' We discussed Rhodesia, which had just declared U.D.I. He said: 'I have been down there and did my best to tell them that our experience here suggests that they have nothing to fear from being ruled by Africans. But they would not listen. We have learnt from experience, and I suppose they have got to.'

I remember especially one talk in Nairobi with a British machinery officer attached to the East African Agriculture and Forestry Association. He told us how in Tanzania 940 British tractors had been imported in a single year. The vast majority of them were now lying idle because of the lack of trained personnel to maintain them and do simple repairs. He himself, after sixteen years' experience, had come to the conclusion that ploughing in many parts of East Africa was more efficiently done by bullocks than by tractor. And he startled us with the information that 80,000 bullock ploughs were imported into East Africa every year. He was now training farmers in the villages how to handle bullock teams for ploughing to replace the hand hoe. He reckoned that to plough an acre of ground with bullocks cost one quarter as much as it did by tractor.

This talk with the East African advisory officer rang true to me.

He was not a political type, merely realistic. He was just sorry that Britain could not understand how so much of her effort to 'prop up African countries' was wasted. To send a tractor to East Africa is useless unless you also send someone who is either going to stay there and work it, or who can get down to teaching Africans to do so.

Later on, back in England, I had an introduction to the secretary of the Agricultural Engineers Association, who had been of help to one of our Herefordshire landowners. I tried to tell him of my concern. He said: 'You and I are on different sides of the fence. I do what is best for British industry.' His job was helping industry to export tractors.

It so happened that while we were in Kenya our host, Michael Low of Narosurra Farm in the Rift Valley, was lobbying Ministry of Agriculture officials in Nairobi to support an on the farm training scheme which he had devised. I went with him on one or two of the visits. He got the needed support, and before we left the decision was made, and the Narosurra Farm Mechanisation Training Scheme was launched.

The whole emphasis of the scheme was on training Africans in simple tractor maintenance, including welding. It ran well for some years, and soon produced a network of grateful small farmers all over Kenya, including a National Ploughing Champion. It made its mark because of the respect and standing with the Africans which Michael, and his white farmer colleagues who were the moving spirits, enjoyed. All had accepted the offer to become Kenyan citizens. Michael and two others, Alan Knight and Wilfred Hopcraft, had already sold a proportion of their farms to some of their best farm employees, by selling them to the government at an agreed price on condition the government resold them to the selected employees. The government, for reasons unknown, backed down from their agreement with Alan Knight after it had been running for two years. But with Michael Low at Narosurra, the agreement gave him a good start with twelve new independent African owner-farmers on five hundred acres of his former farm plus himself on the remaining five hundred acres, all members together of the Narosurra co-operative. Not a bad base on which to start a farm training scheme.

Back home, we arranged a meeting at the National Farmers Union H.Q. meeting hall in Hereford, and with the good support of an old Kenya hand farming near Leominster named Jack Best (the famous escaper from Colditz, as I afterwards discovered) raised a certain sum of money to help the scheme along. The last instalment of this was taken by another well-wisher, Bill Bengry, to Narosurra in person. Bill is a garage proprietor in Leominster, and was in the habit of driving a car in the East Africa Safari motor rally. He sportingly volunteered to drive on to the Lows for a visit and deliver the cash.

We also sent one young farmer from Suffolk, Jim Wigan, to help with the training. A leader of the Young Farmers' Clubs in his district, he was pronounced an ideal candidate by the V.S.O. people who interviewed him. But Jim only wanted to go to Narosurra under the umbrella of Moral Re-Armament, and they felt unable to sponsor him unless he was willing to go anywhere. So he went unsponsored by V.S.O. and the money was raised somehow.

Jim was certainly an asset to Narosurra during his time there. It was sad that not more than two or three years after Jim left the Narosurra Farm Training Scheme appears to have died a natural death, owing to a shift in the Kenyan government's attitude to white farmers. The word went out that white farmers must go, and they had a struggle to get anything like a decent price for their farms. So Michael and others had to go. Alan Knight and Wilfred Hopcraft were just able to stay on. Years later I was with Wilfred in Ethiopia. There he spoke of taking on not only his own country of Kenya, but the whole African continent.

From Kenya, we moved on to Rhodesia, at that time under white control. The governor, who had opposed U.D.I., had been stripped of his powers and placed in a kind of open detention by Ian Smith's party. He welcomed us, listened carefully to what we had to say, and thanked us for what we were 'trying to do'. We visited the owner of one of the 'purchased farms' which had been bought cheaply from the government by their African owners, freehold. There were about eight thousand of them. Visits to him, to the owner of a white farm, plus a couple of government ministers, were among other events laid on for us by our host, Ridley Waymouth. It was only three days, but an unforgettable first glimpse of that country which was later to emerge so miraculously from civil war as the new nation of Zimbabwe.

On to South Africa – South Africa under apartheid, with the white Afrikaans Nationalists in control. Who would ever have thought then that twenty-five years on the leader of the National Party and President of South Africa, F.W. de Klerk, would be making a bold bid to reverse apartheid? On the day I am writing these words (29 January 1991) Nelson Mandela and Chief Buthelezi are meeting to seek a way of overcoming their differences and of enabling them to co-operate in building a new South Africa of free people. But then, in 1966, there must have been very few places where black and white could eat together. At Lawley Road, then the home of Bremer and Agnes Hofmeyr and their family, you certainly could, and we did.

Bremer and George Daneel laid on a trip in a station wagon for our whole party, with George driving, through the Ciskei and Transkei to the Karroo. In Soweto we picked up, by arrangement, Philip Vundla, an African revolutionary and in my opinion one of the great figures of South Africa of that time. First out of their house came Mrs Vundla, with the smallest child, then in ascending order of age the other twelve children, and finally Philip, with his Gladstone bag packed for the journey. Philip talked freely to us as we drove along. One of his sons had left home to join the guerillas in exile. Philip did not want conflict. But he was afraid that the younger generation would not be as 'patient' as his had been. At Umtata we bought sandwiches and ate them in the car. We would not have been allowed into a restaurant together. I asked him what he felt about those whites who were trying to fight apartheid. 'They are heroes,' he replied.

It so happened that there was a parliamentary election on, and at dinner at the Karroo our host Roly Kingwill had invited a few friends including the local parliamentary candidate for the United Party (the official opposition party in the white parliament). He got them, and Philip, to say a few words after dinner. Their faces of dawning wonder as this black revolutionary talked good sense, and made some good jokes, were a study. We understood afterwards that they had probably never met a black man socially before. Philip himself commented wryly next morning that it still hurt him to realise how hard whites found it to accept blacks as human beings.

Promise of the Veld is the title of a documentary film about the Kingwill family on their farm in the Karroo. Made in 1987, it vividly encompasses the change in Roly Kingwill's life way back in the 1930s, how it affected the life of his workers and their families, and how it gave him a shaft of insight into the way he had been exploiting his land as a farmer. Overgrazing by sheep was resulting in the disappearance of edible grass from the valleys. As a result there was no root system left to hold the moisture in the topsoil after rain. The water ate its way down in little runnels into the stream in the valley bottom. The swollen stream poured ever faster down its deepening bed to the sea, taking the topsoil with it. The fertility of the farm was growing ever weaker.

Roly first of all decided to reduce his sheep numbers by one third.

That was the crucial decision. Then he embarked on a long-term programme to reclaim the valley floor. This was being done in the opposite way to what I had supposed it would be: not by catching all the water at the lower end of the valley, but by starting at the top end with a reservoir to hold it in and feed it over on a wide front. Then, in the dry season, build another dam lower down, and so on.

Roly told us all this, and much more, illustrating it on the ground. He made sure we had seen all the various grades of grass: the sweet grass (edible), the sour grass (edible by sheep when they had finished the sweet grass), the edible bush, and the non-edible bush, they were all there. One gathers they were all there before 'modern' farmers arrived. The then 'livestock', namely the wild animals, controlled their numbers and prevented erosion by preying upon one another – what is called the balance of nature. Was it possible that Roly's obedience to the Creator in the matter of how he used his land was a demonstration of how farming can be environment-friendly? He has stuck at it for fifty years, and his sons after him. He is now a recognised farming authority in the neighbourhood, which has a recommended sheep stocking rate of just about exactly the same numbers per acre he felt he should have when he first set out on this venture.

And so, on to Nigeria, that huge country where over one quarter of the whole population of Africa lives.

Hugh Elliott welcomed us, and put us up in his house outside Enugu. Hugh was at that time administrative officer for the Eastern Nigeria Farm Settlement Schemes. In one scheme the first rice had been harvested. There were five other schemes planned. Villages were going up. A standpipe with water gushing up from a hundred feet down was the delight of the new villagers. We sat in for two hours on a most interesting discussion on various issues raised by the people of another settlement.

Eastern Nigeria is the home of the Ibo tribe. Only three years later, after terrible massacres of the Ibos in the north by the Hausas, the East tried to secede from the Federation and form a separate state – Biafra. In 1967 General Gowon, the head of the Federation, declared war and invaded the East. The war did not end till 1970 when resistance collapsed, and General Gowon surprised the Ibos and the world by a generous peace. Astonishingly, the scars of war have since been healed. The African capacity to forget the past and to get on with rebuilding has seldom been more vividly illustrated.

Such was our very brief glimpse of Nigeria. It struck us at the time we were there as potentially easier, on account of the value of the crops, to make a living there on ten acres than perhaps anywhere else we went in Africa. The oil-led business boom which followed the war led to the building of a network of good roads, but has drawn more and more Nigerians to the cities, to the neglect of agriculture – which is only now beginning to recover.

We travelled back to London, spent a day together to assess our tour and agree a report, and went our different ways; Lennart and Ove back to Sweden, David and I back to our Scottish and English estates. Over the years since then I have seen something of all of them, David in particular, and we have at times co-operated on various projects. How has it developed so naturally between us?

I am sure that the shared African experience, was a big factor. We worked all out. I wrote my notes at the end of each day before going to bed, so that I would not forget events as they passed. Most important, we shared with one another the thoughts which came as we laid each day before God and asked for His guidance: this usually happened in the car, driving to our first appointment – the only time we were alone together. I don't remember feeling tired, or anything like that, after the tour.

CHAPTER XV
Farmers and friends

BACK HOME, PAT had become Chairman of the local branch of the National Farmers Union, and a member of the county Executive Committee. His chairmanship of the Bromyard branch coincided with the tenure of the county chairmanship by our friend Harold Herford. Harold, having spent the earlier part of his life in India, was running a successful small farm near us, with the help, mainly, of his large family, male and female. He was at first a bit cagey about us, expressing rather surprised appreciation of our efforts as 'affluent farmers' to focus public opinion on the needs of the small man. But he was magnificent as County Chairman, managing the crowds outside the old Market Hall in Hereford during a farmers' demonstration for a fair deal from the government.

I was an amazed witness of this scene. There must have been over a thousand, even several thousand, people jammed into the city centre. There were several dozen tractors with trailers carrying placards, banners and the like, inching slowly in procession through the crowd.

One of the most noticeable was that representing the Bromyard branch. Pat, as chairman, had laid on a tractor and trailer supplied by a colleague who lived nearer to Hereford than we did. It was driven by its owner, with Pat and his wife Kristin and their house-guest of the time, David Hume of Northern Ireland, manning the trailer. A huge and magnificent plum cake made of stiff paper or cardboard and appropriately painted filled the trailer. The message on an accompanying placard read: 'Help us bake a bigger cake so all can have a larger slice.' This was a sentence from a speech made by Henry Plumb, President of the National Farmers' Union, a few days earlier – hence the 'Plum(b)' cake. Kristin, helped by Erica and David, had been up half the night in our drawing-room at Whitbourne Hall putting the 'cake' together and painting it. I saw Harold burst into delighted laughter as they moved past him, with David doing his P.R. stuff as to the manner born from the back of the trailer.

What I remember best about Harold's speech on that occasion was his point (with which I agreed), that the 'farmers' subsidy', as it was called, was really a housewife's subsidy, keeping the price of food down in the shops. The farmers, whose prices for their produce were subject to an annual price review, did not see any of this subsidy, except as consumers. This was just one factor which at that time steadily drove the farming community into a deep distrust of the government.

It came home to me in another way, when Tim Harris, the Chairman of the Junior Section of the Farmers Club in London, drew my attention to a forthcoming international conference which had been called at Reading under the chairmanship of Dr A.H. Bunting, Dean of the Faculty of Agriculture at Reading University. The subject of the conference was 'Change in Agriculture'. Tim had invited me to speak to the Junior Farmers' Club members on 'How can European Farmers Help African Agriculture?' I had not met Dr Bunting but Tim had a high opinion of him, so I wrote to ask if he would accept me as a member of his conference. He wrote back welcoming the idea of having one or two *bona fide* farmers there. So I signed on and went. Erica came and joined me for the social dinner at the end.

The conference was all about investment in developing countries. Hundreds of experienced men in overseas aid departments of governments compared notes with one another on lessons learnt, and successes achieved. Dr Bunting himself repeatedly made the point that the people in the world who are hungry are the farmers in the villages.

I sat opposite a couple of youngish civil servants in the canteen one day, and they asked me what I was doing. I said I was farming. They looked at me with a priceless expression of wonderment, and one of them said something like 'I don't see why we shouldn't have some farmers here.' I did not meet another person in that conference who was actively engaged, for a living, in agriculture in any way. The overwhelming impression I got was of a vast international army of do-gooders, planning to do more good to the farmers of the world. They seemed to miss the point that the farmers themselves can do the good, if they are shown something that will pay now, not next year or the year after.

It reminded me of a story told by Pat when he was in the VIth form at Cheltenham. The master in charge asked the form what they hoped to do for a career. When he heard from Pat, one of his brighter pupils, that he hoped to go into agriculture, he said: 'Are you sure, Evans? Can't you find anything better?' He did not believe that anyone with a serious desire to do something in the world could choose a static profession like farming.

However, Pat did. He took a BA (Agric) at Cambridge, then got a job as soil adviser in the Ministry of Agriculture, followed by a succession of farming jobs for other people in Britain and France, before settling in to Whitbourne. In spite of being almost a workaholic, certainly no shirker of routine jobs, he never found farming a static job. It did not prevent him speaking and writing on agro-politico issues. In our very early years I remember him startling the N.F.U. membership of Bromyard branch with his interpretation of how the recent moves towards friendship between France and Germany were 'building bridges across the Rhine.' I remember too the rector of Whitbourne congratulating him on his 'excursion into journalism' when a half-page article appeared under his name in the *Hereford Times*.

Pat's many friends included, notably, Philippe Schweisguth, chairman of the board of directors of *La France Agricole*, France's leading agricultural newspaper. Philippe wrote an article in the paper regularly once a week for many years called 'Le Cheval de Devant' ('The Lead Horse'). He was still writing it when he died in 1993. During that tricky period when we were wondering if we could possibly trust the French enough to enter their 'common market', Pat invited Philippe to speak at 45 Berkeley Square, the MRA home in London. It was the evening before the Annual General Meeting of the National Farmers' Union, and we invited all the delegates from all over Britain to come and hear him. I think about a hundred came. It was a jolly, lighthearted evening, with plenty of jokes and banter. Philippe had the perfect sense of occasion, telling the British farmers that as a Frenchman he wasn't afraid of competition from our British sheep. Above all, it was a friendly evening.

I meanwhile had been getting acquainted with my fellow members of the Herefordshire Committee of the Country Landowners Association. I felt quite a stranger among them at first, having been introduced to them by their secretary as the High Sheriff from the opposite end of the county. The Chairman on that occasion made some reference to how the committee had felt the need for some younger blood. As I was then in my mid-fifties, probably well up to the average age of the committee, I must have allowed my jaw to drop visibly. But our senior member, Brigadier Clive, quickly restored matters by explaining that two of the new members were young, while one was an 'experienced landowner already'.

Experienced landowner or not, I was pretty well at sea over many of the matters the committee had to deal with. The division of responsibility for roadside drains between the local authority and the landowner; rights of way; rights of canoeists on the River Wye; gypsy encampments; lots of things. I was interested to see that Archer Clive sometimes seemed to be in a minority of one on matters concerning the River Wye in discussion with his fellow riparian owners. He was not afraid to express what I regarded as liberal views, so when he pressed me to have a go at being one of the committee's representatives on the C.L.A. Council in London, I was already disposed to agree: the more so, as he insisted that the main thing about the council was that one went there to learn. So I did agree, and I became a council member representing Herefordshire for many years. Archer himself, to his surprise and pleasure, was elected National President of the C.L.A. 'The last of the amateurs', he used to describe himself as.

He had invited me to lunch with Erica before I went on my African tour, and two years or so after I came back from it he came and met Michael Low and others at Whitbourne. The Secretary asked me at one of our A.G.M.s to offer a vote of congratulation to Archer Clive on his appointment as National President, which I did with real conviction, saying that I thought he aimed to use his job to serve his country. He said afterwards that this was not true, but thanked me all the same. This did not prevent him later on from ticking me off after meetings once or twice for having lost my thread and waffled.

So I had Archer Clive largely to thank for a fairly painless apprenticeship of two or three years to the committee. Of course, common interests brought us closer together as well. Before long I found myself elected Vice-Chairman, which meant that barring accidents I would be Chairman in three years' time.

In the meantime, we had the chance to show in our dining room at Whitbourne an Indian film called *Galloping Horse*, which showed how the ideas of Moral Re-Armament had begun to take root in the villages there. It was to an invited audience, and one of those I invited was a neighbouring farmer Alec Hutton. Alec at first wrote refusing the invitation, on the grounds that he had enough problems at home to deal with (he was chairman of Worcestershire N.F.U. at the time) without coming to see more problems in India. I wrote back saying that the film would deal with answers, not problems, and I hoped he would change his mind and come. He came, and was much encouraged by what he saw in that film.

Some months later, we had a rather larger event in the dining-room to which Alec came again. I cannot remember the subject, but I remember that the guests included some, and one in particular, who had never to our knowledge heard of Moral Re-Armament before. We had the meeting all planned before I went out after breakfast. I had a busy day, but unexpectedly I was forced by something to wait in Worcester for half an hour. I spent the half-hour quietly in the public library, and there I had the clear thought that we should include in this meeting a 'quiet time' of listening to God. We did, and something seemed to happen to Alec in the quiet time. He said a few words at the end, and I felt: 'Here is a chap who is going to want to fight with us.'

The next thing I recall was that that winter Pat and I were at the N.F.U.'s A.G.M. at the Central Hall, Westminster. The farmers were in militant mood, feeling that their leadership had let them down. 'Bill' Williams, the President, was speaking, trying to talk them round. Suddenly a figure emerged from the throng, left his chair, crept slowly and silently to the side of the Hall, and unfurled a huge placard from the Worcestershire branch, setting out their demands. It was Alec, of course. He quietly took his seat again, and Williams after a slight pause went on with his speech as if nothing had happened. But, of course, it had.

Alec came to Caux the following summer. Erica and I went out with him, and came back before him. While we were visiting the Royal Show a few days later, we went to the Longhorn cattle lines, and a figure waved to us from among the straw bales – Lesley Hutton, Alec's wife. We hardly knew her then. 'What have you done to my husband?' she demanded. 'He's become a different man! We were up talking half the night last night.' That was the first we heard of Alec's change at Caux. What we heard from himself came later.

Alec became, and remains, a firm friend and ally in the battle for new understanding in the world, and especially in the farming world. He has brought with him a shrewd business mind, plus a spirit of 'wanting to affect how things go rather than sitting back and letting things happen' (his own words, or my best shot at how I remember them). He has shown understanding and wisdom to me in some difficult moments. We have gained much from his co-operation – including his sense of fun and down-to-earth quality.

About this time (1967) the vinegar works in Worcester, which had largely provided the sinews of war for most of our goings on, packed up.

Hill Evans & Co. Ltd. was a public company, whose shares were not quoted on the Stock Exchange. Financially speaking, it had been standing still for a long time. My father had been Chairman until his death in 1958. After him, our cousin on the Hill side, Tom Wilson, by then Archdeacon of Worcester, took over the chairmanship. I succeeded him on his death, and was Chairman when the moment for decision arrived.

I had to handle a rapidly deteriorating situation. We brewed and sold vinegar as the main product of our five-acre factory. Cider and British Wines were an insignificant sideline. Firms like H.P. Sauce who manufactured many products were pricing us out of the market. Our position had been bolstered by the fact that half our output of vinegar – about a million gallons a year – was taken by the H.J. Heinz Company. We finished by selling to Distillers, or to their subsidiary, British Vinegars. We sold the business to them. Then we sold the five-acre site, renamed 'Worcester Properties', for industrial use, after a prolonged battle (which we lost) to get planning permission to develop it for offices.

It was all new to me, and I tried to learn the ins and outs, but our advisers didn't appear to know a great deal either! The director who was most helpful was Roy Harrison, a Worcester solicitor of good standing, who was about my age and had been appointed a director at the same time as I had. It was he who made a lot of the running in the policy considerations which led us to the final deal. The actual negotiations of the deal were in the hands of Leonard Jones, the managing director. The price finally agreed enabled us to pay the shareholders 28s in the £ on their shares. I regarded this as a minor triumph for Leonard Jones. The amount on the balance sheet allocated for 'Goodwill' had not varied for well over twenty years. It stood at £48,000. British Vinegars paid us this sum in full.

Fortunately, the employment situation in Britain at the time was good. No one failed to find a job of some sort elsewhere. But that did not make up for the fact that many, probably most, of our ninety employees felt that a life-time of service to the company had been cut off, and something had gone badly wrong. And they were right. The directors had failed to expand the business in the years of success, and when they started to try it was too late. When I addressed the employees and thanked them for their services – I cannot remember what I said, but I kept it fairly matter of fact and brief – what came back to me from them was no feeling of hostility or bitterness, but mainly I think shocked acceptance. That vast single span building, which is still a landmark in the middle of Worcester, was no longer to house the largest vat in the world, made of Oregon pine, and with a capacity of 120,000 gallons. This went elsewhere with a few others of the bigger ones. Many of the others were dismantled and sold as staves to builders.

A few staves found their way onto our estate. I remember taking our estate maintenance man, Stan Williams, to the works to select suitable pieces of timber for us. Stan started getting enthusiastic and wanting to look at all sorts of objects of interest. I choked him off, and told him to stick to the business of selecting material for the estate. This was not a sightseeing tour. Stan afterwards put it around that the boss was 'feeling deeply' about the vinegar works. He was right there, too!

However, in another way it was a bit of a relief to me personally to have the vinegar works no longer round my neck. That winter Norman Green-Price of Wales suggested to Pat that we should start a 'Think and Act Tank'. Norman had made his mark with a wide circle of friends and neighbours for his fresh and outspoken advocacy of farmers in Britain meeting the needs of farmers in developing countries. He had generously supported our visit to Africa of 1966. Now he drove over with two Welsh friends to Pat's, and we had a series of discussions on how to carry the idea forward in a practical way. One of those who came with him was a young dairy farmer called Simon Gourlay, later to be President of the N.F.U. in England and Wales.

CHAPTER XVI
Return to Eritrea

ONE DAY IN about early March of 1969 I had an unexpected phone call from Hugh Elliot.

The Governor-General of Eritrea, His Highness Ras Asrate Kassa, a cousin of Emperor Haile Selassie of Ethiopia, had organised a Conference for Moral Re-Armament called 'Modern Men to make Modern Nations', to be held in Asmara from 25 April to 5 May. His Highness had invited Jim Baynard-Smith, an Englishman who had formerly been A.D.C. to the Governor General of the Sudan, to come over and help his committee. Jim had asked Hugh, knowing how valuable his experience and support would be. Hugh and his wife Bridget and Jim and his wife Sally would all be there. Would Erica and I like to come? They reckoned that we would qualify through our connection with Moral Re-Armament, and that I would also qualify by having taken part in the battle of Keren which liberated Eritrea in 1941.

Part of the background to this was the visit to Caux in 1967 of an Eritrean lecturer on the staff of the Teacher Training Institute in Asmara named Teame Mebrahtu. Mebrahtu was an able teacher, but had a bitter hatred of all whites. At Caux he had a deep experience of change and apologised for his hatred. On his way back at Asmara Airport he met Ras Asrate, who was on his way to London. They talked for half an hour. H.H. Ras Asrate was sufficiently struck by the change in him to start the wheels turning for this conference of 1969. Teame Mebrathu became a member of the Committee of Invitation, and was a key figure during the conference itself.

Another imaginative stroke of the Governor-General was to send Sheikh Surur, a leading Eritrean Muslim, also on the Committee, to attend the opening of the MRA centre at Panchgani in India; following which it was his 'wild idea' (as he called it) to invite Rajmohan Gandhi, grandson of the Mahatma, with a large group of Indians to come over and bring with them the entire cast of the play *The Forgotten Factor* to the Asmara Assembly. They all came.

We went too, of course. We arrived in Asmara on 22 April, and were allotted rooms in the Albergo Italia – a reminder that much of the economic infrastructure of Eritrea was still in the hands of the Italians.

Unlike the rest of Haile Selassie's Empire of Ethiopia, Eritrea had been an Italian colony for nearly sixty years before the outbreak of World War II. After the Italian defeat, Eritrea was administered by Britain, under United Nations mandate. This was from 1942 to 1952. It then became part of a federation with Ethiopia. This lasted till 1961, when the Emperor unilaterally abrogated the federation, and Eritrea became administratively incorporated within the Ethiopian Empire. That was when Eritreans who had not wanted the incorporation first took up arms and the long-running guerilla war, which was still much in evidence at the time of our visit, began.

From 1966 onwards Eritrea had been run by its own quite impressive Civil Service under a Governor-General (Ras Asrate Kassa). That was how it was when we arrived.

As British visitors, we found a ready welcome. The British post-war administration had carried through a programme of educational reform which remained in place after we left Eritrea in 1952, and that was held in our favour. Also, it was widely felt that we had rescued Eritrea from Fascism, for which even most of the present Italian population appeared to be grateful.

One of the practical bonuses for Erica and me was that we were staying in the same hotel as other overseas delegates like Irène Laure and Rajmohan Gandhi, and had a chance to get to know them.

The first morning after we arrived, I headed off on my own and met Ato (Mr) Hateab Haile, Deputy Director in the Department of Agriculture. I evidently invited him and his staff to *The Forgotten Factor* that same evening, and noted his reaction when he came: 'Wonderful! I will come to the next play.'

The following morning Marcel Grandy (Switzerland), Karl Gunning (Netherlands) and I went to address the boys of Hebret High School. I cannot remember anything we said except that Marcel in introducing himself told them his name was Grandy, not Gandhi. But when I stood up to speak, and appeared (I suppose) for a moment at a loss for words at this sea of hundreds of black faces confronting me, they all burst out into roars of laughter, in which I heartily joined.

In the afternoon we met H.H. the Governor-General for the first time at an official reception for conference delegates from overseas. He asked me about Keren, and said he would arrange to send me in his private car with driver the following week to meet the Governor of Keren and look over the battlefield.

On Friday the 25th we spoke at a school for the sons and daughters of officers – a grand occasion. And the opening meeting of the conference took place in the new Expo Pavilion before five hundred people with a further hundred standing. Erica and I met the British Consul, Major John Bromley, and his wife, at a cocktail party they gave to mark the Queen's Birthday. We found that Major Bromley had known Erica's first cousin, Nigel Leakey, V.C., when he was serving in the King's African Rifles. They had stayed up one night in 1941 until 2 am talking about questions of belief and faith. The next day Nigel was killed at the battle of the Bilati River, where single-handed he had headed off a column of Italian tanks. For this he was posthumously awarded the Victoria Cross.

Erica had not seen Nigel since their schooldays in England, when they both took part in some well remembered, and well enjoyed, family camps, run by Erica's mother and aunt in the summer holidays.

On the 26th (my birthday), I told the Assembly the story of our supper party for the ex-Mau Mau men at Whitbourne. In the afternoon we held a riotous public meeting in the grandstand of the football stadium. It was an object lesson to see how Irène Laure handled the crowd estimated at over five thousand, mainly of quite young children. She spoke in French, with an interpreter into English, and then the English was interpreted into Tigrinyan. She shouted: 'Can you say those four standards? Absolute Honesty!' and she stood up and beat it out like a conductor to everyone who could see her, Absolute Purity! A bit louder this time. Absolute Unselfishness! A real uninhibited shout from the audience. Absolute Love! An immediate uncontrollable cheer (in Tigrinyan) of 'Absolute Love'.

I thought those in charge of the meeting must have been by this time a bit stuck as to how to proceed. But fortunately the noise of cheering voices was overcome by a deeper note – the steady roar of rain on the roof of the stadium – long desired and long awaited rain!

The children all spontaneously left to enjoy the feel of the water. They splashed knee-deep into water wherever they found it racing down the streets, reminding Erica of how our boys used to rush into the sea.

Rajmohan's speech had been very brief. He laughed about it with us in the car going home.

But we had heard Rajmohan speak to hundreds of attentive

listeners on our very first evening in Asmara. It was at an Open Air Meeting, outside St Mary's Coptic Cathedral. His theme had been 'Doctor Africa'. 'Some call Africa a patient, but Africa is meant to become doctor Africa. In the spirit of Moral Re-Armament Africa can help the world,' he had said.

Early the following week we made our visit to Keren in the Governor-General's car. We took with us Michael and Margaret Barrett – Michael being an old friend from Oxford days and an ex-officer in the U.S. Air Force – and Wilfred Hopcraft and his daughter Heather. Wilfred was a Kenya settler farmer, one of those who with Michael Low had made over land to his employees before the launching of the Narosurra Farm Training Scheme. It was a real day out for all of us.

At Keren, we were received briefly by the Governor, and transferred to the care of the Deputy Governor, Ato Ahmed Haj Feraj, who was to take us round.

We visited the Keren War Cemetery, seeing the graves of several old comrades. We were asked if we would like to go down the hill to the bottom of the escarpment, under armed escort because of the risk of Shifta (guerillas). We said Yes, and went down. We found the rocky feature where the shell landed and removed half my platoon. We were able to identify roughly the route over which we had to attack, with Mt Falestoh looming large on the horizon. We drove back up the road – that road previously denied to us by demolitions – and we identified Fort Dologorodoc. I would have liked to have got closer, and walked some of the way we actually went – even to the sangar where I was wounded – but there was no time for that. We had a look round a maternity clinic and the market, saw the spot where General Lorenzini the Italian commander was killed during the last days of the battle, took our leave of the Governor, and went.

The Deputy Governor, Ahmed Haj Feraj, and I became good friends. He came up to Asmara and joined in the conference and saw some plays put on by the students. He, along with Ras Asrate Kassa himself and others of our friends, were to be shot in the revolution in which 'General' Mengistu seized power not long afterwards.

On the way back from Keren to Asmara we stopped at a famous show-piece farm called Elaboret, run by an Italian. They had a herd of nine hundred milking cows, mainly Friesians and Ayrshires. Wilfred Hopcraft was in his element, being shown everything by their head man. We saw fields of lucerne, fed by gravity-flow irrigation from a river further up, all green and fresh surrounded by

Signing the book of remembrance at the War Cemetery at Keren, Eritrea. With me are Ahmed Haj Feraj, Deputy Governor of Keren, the war graves assistant, and Michael Barrett

rocky desert. After getting back to Asmara we heard on the radio that the Italian head of the company had been kidnapped by the Shifta soon after we left. He had been released, no doubt after paying a price, which was not named.

Next morning, the subject of the meeting was 'Qualities of Leadership'. I was expected to speak about our day at Keren. But I could not find much to say. I reckon the last twenty-four hours had been quite an emotional experience for me.

I have already referred to Wilfred Hopcraft's speech to the assembly on taking on the African continent. He said: 'My thought is that I should fight for my country under God instead of giving priority to farming. I should be part of a world force rather than of a smaller team in Kenya. Incorruptible leadership is the need. We have to fight for the continent of Africa.' One of the last things I did in Asmara was to go with Wilfred to the War Cemetery where many of his K.A.R. (King's African Rifles) comrades are buried.

After the conference, Erica and I took off by air to Bahar-Dar to

Showing Haj Feraj features of the 1941 Keren battlefield
Source of the Blue Nile at Lake Tana

join the large Indian contingent for a breather at the hotel there on Lake Tana, overlooking the falls which are the source of the Blue Nile. We were taken over the lake to an island monastery, where the priest unveiled for us a seven hundred and fifty year old Bible. It was in the ancient language of Ge-ez, with brilliant illustrations in bright colour. The priest ran us through the whole Bible story. It was printed, or painted, on goatskin, and kept always wrapped up in goatskins. He did not touch it with his hands, but with a forked stick which he kept to turn the pages. We got a good deal of what he said through our interpreter. When he got to the picture of the three wise men who came and brought gifts to Jesus after His birth, I mentioned that we had just acted out that same scene in our own village church at home. We were now, of course, in Ethiopia proper, no longer in Eritrea.

No women are ever allowed to set foot on this island-with-a-monastery in Lake Tana. This caused a minor 'incident' in our party, when one of the ladies, who had of course all remained on the boat while we men, including her husband, were visiting the monastery, was found to be 'missing' on our return. She had 'stowed away' in protest at such discrimination, and only emerged when her husband had started to search. The boatman, as party to the game, watched delightedly!

We spent the final few days based on Addis Ababa. Here we had a meeting with H.R.H. Princess Sarah, Duchess of Harar, who was a daughter-in-law of the Emperor. We gave her a letter from her son, Philip Makonnen, who had been staying with us immediately before we left for Eritrea, being looked after by our son William. She appeared moved and warmed by Erica's stories of Philip at Whitbourne, including playing football in the hall, and cooking pancakes in our kitchen whenever he could find a pretext. I recorded the Princess as 'a most interesting woman, with plenty to her.'

That afternoon we had tea with Sir Thomas and Lady Bromley, the British Ambassador to Ethiopia and his wife. The Bromleys were good friends with our North Herefordshire Member of Parliament Sir Clive Bossom and his wife Lady Barbara Bossom, and we passed on their greetings to them. What a very nice and good couple they were. He was direct, unassuming and caring. We spoke of farming structures. He said that in Ethiopia as a whole all landlords are absentee landlords. The small farmers are their tenants. They give half their produce to the landlord (in Eritrea I had heard it was sometimes as much as two thirds). Eritrea is organised differently:

up to now tenants have had a seven-year tenure of their land; now it has been altered to a forty-year tenure (an obvious attempt to give security of tenure for one generation). Sir Thomas was particularly interested in the play *I Am the Third*, written by one of the students I had got to know called Osman Ibrahim Shum. This play was produced in Tigrinyan, for the first time, in Asmara while we were there. Osman had hopes that it would be translated into Amharic and shown widely round the villages of Ethiopia.

Lady Bromley told Erica how the Duchess of Harar had been sent by her father-in-law the Emperor to Scotland, to be trained to be the

Brigadier and Mrs Sandford on their farm outside Addis Ababa

matron of a new hospital in Edinburgh. This hospital had been built, and, we understood, endowed, in memory of her husband the then Crown Prince of Ethiopia, who had lost his life in a car accident.

Our final day was memorable for a drive out of Addis to the farm of Brigadier Sandford. Sandford was the man who had mobilised the Ethiopian Irregular Forces behind Emperor Haile Selassie on his return from exile in 1940. Working closely with General Orde Wingate, he played a key part in the campaign which restored Haile Selassie to his throne in 1942. Now here he was in his late eighties, leading a contented retired life on his farm. He and his wife welcomed us at their farmhouse just like a couple of old settler hands. He drove and walked us round, enthusing particularly over his strawberries, the great crop of the moment. In a bedroom of their home there were some beautiful old flowered porcelain bowls and water jugs from the Edwardian era, still unblemished and obviously in use.

We arrived back in London on 13 May, having been away just three weeks. I met our C.L.A. President at a Forestry Walk the following week, and he asked me where I had been. I said: 'Ethiopia.' He said: 'How dashing!'

But I had seen enough to realise what a volatile situation we had been in. Ethiopia, including Eritrea, seemed to me, for all its long tradition of Christian culture, to be, agriculturally, the most backward of all the countries I had seen in Africa, and because the most backward, the most vulnerable to revolutionary take-over.

The conference 'Modern Men to make Modern Nations' stirred the consciences of many students, and began to give fresh faith to the middle class of Eritreans and to many civil servants. But, sadly, it was too late for the effect to be felt nationally: soon afterwards a violent revolution took place under a junior army officer named Mengistu, who overthrew the Emperor and ruled by a bloody dictatorship. During the course of this revolution, several of our friends were shot, more imprisoned, and many forced into exile. The authentic story of how some of these survived the years of privation and persecution and are now at work rebuilding their country is only now beginning to be told – as in the book *A Painful Season and a Stubborn Hope*, by Abeba Tesfagiorgis.

It is my firm belief that this revolution could have taken place without bloodshed, if there had been enough landowning families in Ethiopia with real care for the land, and for the people who lived on it and gave their half-share of produce regularly to their absentee landlords.

CHAPTER XVII
Whose job to feed the hungry?

MEANWHILE WE HAD been maintaining our touches with the French. Erica and I had an invitation to go to Brittany and visit a small farmer there and a member of a Co-operative. The opportunity came when in the winter of, I think, 1968 we were holidaying in Jersey and flew over to Brittany for two or three days of intensive visiting. It was the first time I had ever been in France with time to stop and look at the countryside, and two or three days was not much. I learned quite a bit, though. For instance, that when first introduced to a family, it is polite to kiss all the children!

I had been reading in the British press that France, and especially Brittany, was full of inefficient small farmers, who deserved to be squeezed out. What we found were small farmers, indeed, but highly organised, and dynamically motivated to survive. We met a cousin of our host who had a steel plate in his head where he had been hit by a policeman's truncheon during one of many farmers' riots. He was a hero (nearly a martyr), and treated with deep respect. Discussion on farm policy, sitting on benches round a bare kitchen table, was a bit of a challenge to me, though less so to Erica, who speaks French. The only time I can remember being really listened to was when I told them how I had to apologise to a colleague in Birmingham for having been jealous of him, because he was better than I was at handling certain difficult people!

I wrote some reflections on the French visit for the journal *New World News*, as a result of which I received an invitation to address a 'Women of the Hour' luncheon in London. I did so, and it went down OK. Next I was asked if I would write a pamphlet on agriculture and the Third World for Moral Re-Armament. So finally I did that too. I became the author of what I am sure was the first ever MRA pamphlet on agriculture! It was called *Whose Job to Feed the Hungry?*

The pamphlet's answer to this question was: It is everybody's job. But it is especially the farmer's job.

The pamphlet started by giving the proportion of the world's population engaged in farming – in Britain 3%, in Switzerland 8%, in France 16%, in Yugoslavia 50%, and in most countries of Asia and Africa 75% to 90%. It quoted Dr Bunting: 'The people who experience world food shortage and the people who produce the food are to a very large extent the same people.' And it added: 'It seems clear that the heart of the question is: how can those hungry farming families in the developing countries feed themselves, and produce that bit extra to feed the rest of their populations?' After outlining the prospects for various international aid agencies, it gave illustrations from Europe, India, Iran and Africa of progress made, remarking that it was not a matter of politics: it was a matter of change in the character of men. 'Behind such results lies the basic appreciation at Caux that the cause of all poverty in the modern world is selfishness somewhere, and that therefore the answer must he a moral answer.'

The pamphlet also described how Rajmohan Gandhi invited some European farmers to help at the Moral Re-Armament training centre at Panchgani near Poona. 'We asked him what European farmers could do for India. His reply, as a matter of fact, was nothing to do with asking us to impart our knowhow. India has a first class Government Advisory Service of her own. No, his reply was: "Teach us Indians to care for one another, then we will feed one another." Look at it how you like, if you can remember that sentence it will live with you.'

In the final paragraph, on the twelfth of twelve short pages, I quoted from one of Frank Buchman's speeches: 'Human nature can be changed. That is the root of the answer. National economies can be changed. That is the fruit of the answer. World history can be changed. That is the destiny of our age.'

Shortly after the publication of *Whose Job to Feed the Hungry?*, Erica and I were at The Hague with a group of colleagues from Europe to take part in the United Nations World Food Conference of 1970. The conference was a disappointment to me, and to others in our party. It was made noteworthy by a crowd of young people, scruffily dressed, who seemed to assume that no one from the platform could be worth listening to, invited us to fast for the starving millions while we queued up in the canteen, and seemed to be treated with an over-elaborate courtesy by the authorities. In a large upstairs gallery, huge sheaves of pamphlets were to be found on offer for all to read, free of charge. We decided to risk a number of copies of *Whose Job to Feed the Hungry?* They all disappeared that first afternoon, and we decided not to risk any more, hoping for more carefully selected targets.

Erica, meanwhile, had been invited to go on a bus tour of the city with the other delegates' wives. She she had met a Canadian woman on the bus called Janet Munro. They had made good friends, and agreed it was a nice change to have a look at the city after all that talking. That night Mr and Mrs Peter Hintzen, our hosts, arranged to have a party with films a couple of evenings on, to which we could invite guests to hear news of MRA. In the morning we arrived in the enormous conference hall and took seats somewhere about the middle. Who should turn up in the row directly behind us but Janet Munro and her husband Charles! Charles turned out to be a family farmer from Ontario, who was feeling slightly impatient, as I was, with some of the goings-on at the conference. He and Janet accepted our invitation to the party at the Hintzens. We found out that he was actually the President of the Canadian Farmers, and the President of the International Federation of Agricultural Producers as well. He and Janet were due to go straight to another conference in the South of England on their way back to Canada. When we asked them if they'd care to come and have a look at our farm while in England, they jumped at the chance.

So a few days later we drove down to Farnham Castle to pick them up as their conference finished, and drove them across the Cotswolds and back to Whitbourne. Next morning Charles and I walked round the farm with Pat. (Erica took Janet off to Marks and Spencer!) We learned quite a bit from Charles about Canadian agriculture and the I.F.A.P. His heart and soul were in farming and his family. He brought to his public work a dedication born of desire to improve the standards of living of farmers across the world. It strengthened my faith in human nature. The whole episode of how we got in touch with the Munros had, I felt, a touch of inspiration about it. It also got me stretched out onto a wider vision of what we might be meant to do. Previously I had tended to feel 'Don't start anything you cannot finish.' Now I was seeing that if it is God's work you are doing you will never finish it anyway, so why not feel free to start anything, provided He guides.

I had become aware that there was no need to wait till you become an 'expert' before making your contribution to a situation.

CHAPTER XVIII
Anything to declare?

THE WIDER VISION was soon made wider still when, in that autumn of 1970, Erica and I left for Australia, New Zealand, India and Iran. Before we left, I made sure that the outdoor chrysanthemums were covered against frost. A fortnight later, in Melbourne, I heard from Mary Shaw, my acting secretary, that an October frost had finished them. Oh well, you cannot have everything. I just had to hope that they had made a good price in the intervening two weeks.

This was the longest time that Erica and I had ever been away from home together – seven weeks at a stretch. We received the invitation to go from our son Christopher. Our elder son William (now known as Bill) was in the party at breakfast in the library when I opened Chris's letter.

I must make a short diversion here, having mentioned Bill and Chris. The fact that I have said little if anything about them in this account only goes to show how limited it is. It is not in any sense an autobiography. Anyway Chris, having left Bromsgrove and done a year's apprenticeship on a Shropshire farm, had accepted an invitation to join the European cast of a travelling musical show produced by Moral Re-Armament called *Anything to Declare?* His letter said that those responsible thought it would be very good to have someone with an agricultural interest to accompany them, and would there be any chance of us coming out and joining them? The cast were all under thirty. We were around sixty. There were one or two other older people with them, but not many.

Erica and I felt it was right from the word go. I left the forestry to Roly Powell the head woodman, the garden to John MacIntosh (successor to Charlie Greenwood), and the estate maintenance to Stan Williams. Pat and Kristin happily agreed to be in overall charge.

We arrived just at the end of the showings of *Anything to Declare?* in Australia. Almost our first event in Melbourne was attending the Agricultural Spring Show. This was, and I am sure still is, a major national event. There was a relaxed good-humoured holiday feeling about the crowd. They roared their applause when a little red steer went trotting round the ring with a straw boater on its head, leading the parade of cattle. That never happened at Stoneleigh.

We made the acquaintance of the interesting and impressive team of men and women who had invited *Anything to Declare?* to Australia. Among them was an ex-English Australian whom I had known well in early days with the Oxford Group in Worcestershire, Stanley Barnes. He had managed a dairy in Moreton-in-Marsh, then been appointed technical adviser to reorganise the milk supply of Malta, married an Australian girl there, and after the war decided to give his children schooling in Australia and become an Australian citizen. Then he spent several years in Asian countries starting dairy schemes for the Australian Dairy Development Board, and had been awarded the MBE for services to the dairy industry. Now here he was, already, sadly, a widower. But there was no doubt of his commitment to Moral Re-Armament and to answering hunger in the world.

In New Zealand, the show was put on in Wellington, Christchurch and Auckland. Erica and I were delighted with it, and the cast, and Christopher's whole-hearted participation in it. I remember particularly a cossack-style dance led by Michel Orphelin, the French mime artist, with Christopher on one side of him and someone else on the other. Also a song by the Swiss soprano Sylvie Haller called 'The Kiwi Learning to Fly'. And, sung by the whole chorus, that

Cattle parade at the Melbourne Spring Show, Australia

glorious *Haeramei*, the Maori song of welcome. Life consisted of a mixture of supporting the show and being sent off by our hosts on forays to meet people round the countryside.

After the Wellington showings, we stayed with Robin and Enid Prickett on their farm near by. Robin, like Stan Barnes, was another ex-Englishman, only this time a New Zealander. Fed up, as a young man, with working in a bank in Britain, he had come out to New Zealand to farm, and made a success. A keen member of the National Party, he had become a trusted friend of Keith Holyoake, the Prime Minister. At one point Mr Holyoake's government was under pressure to authorise the growing of sugar beet in New Zealand in order to revive the fortunes of New Zealand farmers. Robin and his friends urged him not to do this, because though it might have helped New Zealand's farmers it would probably have destroyed the cane sugar industries of Fiji and other South Pacific Islands. Holyoake decided not to go ahead with the plan. It was a moral decision, taken out of consideration for a neighbour. Fiji has had her troubles since then. Who knows how much worse they might have been if New Zealand had not held back from striking her a blow at this time?

New Zealand is a unique temperate-climate country. From Auckland to the end of the North Island it is semi-tropical. Round Invercargill at the southern end of the South Island you can get sharp frosts. In between there is a very large area where the weather is similar to Britain's on an average day, but without the extremes of fog, frost or drought. Much clearer and less muggy, though rather more windy. Grass will grow the whole year round, even on quite high hills. Farm implements can stay out in the open. The only building you need besides your house is a woolshed for shearing the sheep, and perhaps a milking parlour for milking the cows. It was in a way a farming paradise. 'Exotic' trees – trees introduced from abroad such as pines and firs, but also poplars and other deciduous trees – will grow at three times the rate that they do in Britain.

We were sent on a tour of the South Island early on. It must have been during a break in the shows, because Chris was with us. We were royally entertained by Alpheus and Anna Hayes in their spacious home in the Hakataramea Valley on the Waitaki River. Alpheus had become totally blind, I think from glaucoma, but he would look towards you and have a conversation round the crowded dinner table, joining in fully, and it was hard to believe that he could not see a thing. Then he would tap along with his stick past familiar landmarks, showing you the farm, and discourse on what life had been like building it up.

It was Chris's birthday on 13 October, and after some discreet lobbying by Michael and Margaret Barrett who were also staying with the Hayes' at the time, Erica and Chris and I found ourselves setting off in a car with rods and tackle borrowed for us by Anna from a neighbour to fish a reservoir for trout. Erica settled down to paint, and left Chris and me to it with the car. We headed off and fished the area at the opposite end where the breeze blew the water inshore. In the afternoon we drove round to rejoin Erica, and we enjoyed her amazement on opening the boot of the car to find three nice trout in it, almost as much as we did catching them!

Back home, the Hayes' were as surprised as Erica that we had scored. Alpheus felt the fish up and down and assessed their weight. Anna gave us a raspberry for not having cleaned them properly down the inside of the spine. It was a healthy home scene. To us three the only thing missing was Bill. It reminded us of those various fishing holidays we had had with both the boys when at school, usually in Scotland. What fun they were!

It was the Hayes's son-in-law, Robin White, who gave me my first understanding of the different approach to lambing by New Zealand and British farmers. In Britain we managed our lambing ewes intensively, usually in buildings, visiting them every night, aiming at a survival rate that averaged one and a half lambs per ewe. In New Zealand they did the opposite, letting nature run its course. The ewes ran out on the hills, grazing the grass and throwing and suckling their lambs without assistance. You visited them once or twice a week. You accepted a proportion of losses as natural. You were pleased if you were on the right side of one lamb per ewe.

Back in the North Island, we had a happy visit to the Gilbertsons at Hawkes Bay, on their sheep and cattle ranch. They were definitely in the 'grass-all-round-the-year' part of the country. Stewart seemed to have very few workers but he had a motor bike, on which he would roar off across country to pretty well any part of the farm. And he had dogs – beautiful, well-trained, eager dogs. One of them specialised in long sight. He could see a ewe 'turned' on her back half a mile away, and on a word from Stuart would gallop off and then gently nose the ewe upright again and gallop back, mission accomplished. Another dog, looking every inch a dingo after his quite near ancestors, was adept at helping his master select sheep when they were herded together in a pen. Stuart would indicate with his long

ANYTHING TO DECLARE? 171

Stuart Gilbertson ready for take-off round the farm, Hawkes Bay, New Zealand

With host Bill Coffey looking towards the old Parliament Building, Canberra, Australia

staff which individual sheep he wanted and the dingo would trot calmly over dozens of sheep's backs, causing no disturbance at all, till he got to the right one and in no time he edged it out to the outside of the pen where it could be handled by Stuart's man.

It turned out that the Gilbertsons were near neighbours of an old friend of mine who had visited Whitbourne in 1935. His name was Ian MacPhail, and we had an enjoyable reunion with him, also meeting his wife, in their farmhouse. This was made memorable by the fact that when we were all seated at dinner, the floor beneath us began to rock, and queer scraping noises issued from under it. It was our introduction to the opossum, a creature given to making its home in embarrassing proximity, sometimes, to humans.

Back to Australia. (I am going to give a short summary of some main impressions.) A trip from Melbourne to a country show: everyone's children entering for a competition such as 'Best Dressed Pet', etc., and every child getting a prize of some sort. Stands at the show with expert boxers offering the privilege of trying your skills against them for so and so many dollars a time. A Rodeo, with local riders entering and frequently falling off. Delightful and dignified. Afterwards our hosts took us through a dry grassy area where they hoped to show us a rattlesnake, but no luck.

Geelong, and its vast grain stores at the dockside full of wheat ready to be shipped to China. The immensely moving Anzac War Memorial at Canberra. The sheep station in the outback near Broken Hill, where the stocking rate was one sheep per hundred acres, and when we came upon some of the flock gathered to drink from the dam they took fright and disappeared over the horizon. Meeting farmers with Stan Barnes, including one who had had to pull his farm round after a bush fire. You could see the charred stump of a fruit tree hardly ten yards from the house. The fire had destroyed everything on hundreds of acres. They were a normal yearly hazard.

Finally, at Perth, being entertained by Kim Beazley, Cabinet Minister and pioneer of human rights for the Aborigines, and being shown round the university by his son, also Kim, who later became Minister of Defence in the Labour government. I must mention also Allen Griffith, our host at lunch in Canberra, who became for many years the adviser on foreign affairs to Malcolm Fraser, the Conservative Prime Minister.

From Perth we flew to Bombay, to take up an invitation from R.D. Mathur to visit the new MRA training centre at Panchgani, Maharashtra. 'R.D.' was a graduate of Delhi University where he had been president of the United Nations' Students' Union. He had joined Rajmohan Gandhi, grandson of the Mahatma, while the process of building the centre at Panchgani, his brainchild, was still going on. The two of them had been joined by Niketu Iralu, from a hill village in Nagaland, the former Assam, now part of the modern state of Megalaya. These three carried the ultimate responsibility for 'Asia Plateau', as the centre at Panchgani was called.

From the start they made the centre an ideal spot for Europeans and Asians to meet on Indian soil. They accepted the help of an Australian architect to draw up plans, and invited the then Secretary of Moral Re-Armament in Britain, Roland Wilson, to come out and open the building when it was finished. They also engaged dozens of local stone-masons, many of whom we saw at work. No bulldozer had ever seen the place; there was an army of donkeys to shift the earth, controlled by villagers. The scaffolding, as I found out everywhere I went, was all timber laths lashed together with rope by hand.

The result is one of the most beautifully laid out conference centres I have seen anywhere. There was a farm attached, reclaimed, by terracing, from the hardest of soils, and starting to grow crops like lucerne. As farm manager, John Porteous, a dairy farmer from New Zealand, supervised a small dairy herd, based on animals sent from Australia.

I went with Niketu to see the Indian Minister of Agriculture. Asked by us what he most hoped for from his office, he replied: 'to see the green revolution extended to the villages.' We also saw Mahinderpal Singh, rated as the world record holder at that time for wheat production (3.7 tons per acre). His farm was a few miles outside Delhi. The green revolution had helped him produce the crop varieties, and his own entrepreneurship in water management had produced the conditions under which those crops could grow.

India had first class agricultural technology and a first class agricultural civil service. She had moved in a few short years from being a poor country, dependent on countries like the USA for vast amounts of annual food aid, to self-sufficiency in wheat and a surplus to export.

We were overwhelmed by the sheer numbers of the people, often overflowing into makeshift dwellings in huge concrete drainage pipes with electricity laid on. In the outskirts of Bombay there were thousands living like this. We spent useful days in Delhi with John Porteous. His son David had been with the cast of *Anything to*

Haryana Agricultural University, Punjab, India; Vice-Chancellor Fletcher and students welcome Australasian and British visitors. The Vice-Chancellor is standing centre front, John and Annette Porteous (New Zealand) are centre r. and David Lancaster (Australia) is just behind

Frank Garner, Principal of the Royal Agricultural College Cirencester, England (l), with (l–r) Robin Prickett (New Zealand), a friend and Stanley Barnes (Australia)

Declare? We also found Garfield Hayes, son of Alpheus Hayes of New Zealand, taking responsibility in Delhi. I particularly appreciated a long talk with him, in which he told me he was considering returning to the family farm, which he shortly afterwards did.

A lasting impression I got of Australians and New Zealanders on that tour was that they appeared closer to Asians, and to have a more instinctive understanding of how to meet their needs in terms of trade and aid, than did we Europeans.

In December we exchanged the heat of India for the freezing cold and snow of northern Iran. Dr Abulfazl Hazeghi, a Member of Parliament, had invited us there for a few days. Hazeghi was a longstanding friend of my brother-in-law Francis, and had become a friend of ours too, and a visitor to Whitbourne. Erica caught the father and mother of a cold the day after we arrived, but Hazeghi, who was temporarily without his wife – away visiting one of their sons in Paris – looked after us splendidly with powerful pastilles and a marvellously efficient heater in our bedroom. He also lent me a warm overcoat, and when we left he insisted on giving it to me, swearing that it was no longer any use to him. I went on wearing it for quite a few winters in England.

He was a most generous host. He introduced us in a short time to a number of people individually and in a seminar. I usually had to say a few words, hardly knowing who I was speaking to. But there was much warmth shown towards Erica and myself. We glimpsed something of what Hazeghi had been through as a younger man in his efforts to support the then Shah.

CHAPTER XIX
Landowners and tenants

WHAT STANDS OUT from our time in Australia, India and Iran is the memory of friendships made with people who were in their own way affecting their countries' histories. All of them could have books written about them. Many of them, like Stan Barnes, have already written books themselves.

I was not in the business of writing books, but I was interested in working together with others to affect the history of agriculture, also I had learned that it is easier to make friends if you let people know you as you are. If you do have a conviction, and are open about it and ready to be proved wrong, it goes a long way with people.

This was so with the Herefordshire Committee of the C.L.A. Soon after I became Chairman in 1971 some quite tricky things came up. One was that a new secretary had just been appointed, and was to cover not only Herefordshire but Worcestershire and Gloucestershire as well. Accustomed as we had been to a secretary serving Herefordshire only, several committee members objected to this and a resolution was carried asking the Council to reconsider. There were three of us on the Council and as Committee Chairman I was now the senior one, so it fell to me to put the resolution to the 120 or so present at the Council meeting in London. I did this as best I could, knowing that it hadn't a chance of getting through, and it didn't. I found no supporters. The Chairman offered a few words of sympathy to Herefordshire at having lost an outstanding secretary and finding it difficult to settle down under a new regime. We moved swiftly on to other business. Poor Maurice Rea, our new secretary, had to sit and listen. But I think the committee at home felt that their case had been put; or at least that the man mainly responsible for our resolution did.

I was not quite so sure about Sir Richard Cotterell, our Branch President. I sensed from the way he wanted to go up to London specially to some meeting on grey squirrels and sound the warning about the damage they could do to oaks, that he felt I could not be trusted to do it adequately. However I consulted him about the subject for which I proposed to find a speaker for our first A.G.M. of my chairmanship. It was to be 'Is there a future for small farmers?' and the speaker was to be a Welshman called Thomas, from ADAS. Richard said 'That sounds interesting.' Unfortunately Mr Thomas fell sick, and I had to find a replacement at short notice. By a remarkable coincidence, or it may have been God's way of arranging events to stop me making too much of a meal of getting these meetings right, Robin Prickett was in London. He gamely agreed to step in as speaker.

We all arrived at the Royal Oak, Leominster, where the meeting was to take place, and I started introducing Robin to members assembled round the bar, making a point of having him meet Richard Cotterell. Then the business of the meeting began, and at the end of it Robin was introduced and started in. I was nervous, but I need not have worried. He had the audience thoroughly relaxed and enjoying it all, as he expressed the great honour he felt it was to address them; he couldn't, he said, talk adequately about the problems of British agriculture, but perhaps they would like to hear about how farming in New Zealand had gone for someone like himself who had gone out there as a young man with no assured future?

The *Hereford Times* (T.J.C. Court, Farming Diary, 28 July 1972) reported: 'The story of New Zealand's reaction to ten years of great uncertainty born of Britain's intention to go into Europe was told by Mr Robin Prickett, a leading New Zealand farmer with close ties with his country's government. Over these ten years New Zealand set herself targets which raised her sheep population from 47 million in 1961 to 60 million by 1971, and her cattle population from 6 million to 9 million. 'We wanted to be certain that if we were forced into other markets we also had a very big moral tag on Britain,' said Mr Prickett.

'Way back in the 30s, 82 per cent of New Zealand's exports came to Britain. At the beginning of the Common Market negotiations the figure fell to 54 per cent. And today it is 35 per cent . . . Cheese exports to Britain will be reduced by 70 per cent immediately she enters the E.E.C., and New Zealand faces a 20 per cent tariff on her lamb and tough negotiations over butter at the end of the transitional period.'

'"But we have a good deal of confidence in the ties which exist between us and the British Government and people to help us through these negotiations," said Mr Prickett, who paid tribute to the way our negotiators had worked on New Zealand's behalf.'

When at the end of his talk Robin mentioned that he had a yacht at Auckland, there was a sort of satisfied grunt from his audience – as much as to say 'And you deserve it'. He sat down to warm and sustained applause.

Richard Cotterell took quite a liking to Robin, and invited him over to his farm. I felt I had taken a gamble, and it had come off.

A love of forestry was one thing which Richard and I had in common. I well remember my first visit to his estate at Garnons near Hereford, organised by the Royal Forestry Society. Both the mature oak (especially in Caroline's Copse) and the young plantations were a sight to behold. Richard had the reputation of knowing every ash tree in his woods, almost by name! He would discourse in detail on what it takes to grow young ash in mixtures with other species, and always gave a buoyant picture of successful marketing to anyone like myself who was on the lookout for what was to be learned. In speech and manner he was very much the aristocrat. Yet on these occasions when he enlarged upon his efforts to care for his beloved woodlands, his sheer human exuberance would win through and reach all hearts regardless of status.

As I got to know him better, I came thoroughly to enjoy his style of leadership, including his sardonic remarks on what he felt were mistaken points of view. I remember him once ruminating on where all this 'efficiency' was going to get us: who would be left to do the clearing up and trim the hedges and rides? When he came to lunch at Whitbourne with Lady Cotterell, before having a look at some of our oak, it happened that my mother, by then fourteen years a widow, was at the table. Richard shot round to the other side of the table and pushed my mother's chair in for her – a spontaneous act of courtesy and respect for age. When he came with me after lunch to see the oak, he burst out with 'Magnifico!' His oak were famous, I would almost say, in forestry circles, world famous. It did give me pleasure to show him those oak of ours!

As President of our branch of the C.L.A., I felt he was always a bit inclined, at A.G.M.s, to underrate my chairman's report, and press on to the main business of the evening, namely the guest speaker. So I would be told to cut short my remarks. I would cheerfully insist that some of them were important to the membership. This became quite a popular act by the time we got to our third A.G.M.

To revert to year one, when Robin Prickett replaced the ADAS spokesman who fell ill: it still left the question of small farmers not properly covered. This question was linked to the view I took that

One of the Whitbourne oak planted about the year 1800 during the Napoleonic wars, almost certainly as part of a response by woodland owners to grow more oak for ships of war. In fact the parcel including this one went in 1972 to Hull, where it was used to manufacture keels for fishing vessels. Two forty-foot lengths of similar straight oak spliced together could make a keel. This photo was taken and sent to me by the purchasers, Barchards of Hull

Full-time maintenance man on the estate for 26 years; Michael Davis in action

Michael Finch, our full-time farm worker who sees it all through

Sheep dipping. In the background, silage clamps covered by plastic sheets held down by old motor tyres

the A.G.M. was our one chance in the year to say something to the members, who numbered about 900 in the county, and about 39,000 in the country as a whole. I had done a bit of research on my own account into the current wisdom that because only thirty per cent of the farmers (the big farms) produced seventy per cent of the food in Britain, they were more efficient than the main body of smaller farmers who only produced thirty per cent. I reached the clear conclusion that in fact the thirty per cent who produced seventy per cent of the food did so on seventy per cent of the acreage. The remaining thirty per cent was produced by the large mass of small farmers on only thirty per cent of the acreage. In other words, there was no difference between the two types of farms as regards output per acre, and this in spite of all the expensive machinery etc. that the big man had to offer. I discussed this with one of our tenant farmers on a very small (28-acre) farm. He said: 'Well, it stands to reason, doesn't it? The small man is bound to pay more attention to detail.' Stands to reason? The words had a simple ring of truth about them. But they were not the general view.

Anyway, the secretary, Maurice Rea, and I took the view that we should hold a major public meeting in the county, and try to attract to it the great body of members who never came to any meeting, not even an A.G.M. We hit on a particularly sore point: the inclusion of land in capital gains for taxation purposes. The Treasury appeared to treat land as capital to be taxed, in the same way as business capital; whereas we said land was the raw material with which we had to work. The sudden steep rise in land values, which was beginning to take hold at this time, could bring even modest owner-occupiers on 250 acres, of which there were many in the C.L.A., well within the capital tax bracket. The time seemed ripe, people were anxious, so Maurice booked the biggest hall he could find in the county – a recreation hall – and we set out to find a speaker.

The speaker came from the C.L.A. Taxation Department, which we knew as one of the most effective of all the departments at C.L.A. headquarters. Maurice Rea saturated the county with notices of the meeting, urging all to come and hear the answers to their problems. We went along, not knowing what to expect. The size of the crowd astonished everybody. The official count made it 603 people in that hall. I welcomed the huge company present, which included four national presidents or ex-presidents of the C.L.A., and the speaker launched in. He was listened to with expectancy at first, but as time went on it became apparent that he had nothing really new to say except that he recommended everyone to consult their professional adviser. The applause at the end was polite, warm even, but not enthusiastic. I wondered if there would be any questions. Luckily there were – just about enough to keep us going for the required time till the vote of thanks. In conversation afterwards our much respected N.F.U. Secretary kept repeating in a tone of wonderment: 'He never told them what they could do.'

In spite of some of the nice things said – 'any branch that can get six hundred people to a meeting cannot be dead' was one of them – we had to face the fact that in our keenness to get something across to the ordinary member we had neglected to make sure that we had a speaker who could 'deliver'. Probably our notices about the meeting were not well-judged. They raised expectations too high, and in the event members were sold short. Not that the membership went down. It stayed roughly the same, numerically.

Meanwhile, Edward Heath took us into the Common Market. The referendum on Britain's entry into the E.E.C. came in 1975, but as early as 1973 we had experienced the unique pleasure of a major jump in farm prices. Suddenly at harvest time we found ourselves getting substantially more money for wheat and barley than we had ever done before. The same thing happened with beef cattle and sheep. I wish I could say that it was the beginning of an upward process, but it wasn't. It was a once-off affair, in which we jumped in one go from the pre-European price to the European price. Our net profit on the farm rose to £9,000. But by the next year it had sunk to a mere £2,000 or £3,000 again. However, for a time we felt a lightness in the air, and an enhanced possibility of cooperating with our colleagues in Europe.

We could now see that Britain was connected, agriculturally, with Europe. Was Europe connected similarly with the wider world?

The man who at this time became most helpful in clarifying my mind on issues of the developing world was Asher Winegarten, chief economist and director general of the National Farmers Union, while Henry Plumb was president. On two or three different occasions I went and sat with him in his office in London. He was genuinely interested that a substantial body of farmers with no particular axe to grind should be concerned with farming in Africa and Asia, and was as keen as I was to find the appropriate phrase to express what we wanted to say, as well as of course making sure we had our facts right.

When the next U.N. World Food Conference came round in 1974 in Rome, we attempted to put our ideas in the form of a letter to the Secretary-General, in the drafting of which Asher Winegarten gave considerable help. Of the 22 signatories whom Pat and I asked to sign this letter, a good half were or had been county chairmen of the N.F.U. or the C.L.A. in England or Wales. They included my immediate predecessor and successor as C.L.A. Chairman in Herefordshire.

Our conference delegates were Bill Lang (manager at Hill Farm, in Suffolk), Pat and Kristin, and Peter Anderson, recently retired from farming in Kenya. From what I gathered from them, the F.A.O. (Food and Agriculture Organisation of the United Nations) seemed to have learnt a thing or two since the previous conference in 1970. The 1974 Conference set up for the first time a 'World Food Council'. It marked the emergence of N.G.O.s (non-governmental organisations such as Oxfam) as a force capable of combining and beginning to have the ear of governments in matters of food policy.

Bill Lang said he found our letter a most useful 'visiting card' at the conference. The letter did not represent the last word in British agricultural thinking at the time. But I felt it did show the way the wind was blowing.

The letter was as follows:

The Farmers Club,   November 1974
Whitehall Court,
London, S.W.1.

To: Sayed A. Marei, Secretary-General,
    United Nations World Food Conference, Rome

Dear Secretary-General,

We, who make our living from farming in Europe, send you our best wishes for the success of the United Nations World Food Conference.

All of us have held office in farmers' organisations, and have taken part in efforts to secure farm prices which can enable us to survive, and to expand. We want to expand, but we are not content merely to fight for what we can get for ourselves. We would like, with you, to fight for an expansion of agriculture all over the world, to meet food needs. E.E.C. farmers, through COPA, have already put forward a plan outlining how this might be done.

1. We suggest that this Conference ask Governments, in consultation with I.F.A.P., to invite farmers to participate in decision making.

2. We submit that the answer to malnutrition in the world can come not only from 'Aid', but mainly from a new pattern of international Trade. Aid cannot succeed as long as trade works against it. It can succeed if it becomes a part of trade. We think the need is for international agreements on trade in agricultural products, designed

to assist the economies of countries with differing living standards. Within this framework any special treatment given to needier countries could be roughly comparable to that given to the 'mountain and difficult lands' in Europe within the framework of the Common Agricultural Policy.

3. <u>We would welcome</u> a new spirit of co-operation between governments, issuing in plans which can be understood by every producer and every manufacturer of food. As we see it, this will involve not so much new plans as a new determination to make the best plans work.

4. We as European farmers for our part <u>undertake</u>
to accept our share of the moral responsibility for helping the poorer countries to develop their own agriculture, including
(a) an extension of activity under the World Food Programme, and
(b) a reduction of our call, as a richer area, on other countries' production to meet needs which could be satisfied from within the Community:

on our own farms, to put the needs of those who work with us, and the conservation of the land, before maximum profits:

to seek through the natural bond existing between farmers all over the world, to make co-operation between our countries at government level easier.

With best wishes and regards,
Yours truly,

G.H. Ballard	A.G.W. Hutton
John C. Bowerman	Elliott Jeffrey
L.A. Dickson	E.A. Lane
T.R. Dunne	W.A. Lang
E.S.F. Evans	Sir David Lowe
P.H.B. Evans	James Main
Nigel Finch	R.B. Morgan
S.A. Gourlay	Sir David J.W. Ogilvy, Bart
Douglas V. Rennie	George B.R. Gray
N.P.D. Green-Price	T.C. Skyrme
B.A.F. Hervey-Bathurst	Robin White

The wind of change in land values blew pretty powerfully, at the same time, on the Whitbourne estate. We sold off three tenanted farms, with a total acreage of about 450 acres. They were the three farms which were entirely served by the hydram for water. The basic reason for the sale was financial. Capital taxation was so high that there was no advantage in owning a lot of land. By completely unforeseen chance our land was now worth about twenty times as much as it was when I took over. My brothers and sisters, as co-owners of the land in question, could also be compensated for their years of unselfish giving to keep us going.

Our advice, via Ted Rayer, was that the acreage we were contemplating selling was probably large enough to qualify for the premium price which it had become normal for large corporations to pay as a long-term investment in such things as pension funds. This would mean about £600 or more per acre, as against little over half of that for a sale to the tenants.

Not many years earlier, I had sought the advice of a well-known London firm of estate agents on whether there was a case for rationalisation of the structure of the estate. Their man came down and I showed him half a dozen farms, and we studied the maps and records of work done. My question to him had been: 'Do you think we ought to amalgamate some of these farms and centralise the buildings, making only two or three farms where there were six at present?' His answer surprised me. He said 'No.' 'Why?', I asked. 'Because I believe that people matter more than buildings. Because I think it might destroy the character of the farms, with their compact farm buildings round the homesteads.'

I was glad at the time that he had given this advice. But now time had moved on, and I suspected that his firm had probably been responsible for quite a few deals by which land had changed hands at a premium price. People were pointing to companies like the Prudential, who had bought estates and brought the dwelling houses and buildings on them up to a higher standard of modernisation with comfort, plus productivity, than landowners like us with limited capital resources could ever expect to reach. It was not necessarily wrong in our case to go for the big money. And of course the whole idea was to get some cash. I hoped it would be a once-off deal and not have to be repeated.

Anyway, after getting the family's agreement in principle, I first went and saw the tenants, all on the same morning, on their farms. I told them of my intention to sell their farms, stressing that their future was secure, under the Agriculture Act, as tenants of any future landlord, and trying to reassure them that any potential buyer would be much better able than we could to look after them and do things for them. Reactions varied. Brian said: 'Oh, don't sell us off to someone else. We're just getting used to you.' Bill said: 'I'll buy it from you any time. Sell it to me.' Roger said: 'I never thought I would hear that from you. Losing land, it's like losing your right arm.'

I thought of those three men: Brian, living with his wife and small daughter in a big stone house, a highly skilled shepherd, often in the prize money at local shows and beyond. Bill, a passionately keen farmer and countryman from a large local family, who took over his farm in a pretty scrubby state, and reclaimed it by sheer hard work. He turned over his tractor, and escaped with his life, twice, on the sloping ground. Roger, youngest of another big family, who reckoned when he got his farm that he had got a 'plum'. A sportsman and an athlete reared on a smallholding on the estate, I remember he had said of National Service that it was a good thing because it 'pulled us all up together a bit.' I had good memories of all of them.

The next step in my exploration of how to do the deal led me up to London for a consultation with Colin, our solicitor. I told him of my touch with the tenants and of the regret I felt at giving up my dream of turning them into landowners, as I felt they would not be able to afford the price. I cannot remember the detail of our discussion but I remember that Colin followed me out into the street afterwards and said that the Duke of Westminster had had just the same problem. He put it to all his tenants and they offered (I think) £400 per acre, each for his farm. But a large company had offered £745 per acre for the whole. He felt he had to accept it, and the tenants were quite happy.

Then came what I saw as the moment of truth. Moral Re-Armament were putting on a national review called *G.B.* at the Westminster Theatre. It was brilliant. Funny in places, moving too, at times satirical. A scene which threw out a barbed hook caught my attention. In it the chorus sang: 'We worship the Great God Growth.' Was it possible that growth, in the economic sense, might be a good deal less essential to the nation's well-being than most of our economists and industrialists seemed to think? In my mind, I equated growth with more return on capital. For many people it was an axiom, almost a moral imperative, that you made the maximum return on capital that you could. But I saw that in God's mind this was probably not true at all, or certainly not always true.

So my thinking shifted into another gear. Steadily the conviction grew that I should after all sell to the tenants. And with Ted Rayer's help, I did. They offered from about £400 to £440 per acre. As a result of the deal, the family were able to receive a lump sum of £25,000 each. Three of them bought their homes for the first time. I was able to keep just enough to build Dial House, the alternative to Whitbourne Hall, two years later. We felt that the tenants had been given a chance to start as landowners, on land that looked set steadily to appreciate in value.

As to what the tenants did with their 'chance', it taught me an interesting lesson. Brian soldiered on as an owner-occupier farmer, assisted by his wife Ann. Roger re-sold his farm lock stock and barrel to someone else and went for a job as a farm manager not very far away. Bill sold off his land in bits and pieces, and finished off by selling the big farmhouse and developing the farm buildings into a most attractive set of bungalows, including one for himself and his wife and family. In the process of doing this, he demolished a new covered yard I had put up for him over the old muckyard, and turned the area into an open precinct with the dwelling houses in lieu of farm buildings behind it.

My 'dream' of having given the tenants a leg up the farming ladder seemed somewhat shattered. In fact, for a short time I was furious with Roger in particular, and pleased when I heard that his brother who was working elsewhere but lived on the estate was also annoyed with him for having thrown away this golden chance. But God spoke pretty clearly to me about this. He said: 'Hey! He's only doing as a landowner what you have been doing – getting rid of some land for family reasons.' So I calmed down. Roger had, after all, been given the freedom to do what he liked with his farm. And I knew that interest rates had gone up to record levels of I think 13 per cent at just about the time that he had to put down the sale money.

As to Bill and his residential precinct, I now enjoy it and feel proud of it on his behalf!

I am bound to say, however, that the experience of selling off those three farms, judged in terms of the result on the ground, has made me wary of doing it again. It has strengthened rather than weakened my belief in the landlord/tenant system; and, on the whole, in the way the C.L.A. seeks to support it.

CHAPTER XX
The estate's second home

FOR US AT least the sale of the farms opened up a new prospect. Now for the first time we had the resources to consider seriously an alternative to Whitbourne Hall from which to run the estate.

The Hall was owned entirely by me. Erica and I had lived there happily for more than a quarter of a century, with the help of countless friends as well as members of our families. It was hard work of course, especially for Erica. If you took a look at the sort of house we needed to run the estate from, Whitbourne Hall was the last thing that we wanted. The boys had grown up and left home. My mother, aged 90, was still with us. She was keen for us to find somewhere new. She said getting rid of Whitbourne Hall would be like 'harvesting it'! She set the pace by insisting on leaving for sheltered accommodation in London, near Gwen and Mary, before we did move out.

I remember, for a start, walking round the north-west corner of the house, looking into the billiard room, out into the conservatory, on to the terrace beyond. Could we adapt something there inside or by an extension outside or even a separate small dwelling? We concluded that anything we did there would probably militate against a satisfactory use for the Hall in the future. Finally I decided we would have to build a new house somewhere. The decision came after I had asked Bill and Chris if we could listen to God together, and see what He had to say about it. We did, and Bill said 'I think you should build.' Chris agreed.

The next question was: what to do with Whitbourne Hall?

First, I offered it to a representative body of people responsible for the administrative side of Moral Re-Armament. Would they be interested in it as a conference centre? They were not.

Next, after consulting Hugh Elliott, I wrote to Chief Anyaokwu of the Commonwealth Office. Would the Commonwealth perhaps be interested in it as a conference centre? We asked a friend in the Foreign Office, who had organised Prime Minister Callaghan's conferences overseas, whether the Foreign Office might be interested.

(Photo: courtesy Berrows Newspapers)

Outside Whitbourne Hall

She suggested we go to the Anglo-American Foundation at Ditchley and talk to them. All these proved impracticable.

We then got in touch with Mutual Households Association (M.H.A.), who ran a number of large country houses as homes for retired people. They were interested, and we decided to go and see one of their establishments, at Aynho near Oxford. We asked Bill, who was working in London at the time, to come up and meet us there.

Aynho had a style and ambience quite reminiscent of Whitbourne, with a well-stocked library and a big billiard room. But it seemed rather empty of people, and those very few whom we saw in the distance were definitely elderly. We went to a café afterwards to discuss it, and Bill burst out with great feeling that we could not do that to Whitbourne; he asked me and Erica if we would consider letting him have the Hall, and try to do something similar in it for a younger group of people. I was pleased at him wanting to take it on, though I didn't see how the devil he could do it. However, his conviction carried the day, and we said 'OK. Yes, you do it.'

How Bill succeeded in building a community at Whitbourne Hall is quite a story. But it is his story, and I am not going to attempt to tell it here. Suffice it to say that today twenty families, many with children, each occupy a flat in the building once intended for a single family. The immediate question for me was: what sort of house were Erica and I going to have built for ourselves to live in? We wanted it to be above all an appropriate and convenient house from which to manage the estate in the future.

We decided to consult Tony Peacock, who had helped me with several modernisation plans on the estate. He suggested we come up to Preston and meet the chief architect of his company, Building Design Partnership. The architect's name was Keith Scott. I had already formed the opinion that we wanted a modern house, a contrast to the many lovely old black and white houses on the estate. Keith showed us some of his work in Lancashire – new cottages, public buildings in Preston. We asked him and his wife Dorothy down to Whitbourne to see the Hall, and see what they thought of our suggestions for a site for a new house. Keith naturally jumped at the chance of designing a house in an open field, with only trees and no other houses to contend with his design. He at once chose a site which I had not thought of – right against the Pool, in a field which we had always called 'the paddock'. Erica saw right away that his site would be more private than the one I had had in mind, which was near the farm road, with tractors going by every day. I saw that the new site would be more sheltered from the north and east. So we gave it the go-ahead.

When it came to the actual design of the new house, we had reason to be thankful that we had an architect who was by temperament an artist, an entrepreneur of considerable enterprise, and a man who had genuine consideration for his clients, especially an awkward old couple like us with our own ideas of what we wanted. At one stage he produced a drawing of a regency-type mini-mansion with battlements, but said he soon rejected that after he had shown it to his sons! He graciously accepted Erica's drawing of what we thought the house should look like from the north-east. The final result bears many distinctive features, chief of which are the big 'prow' windows facing two ways, which I believe are the first ever in an ordinary dwelling house. At any rate, I think it is a thing of beauty. It is certainly convenient, easy to keep warm in all weathers and cool in summer. A model was made of the design, and we awaited planning permission.

A few weeks later I met the chairman of the District Planning Committee in the street outside the Shirehall in Worcester. He started telling me how the plan of our house had been recommended unanimously by his committee. 'Here at last,' he said, 'We have the ideal gentleman's residence.' I said: 'Thank you, but I am afraid the County Council have now turned it down. What do you know about that?' He swore a two-syllabled oath, and stared at me. It was true. The County Planning Committee, none of whom knew our place at first hand, had turned it down because it did not fit in with the existing 'expansion' areas laid down in the structure plan.

As our architect, Keith Scott was associated with a large number of professionals with wide experience in planning matters. Together we worked out a plan for an appeal against the County Council's decision. It was agreed, first, that I should write an outline case for the appeal, and carry it through in my own name without any official involvement of Building Design Partnership. And next, that we should go for a judgement by arbitrator, rather than an appeal in open court. My appeal was based on agricultural grounds; that the proposed new estate house, located as it was next to the estate yard, was a necessary and suitable building from which to manage the estate in the future. I sent it off to the Ministry of the Environment in April 1975.

Meanwhile I was invited to visit farmers and farmers' organisations

THE ESTATE'S SECOND HOME

in Canada, an invitation which I gratefully accepted. The trip was worthwhile, good fun and a refreshing break. It was noteworthy for the teamwork between our team of four men – Paul Campbell, who had invited us, John Sainsbury, Dickie Dodds and myself. Paul rushed us in and out of the offices of distinguished people, which I sometimes entered just at the very moment when I had managed to clear my mind on the subject of whom I was about to meet. John Sainsbury kept on carrying my suitcase for me to keep the tempo up. He insisted on referring to some essential reference books in it as my 'soil samples'. Dickie was fresh from Michael Manley's farm development programme in Jamaica. He is best known as a cricketer, but had also been a successful army intelligence officer in World War II. Ever since that journey through Canada he has found time to stick with us farmers, and to share our vision in a most helpful way.

Erica arrived in Canada to join us just as we arrived in the west. I met her at Calgary airport. She and Kristin had been engaged in a remarkable *tour de force*: a meeting in the Royal Festival Hall in London, to mark International Womens' Year. At five weeks' notice they had filled the hall to launch the 'Housewives' Declaration', which went round the world and was adapted by many countries for their own use. As soon as the meeting was over, she got on an aeroplane and came out. This all happened on the night before the national referendum in Britain, in which we finally voted to join the European Economic Community.

We arrived back in Britain in June. In July I heard from the Department of the Environment that they had appointed an inspector to decide on our appeal. He came in August, and gave his decision, in our favour, in September.

Meanwhile, the cost of building any house had risen sharply, and we had to cut down the new house, cutting out a bedroom, bathroom and flat suite in the north-east wing. This was managed quite smoothly without altering the character of the house, and without the necessity for any fresh planning permission. Building Design Partnership went to tender on our behalf with the revised plans.

It was rather a thoughtful and subdued Keith Scott who rang me up to report the tenders received. They were all about thirty per cent higher than he had forecast, and, I felt, led me to expect. Keith however insisted that all was not lost. He could see some economies which could be made, and so on. I said: 'Do you really think there is a chance we could bring it down to somewhere about the target level?' He said: 'Just a chance'.

So a conference was arranged at the B.D.P. offices in Preston. Erica and I drove up for the day and met with Keith, Tony Peacock, the managing director of the building firm which was our choice from those who had tendered, and sundry assistants. Keith outlined all the economies he thought could be made in the design without spoiling it. It came to the point when I remember saying: 'Well, thank you very much, gentlemen, for the efforts made. But am I right in thinking that it will not be possible to go any lower on the present design? If so, I am afraid we shall have to call it off, and start all over again.' The builder then indicated that he would like the contract, and would not mind having one at the price I had suggested. Keith asked if Erica and I would like to leave the room and talk over whether we could accept this offer. We did, and we did not keep them waiting long. We came back and sat down, and I said 'All right. We accept.'

Keith said: 'Well, there won't be any profit in it for us. But I have felt all along that there was no other competitor in the background, and I would like to do it.' The builder commented it had been 'a remarkable meeting; there was scarcely a dry eye round the table!' Tony Peacock's version later on was: 'It was the night of the long knives.'

It certainly was a remarkable day.

I must say that when it came to building the house we found that we had been fortunate in our choice of builders. We were fortunate, too, in having a member of the staff of B.D.P. as an acting Clerk of Works. He steered us through the inevitable teething troubles. One unforeseen one was that the firm from whom all our carefully chosen kitchen equipment had been ordered went broke after building had begun. The Clerk of Works, George Bell, borrowed our estate truck and driver, drove to their head office with my cheque for £1,000 and came back with the lot. He became a good friend. He brought his wife, who was sadly dying of cancer, down to meet us. And later on we met the lady who, happily, took her place.

We moved in in September 1977. It was a happy time, less than a fortnight after Chris and Anne's marriage at Leeds.

Chris, back in London now from his Asian travels, had been 'seconded' for two years from his full-time work with Moral Re-Armament to help Pat on the farm. The first year he spent doing all sorts of jobs to help out. Then he got married. Then he and Anne lived on for another year in the flat they had created above the garage in the farmhouse. During this second year they held the fort while

Dial House. Photo by Erica. Two grandsons kept the cattle at bay while she was up the stepladder

Pat and Kristin were away for eight months on their longest ever world tour. Those two years cemented Chris and Anne into the village, where they made many friends, including among our own work people and their families. There was never any thought in their minds or ours that it would become a permanent arrangement. But it certainly helped while it lasted. And it still helps a lot, as Chris keeps abreast of Bill on matters affecting farm policy, from his experience gained in those two years.

One of our last events at the Hall was a party to celebrate their engagement. Our doctor, who came to the party, later on saw Dial House blending subtly into the landscape between a large chestnut and a group of old yews. We said: 'We have obeyed your instructions, and moved to somewhere smaller.' He said: 'I did not mean something like this!' But it was a move at the right time for both of us. Erica had three major operations in our first year at Dial House – one a replacement hip, and the other two cataracts. She finished the year in good working order. I finished it a little more experienced in cooking, and beginning to lose that crick in the neck which comes from looking at roofs and wondering if they are leaking.

Friends still ask us sometimes why the house is so quaintly named. It shows signs of becoming 'The Dial House', because, I suppose, people think that is more dignified. What actually happened was that

Roly Powell. For 32 years he served the estate as woodman, becoming my unofficial forestry adviser. Now we share the pleasure of watching the growth of the thousands of trees which he has been responsible for planting from 1956 onwards

we could not think of a name that suited, so we studied the old maps. We found that the paddock on which the house is built was part of an enclosure called 'Wetlands'. Another feature of the paddock incorporated into our garden was known as 'The Drinking Place'. Neither of these seemed any good. The big field across the pool, however, was called 'Dial Park'. Why? Research by a member of the family came up with the theory that probably dial was a corruption of dale, a good old English word meaning the opposite of a hill. So we settled for Dial House. We knew we meant 'the house in or of the dale'. How could we blame anyone who did not get this at first glance?

CHAPTER XXI
Forestry first

BY NOW THE forestry had reached a key stage. It was twenty years since we had clear-felled and re-planted our first plot of ground in the woods. Add to that the nineteen or so other plantations, small and larger, since then, and you had about seventy acres of young plantations to look after, with the number increasing year by year.

I spent a lot of time selecting and marking young trees for thinning, and that was going to increase too. There was one particular plantation of larch which we had hoped would bring a comparatively quick return. The sort of time-scale I was expecting for trees to become saleable from the date of planting was Larch 30 to 50 years, Ash 60, Norway Spruce 70, Douglas Fir 80, Oak 120 to 150 years. I lurched about among those larch, loving the job of selecting them, sometimes with paint pot, sometimes with aerosol sprayer, and getting quite tired.

Now our senior woodman, Roly Powell, had to retire on doctor's orders. Roly had carried the main responsibility for the woods ever since he left the army after World War II, first under Frank Davis, and then for many years on his own, as senior to several assistant woodmen. He had absorbed the shock of new tools such as the chainsaw, various mechanical ride-cutters to replace the old hand hook, a mechanical hedge-trimmer, and later a low-cost forwarder for the tractor to pick up and carry thinnings. He was a tremendous help to me, in that I felt that his judgement was always sensible and firmly in line with that indefinable something which I will call local opinion.

He gave me genuine friendship. In our early years after the war I remember him and Frank saying once 'You know, Sir, we think you ought to sell yourself more.' But later on he had to remind me that I was not being fair in paying a bonus to the gardeners for foliage from the woods which they had taken to market, when the woodmen had grown and nurtured the trees that gave it. From then on I paid the foliage bonus to the woodmen. Roly could be completely relied on to do what was necessary in the woods on my occasional absences abroad. I often catch myself realising how much the estate owes to men like him, who love their work, love nature and the countryside, and love sport too.

So Roly had to go. But the good news was that Bill came to see me and asked if I would consider taking him on full time in the forestry as a replacement! Would I?!

It was a surprise. I suppose I might have realised that Bill felt there was a future for him on the estate, and he might as well start young. But the timing could hardly have been bettered. Of course he took a big drop in salary, after his planning job at Redditch. So Bill started off as assistant woodman to Ernie, who had been Roly's assistant. Once I realised that he was permanently with the estate, I gave it out that I proposed to retire at seventy and hand over the estate to him lock stock and barrel.

He was already launched on the experiment of starting a 'community' at Whitbourne Hall, and this came to a climax one evening in the summer of 1979. Bill told us that he was calling a meeting to reach a firm decision on whether to go ahead and start a Company. The Company would be formed to acquire the Hall from me. Membership of the Company would be confined to the owners (or lessees) of the flats into which the Hall was to be divided. The Company corporately would hold the downstairs rooms, main hall etc., and the garden and grounds. He would ring us up at 10.30 p.m. and tell us if the plan was going ahead. If he did not get at least seven takers to form a nucleus to start with, the whole thing would probably be off, and he might have to hand the Hall back to me. As you can imagine, we had no idea what would happen.

Bill rang at about 10.30 p.m. and said he had got exactly seven takers, and the scheme was on. Actually he had six, but there was one person missing who came on a telephoned reminder and voted as the seventh man!

The Community invited me up to discuss terms, and made me an offer, subject to contract. I asked for 24 hours to consider it, and accepted the next day. There then followed a correspondence with our solicitors on the comparative merits of a lease and an outright sale. They felt bound to put to me the advantages of a lease, so that in effect the estate would not lose overall control. It could be for 99 years, or even for 999. The difference would mainly be that with a lease you could have 'positive' restrictions written into the conveyance, but with a sale you could only have 'negative' restrictions.

For a time I thought our solicitors' advice must be heeded, and sought to prepare Bill for a decision this way, though I could see he was not in his heart convinced. We met with myself and our solicitors, and the Community and their solicitors, in their Worcester office. Separating for a sandwich lunch, the two sides consulted privately, and Colin to my surprise said: 'Do you think we ought to go along with what they really want, and make it an outright sale?' He was evidently quite favourable to the idea. We decided to agree to it. So in 1980 I sold the freehold of Whitbourne Hall to the newly formed Company, The Whitbourne Hall Community Ltd. Colin, looking back on the agreement afterwards, said that on behalf of our family he was 'thrilled' by it.

Sitting here, looking back after eleven years, I cannot say that thrilled was what I felt. But I did feel a quiet certainty of God's leading. I think Colin may have felt that Bill's preference for a sale was a strong factor. Certainly I was warmly grateful to Colin for his friendship and understanding over the years. And I have often since then thanked my stars that we were not landed with the responsibilities of being a lessor!

However, losing Whitbourne Hall did feel a bit like dying. Perhaps sorting out so many of great grandfather's papers had something to do with it.

But then, I haven't really lost it. There it is, looking quite good, and in some respects better than when we lived there!

Quite a lot of things happened in 1980. To begin with, I was diagnosed as being a diabetic, and from then on have been living my life under strict medical rules. I have had to adjust to a daily routine with a limited output of energy. Fine in the morning, sleep after lunch, another go in the afternoon after tea, but not much activity left in the evening – with variations.

Then on my seventieth birthday, 26 April, I handed over management of the estate to Bill.

That June on a Sunday afternoon, the Timber Growers' Organisation held a magnificent Forestry Open Day on the estate. To me it seemed like a sort of harvest festival of my forestry years, and my association with the Royal Forestry Society and the Timber Growers Organisation (T.G.O.). The R.F.S. walks had taken me round most of the other Herefordshire and Worcestershire estates as well as our own, and I had spent many a happy day revelling in the beauty of them and learning from them. The T.G.O. was set up in the early 1960's to do for woodland growers what the C.L.A. was doing for landowners: to look after our interests on matters of policy and economics. It was from the start an independent body financially. But it did have an arrangement with the C.L.A. which I found helpful, namely that C.L.A. members who joined only had to pay one subscription – that to the T.G.O. – on their forestry acreage. So I joined the T.G.O. early on.

I used to trot along to T.G.O. committee meetings without much to say, but when I got onto the Executive Committee in London it became more interesting; and when the Treasury published a quite outrageous report on forestry written by a group of their 'experts', it got pretty lively. The T.G.O. began then to make the wires hum a bit. It is connected in my mind with the appointment of Lord Dulverton as President. Hitherto the leadership had seemed to me to be a little too 'laid back'. Tony Dulverton by contrast was crisp and forthright. He wrote to me, as a 'worried forester', appreciating a letter I had written to *The Times* – a letter, incidentally, which had brought a phone call from the BBC at Pebble Mill asking me over for an interview. Lord Dulverton's estate is near Moreton-in-Marsh on the way from Worcester to London, and we sometimes met and talked in the train during the period when I was chairman of the Western Region of the T.G.O. for the years 1975 to 1978. He came and spoke to our A.G.M. Erica and I went to one of his open days at Batsford.

Those years in the T.G.O. had made me keen to do something to get the British public to understand forestry. We talked about it a bit in committee, and Patrick Lee, our Secretary, kept gently nudging me to have an open day at Whitbourne. Finally I came to the conclusion that we ought to go for it. And under Charles Griffin, my successor as chairman of the region, aided by our newly-appointed secretary, Colonel Peter Winstanley, go for it we did on this Sunday afternoon in June.

I think the success of the day was largely due to the team work between Peter Winstanley and myself. His enthusiasm and buoyancy about the whole project, plus his military no-nonsense approach, were a delight. There was a slight tension between us, in that I was determined that this was to be essentially a T.G.O. open day, with the T.G.O. fully responsible for every detail (provided of course that I approved of it); while he seemed anxious to throw the emphasis on the initiative taken by the estate. However, he certainly did most of the preparatory work, including above all securing the participation of all my fellow landowners in the R.F.S. They were essential to the success of the afternoon, as guides to the members of the public who were to come. I may say that five hundred or so of the public turned up, a figure which astonished a lot of my colleagues from the western side of the county. This in my opinion was largely due to Bill's original idea of advertising the day in *Worcester Source*, a leaflet through the letter-box service, which was reckoned to have brought a lot of people.

Peter and I had the brilliant idea that it would be best to hold the briefing of the guides for the 'demo' in the woods on the same Sunday morning as the event itself. The briefing was set for 11 o'clock, and the public were invited for 2 p.m. This avoided having to make anyone come twice. I could expect to do all my explaining to my team of guides (sixteen of them) in one go on Sunday morning. They would all bring sandwiches. We would not have to try and give anyone lunch.

This morning briefing seemed to go perfectly, and at 3 p.m. I went out again to see how the guided tours were going. There was a good double line of cars parked in the narrow field between the farmhouse and the road. Peter was still there, but only just. More than a dozen loads of men women and children had been sent off in our transport on the half-mile drive to the first wood. The transport consisted of (1) our own tractor with low-loading trailer and straw bales to sit on, and (2) a hired minibus. These shuttled to and fro beautifully without anybody having to wait much. I said to Peter, 'I'd better take a party round, hadn't I?' He said: 'Yes, I wish you would.' So I got up with the next load and we set off.

A great feature of this demonstration in the twenty-acre wood known as Longfield Coppice was that there were seven separate stands, all out of sight and earshot of each other, and yet so close that no one could get tired walking between them. Of course we had cut the rides, and cut small extra drills through the undergrowth where there were no rides.

'Stand' no.1 happened to be the Cundey Peeler, a mobile tool which peels the bark off small softwood thinnings. This was exhibited in action by Western Woodlands Owners Ltd, our forestry cooperative, headed by Patrick Lee. The timber was being brought to it by our own estate tractor and winch, operated by Bill Evans and Steve Bartlett, our woodman. In the background was Bromyard Sawmills, represented by Norman Redfern and his son, actually thinning the Norway Spruce which were being peeled. Stand No.3 was occupied by a senior buyer from Pontrilas Sawmills, a cheerful Welshman who had taken his stand by a nice young ash – 'just the sort I'd buy' –

The T.G.O.'s Open Day at Whitbourne, 1980: briefing the guides. To right of picture nearest camera: Michael Roberts, next to him Charles Griffin

and who showed people a set of cricket stumps belonging to the M.C.C. which they had supplied from a similar tree. About fifty yards on, at the ride-side, stood Roly and Ernie, our woodmen, in front of a lot of young oak less than one foot high which they had grown from planting acorns. On to the outside edge of the wood, where it was all big oak. There our group looked up and saw in the branches of an oak a man in climbing tackle with a chainsaw. He was a tree surgeon, cutting off some lateral branches of the oak which were thought to be protruding too far over a field of wheat. Then back along the ride inside the wood to a specially selected specimen oak, where Paul Venables, a member of the firm of Henry Venables of Stafford, gave us a talk on oak veneers, and how they were made. Finally, to Michael Roberts and his team, exhibiting ladder-making tools beneath a large standing Douglas fir.

It was good to see Michael Roberts so obviously relishing his part. The first member of the family I had known had been Michael's grandfather. My mother used to get me to take my first pony, Brownie, up to his smithy to be shod. He belonged to the horse age. Then there was Jack, the mechanic, under whom the business developed into agricultural machinery. Jack would drive out with his oxy-acetylene gear and repair machinery in the field for you. He it was who advised me to start with a simple tractor winch for pulling out thinnings. And Mrs Jack too: she ran a sub-Post Office for years in their home, and once on a busy spring morning let me sit and watch the Oxford v Cambridge Boat Race on her TV! Now their son Michael, big bearded and red haired, has built up a major farm buildings contractor's business. He put up the latest and longest all-purpose cattle shed on our farm. And he can still make a ladder and shoe a horse.

Back in the transport we invited all who wanted to come to the second wood. Here the most noteworthy thing I remember showing them was the spring which rose inside the wood. We had channelled it into a small brook which ran along the outside, draining what had been an acre or more of swamp. (This was featured afterwards by the periodical *Forestry and British Timber*.)

Reactions after the day were quite interesting. One distinguished surgeon living in our village remarked with enthusiasm, 'I've learned a hell of a lot today.' A Midlands school teacher wrote to our secretary in London thanking him for a wonderful example of how townspeople could be educated in country ways. The talk in Bromyard, emanating largely from the Roberts team, was of how the Whitbourne estate had really 'put itself on the map.' Steve, our recently employed woodman, said: 'It was really good. We ought to do it every year!'

A popular feature of the day was the appearance of a young lady on a grey pony who went round the stands in the afternoon dispensing cups of tea to the helpers. This was Julia, who had just become engaged to Bill, and was meeting one or two of her customers for the first time. There were some merry greetings. The pony, Sparky, who had been shod a few times by Mike Roberts, added panache to the occasion. Bill and Julia were married in the village of Cranham, Gloucestershire, six weeks later – another great event of 1980!

I have no memory of any other events of 1980. But I cannot resist a brief reference to one final occasion in 1981, which will bring this account to an end.

The Royal Agricultural Society of England (R.A.S.E.), who run the Royal Show at Stoneleigh, Warwickshire, every July, run an annual competition between landowners all over England for forestry. A group of six counties are taken each year, and it was the turn of our group of counties in 1981. I decided to enter, and with Bill's assistance we spent a morning showing the judges round the relevant

At the Forestry Commission's stand at the Royal Show 1981; (l–r) Bill, Ernie and Steve with the trophy and citation from the Royal Agricultural Society.

> The Forestry Commission operates under two hats:
> 1) As an independent organisation growing trees on its own land.
> 2) As an arm of government regulating private forestry.
> In its second capacity, private woodland owners like ourselves have had a long and happy association with a succession of forest officers of the Forestry Commission. We plan our woods in accordance with a succession of 'five year plans' which have to be approved by them if we are to receive any Government grants

parts of our woodlands, and supplying them with records of income and expenditure on each plantation since 1956.

They gave us the R.A.S.E.'s Silver Medal Certificate for the best managed medium-sized woodland estate in the six counties! It now hangs, proudly framed, in our office. What added quite a bit to the pleasure of this success was that the two judges happened to be, first a partner in a firm of estate agents who had once acted for me in a dispute with a timber merchant (the only serious one I ever had, and I was glad it did not prevent the said merchant from making me an offer for a later parcel of timber), and second a forester from the Queen's Sandringham estate. One of the latter's comments was 'If you can manage to keep up with your brashing, you'll probably be all right.' 'Brashing' is the shaving off of lateral branches from young trees up to a height of about 6 ft or so. They said kind things about us and the estate in their report. I was so delighted with this success that I must have given an exaggerated impression to some of my friends of the significance of the award. Dickie Dodds said 'You must feel like I would if I had been asked to play for England.'

That July Erica and I, Julia and Bill, and Roly, Ernie and Steve were all present at the forestry section of the Royal Show, and watched Bill receive the award on our behalf. The family were then entertained to lunch in the C.L.A. pavilion by Elizabeth Johnstone, of the Trewithen estate in Cornwall. She had been a frequent visitor to Whitbourne at Royal Show time, and now insisted on doing the honours. Elizabeth was an old friend of both Erica's and mine. She inherited from her father a large and a beautiful house and garden, which she managed for years with the help of agents. We both knew something of the battles she had fought to steer her estate both technically and humanly into the modern age.

But we had not fully realised then what national regard she had won. A short time after the lunch she gave us at Stoneleigh, we were bidden to a ceremony there – and this will really be my last story of this account – in honour of Miss Johnstone of Trewithen, to celebrate the award to her of the Bledisloe Medal for Landowning. The Bledisloe Medal is recognised as the most prestigious award a landowner can win. To qualify, you must have achieved excellence both in some technical aspect of management, and in the quality of human relations on your estate. I believe it had not been awarded in recent years because no one considered suitable had caught the judges' eye. But now it was, and the company gathered with Elizabeth at Stoneleigh included most of her sisters, nephews and nieces, and practically the whole of the tenantry from her estate, most of whom had never seen the Royal Show before. Also present were the Presidents of the N.F.U. and of the Agricultural Workers' Union, and many of the establishment of the C.L.A.

Elizabeth made just one point in her brief speech of thanks. It was that in everything she had done in her houses and cottages on the estate, her aim had been to make them into places where any member of her own family would have been proud to live. I was standing next to Henry Plumb. His comment on the speech was: 'That's what it's all about, isn't it?'

CHAPTER XXII
The richest country in the world

IT IS NOW more than ten years since I retired. But there is one final chapter still to write.

During those ten years Erica and I made one further visit of interest, to that great agricultural country, the United States of America. We went on 26 April 1984 and were there for six weeks.

I had been concerned about the possibility of a trade war between America and the E.E.C. We had gone to the U.S.A. to meet farmers and to look for ways in which we could work together to overarch the growing confrontation between U.S.A. and the E.E.C. with a wider world aim.

They were only too ready to respond. Four years after our visit, in March 1988, there took place at Farmington, Minnesota, a weekend consultation between U.S. and Canadian farmers on the theme 'Factors Affecting the Future of Agriculture'. From that meeting a message of support was sent to the World Food Conference then being convened in Brussels by the President of the European Parliament. The message read, in part:

1. We believe that the first task of the world agricultural community is to assure that everyone in the world has enough to eat.
2. The nation is best served the more the producer can decide himself the best use of his land and his efforts rather than be forced to rely on support from his Government.
3. It is clear that we have to learn to work with people with whom we do not agree.
4. From our experience, we note that a first requirement in aid to the Less Developed Countries is a greater effort to help people on the land meet the basic food needs of their own country. Also, seeing that they must sell what they produce in order to be a market for agricultural products, we seek to help them produce well what they have the potential to produce.

The friendships we made on that American tour were no flash in the pan. Only last month (November 1992) John and Louise

Morrison of St Paul, Minnesota, our host and hostess for the first half of our visit, were staying with us here at Whitbourne. It was with them that we first met two of the signatories to the above statement, Dr Jesse Williams and Merlyn Lokensgard.

Jesse Williams, a veteran of World War II, worked in the Agricultural Extension Service for the University of Minnesota, and as a professor of animal husbandry was in charge of projects on their experimental farm. He explained to me that in the United States the Extension Service to farmers – roughly the equivalent of our Agricultural Advisory Service – is all university-based, state by state. With him I saw for the first time ewes being kept to produce milk for human consumption. He and his wife Ann have since visited us twice at Whitbourne.

Jesse had also worked for many years for the U.S. State Department, as a project leader in USAID (the US Agency for International Development), and had just completed a twenty-month assignment in Syria. Since then he has attended Lord Plumb's World Food Conference in Brussels in 1988 and put in two long-stay spells at Coolmoreen, the Moral Re-Armament farm-based training centre in Zimbabwe.

Merlyn Lokensgard was a farmer. He was also the former President for the State of Minnesota of the Farm Bureau, the largest of the farmers' organisations in America. He had met Louise Morrison and then exchanged letters with her. On the strength of these letters Louise arranged for herself and John to drive Erica and me over to the Lokengards' farm to meet them.

We left them firm friends. Lokensgard said to me he had been looking for ways in which he could get his members to do more for Africa. His rapport with the Morrisons, and his concern for Mid-Western farmers in what were very difficult times for them, were apparent. But he gave an impression of quiet strength and imperturbability all the same. We saw perhaps some of the qualities which had caused him to be voted 'Farmer of the Year' for Minnesota. Two years later he led a farm group from the United States to Europe, and they spent a day in consultation with French and other European farmers which my brother Pat also attended, in Paris. He gave us several useful introductions to people at Farm Bureau H.Q. and in the State Department in Washington.

In Washington, our hosts Richard and Evelyn Ruffin set to work with a will to get us together with politicians and civil servants in the farming interest. One young lady, who was to play an important part in our next adventure, was a staff assistant to Secretary of Agriculture John Block. After listening to our summarised introduction of what we had come for, she said: 'Excuse me', left the room for a short minute, and came back saying she had cancelled another appointment in order to talk longer to us. She insisted that Secretary Block gave priority to helping agriculture in the Third World. She invited Dick Ruffin to brief a party of U.S. farm women before they made a visit to Europe in the coming September.

Back in Whitbourne, some time in June, we heard that these farm women were indeed coming to Europe in September. They would be in Britain first, then the Netherlands, Belgium, Germany and France. They would be only two days in Britain, one in London and one in the country. Erica and I thought we'd like to repay the Americans' hospitality, so why not ring up the U.S. Embassy in London who were arranging the tour, and offer them a visit to our farm? So Erica rang, and was put through to the Agricultural Attaché, Taylor Oyloe. Next thing we knew, Oyloe sent up his assistant to visit us for a look-over, and after that the deal was on. The American party spent the whole of their only day in the British countryside looking at farming life as lived at Whitbourne, accompanied by the assistant attaché.

There were twenty-one women in all, all leading professionals. It was the first delegation of its kind ever to visit Europe, or anywhere else, representing the Government of the United States. They included the Presidents of five Women's Farm Organisations, listed as follows: 'Women Involved in Farm Economics', 'The National Extension Homemakers' Council, Inc.', 'American Cow Belles Inc.', 'National Porkettes', and 'The National Wool Growers' Auxiliary'. Others included the President of the Farm Bureau for the State of Connecticut, and representatives from the National Councils of many bodies, covering wheat, tomatoes, corn (maize), electricity and cotton.

First, we arranged for them to be accompanied on their chartered bus from London by two good friends of ours, David and Suzanne Howell. David, a former market gardener and a bomber navigation officer in World War II, could explain who we were and point out landmarks on the way.

Then, in the morning they visited Bennetts Dairies in Worcester, a family business built up in two generations from a dairy farm. There they met members of the Bennett family and their staff, and had a close look at some of their operations. I think it was the best possible introduction to the dairy industry in Britain that we could have given them.

They arrived at Longlands, the heart of our farm, for lunch, hosted, cooked and served by Pat and Kristin and helpers. After lunch there was a short period of speeches, including a welcome from Pat, and one on wheat by Richard Steel, a prominent local wheat grower and former Chairman of the National Farmers' Union for Worcestershire. Then there was a talk by Whitbourne farmer Phyllis Williams on her recently published book *Whitbourne – A Bishop's Manor*. Phyllis is a local historian of some repute, and her few words on the book, covering as it does a span of eight hundred years, caused quite a stir and sold a few books as well. Finally, we found just the right person to introduce the Americans to that most deeply established of all womens' rural organisations in England, the Women's Institute; she was Mrs Hammond, from our neighbouring parish of Suckley, who was the President of the Worcestershire County Federation of the W.I.

Then came the moment we had been waiting for. The whole party were let off the leash to visit farms. They were whisked off in small groups of two or three in landrovers or farm trucks by their hosts or hostesses, to spend the next hour and a half being entertained by them in whatever way they liked in their own homes and on their farms. They were all driven back to Longlands – mostly only a mile or two – in time for a cup of tea and an exchange of gifts and farewells before boarding their waiting bus to London, in time for an early flight to the Netherlands the next morning.

After they had gone, we were saying goodbye to Ron, a long-standing tenant farmer, brought up on the estate. Ron said simply: 'Well, I don't remember when I have ever enjoyed a day more. They were such interesting people.' He and his wife Marjorie had had them in their home for just an hour and a half.

Indeed our guests made the day for everyone. They were a wonderful warm hearted crowd, fascinated with all they saw and heard and ate (including Kristin's summer pudding at lunch, which evoked tremendous demand for the recipe). They were also pretty sharp with their questions, and unfailingly courteous in the way they listened to any answers.

(Opposite Top) *Pat and Kristin at Haytons, their new home. Pat retired as Farm Manager in 1986*

(Bottom) *Pat, as Chairman of British Farmers for International Development, with Herefordshire farmers David and Janet Legge and guests from Poland: Jan Brodowski, farmer, and Adam Koprowski, chemical engineer*

THE RICHEST COUNTRY IN THE WORLD

The assistant agricultural attaché wrote to us afterwards expressing delight at the welcome given to the women, and inviting Erica and me to lunch at the U.S. Embassy in London. We went, and saw the – it seemed to us – huge premises with portraits of Presidents along the corridors. At lunch I took the chance of expressing our regret that the Farm Bureau had opted out of I.F.A.P. (International Federation of Agricultural Producers). Not long after, they rejoined.

Meanwhile in the U.S. Congress the Agriculture Act 1985 was steadily being forged. Agriculture Acts in the United States are timed to coincide with the first year of a new President, and their provisions last until the first year of the next President. So there is a Bill every four years. This four-yearly Bill seemed to correspond roughly to our annual Farm Price Review in the E.E.C. There is no automatic annual review in U.S.A. But each year, under pressure from various interest groups, adjustments – sometimes quite major adjustments – tend to be made.

At any rate, for whatever reason, conditions certainly improved for U.S. farmers over the years 1985–88. I can only assume that the natural resilience of the farming community, and their network of contacts with their politicians, had done the trick. I rejoiced on their behalf.

In 1989 Pat and Kristin made a six-week journey through the United States, visiting old and new friends in the farming industry. Pat wrote a report, which was circulated to a certain number of European colleagues. The 'conclusions' in this report are remarkably clear, and will stand reading again today:

Conclusions:
Our journey drew a clear distinction between farmer opinion at the grass roots, and the policy makers in Washington.

Farmers. As farmers we shared a lot of common ground with all those we met in Minnesota and Iowa. Virtually all felt the need of some Government support, of some measure of responsibility towards farmers in other parts of the world, and to have conservation and sustainability as part of the modern farm scene. There is an instinctive doubt about excessively large-scale operations, and a clear belief that too much pressure to produce has negative effects on family life and the quality of society. In short, farmers consider their calling to be both a business and a way of life – and it is a way of life for which they are ready to pay quite a high price.

Policy makers. Policy makers cover a wide range of opinions, and a varying vision of what America's destiny should be. Those who think widest are looking at a world view of agricultural policy, a partnership in achieving it, and a care for people and the environment.

Those who are predominantly concerned with America's current situation tend to remain with the modern dream that equates money with power. They have not come to terms with the fact that since the war America's share of the world's production has fallen from fifty per cent to twenty per cent, which puts it on a par with Western Europe. Nor are they ready to believe that there are values which are more important to many societies than economic values.

When George Bush talked about a 'kinder, gentler America', many people thought they liked the sound of it even while wondering exactly what it meant. Certainly, in an interdependent world competition has its limitations. Europe and America have still to discover the essential basis on which they can face a future where Communism is no longer perceived as the greatest danger, and where poverty is only partly alleviated by advancing affluence.

Of one thing I am certain. The need for the well-off, powerful nations of this world to agree with one another for the sake of the other, less powerful, nations, is far more obvious at the end of this twentieth century than it was at the beginning.

The world has learnt to rush food to disaster areas to save millions of people in country areas, farmers and their families, from starving.

Has the world listened to the survivors?

Yes, the world has listened.

Sustained long-term agricultural development has now become the accepted wisdom of the West as the answer to starvation.

It looks as though statesmen are realising that they can call on the experience of farmers everywhere who would really like so to farm that permanent solutions can be found.

This is a process going on in the world which gives me hope. I have been privileged to get an insight into some of it. I have seen it happening through the vision and commitment of men and women at the grassroots. Some of them I have mentioned in these pages. Many more I have not, though I know them by name – and large numbers again I do not know by name.

I thank God for every one, and I dedicate to all of them this story, grateful to have had a part with them in the remaking of the world.